EARLY HISTORY OF THE SPREAD OF BUDDHISM AND THE BUDDHIST SCHOOLS

EARLY HISTORY OF THE SPREAD OF BUDDHISM AND THE BUDDHIST SCHOOLS

By

NALINAKSHA DUTT

COSMO PUBLICATIONS

2021 New Delhi

EARLY HISTORY OF THE SPREAD OF BUDDHISM AND THE BUDDHIST SCHOOLS

Published by COSMO 2021

ISBN-81-3070-092-1

Published by
COSMO PUBLICATIONS
for
GENESIS PUBLISHING PVT. LTD.
24-B, Ansari Road, Darya Ganj,
New Delhi-110 002,
INDIA

Printed in India

TO THE MEMORY OF

THE LATE **Sir Asutosh Mookerjee**

THE CHAMPION OF THE CAUSE OF HIGHER EDUCATION

THE TRUE FRIEND OF SCHOLARS

THE INITIATOR OF THE STUDY OF PALI IN BENGAL

THIS HUMBLE WORK IS DEDICATED

AS A TOKEN OF THE AUTHOR'S DEEP GRATITUDE AND ESTEE

FOREWORD

The first portion of this work analyses the forces that helped the propagation of Buddhism in India, and delineates the missionary activities of Buddha in detail. There are scholarly biographies of the great Teacher touching incidentally on topics connected with his missionary activities, but a biography cannot give the fullest scope for the presentation of such an account. It is only a book devoted exclusively to the subject that can do justice to its treatment, and so Mr. Dutt's work is welcome as a compendium where all information connected with the progress of Buddha's missionary work is available in a well-ordered form. Such a sketch, the details of which have been laboriously collected from the Buddhist scriptures and arranged in such a way as to enable one to see the large masses of details about Buddha's career in their logical and chronological relations as far as possible, has certainly a value in the eye of scholars interested in the history of the spread of Buddhism. The attempt on the part of Buddha and his disciples to preach the doctrines of the religion and propagate it far and wide involved arduous work from village to village, and district to district, each locality presenting problems which had to be solved as best as they could by bringing to bear on them the application of the best qualities of head and heart that the personalities of Buddha and his disciples possessed. These and similar points can be properly tackled only in professed accounts of the spread of Buddhism and not in biographies of Buddha, where they may not find at all a logical setting. The degree of influence of Buddhism at a particular centre, the volume of patronage offered to the religion, the nature of collisions that took place between Buddhism and various other religions and such like can be treated with adequate justice to their importance only in a treatise directly and expressly devoted to the delineation of the subject.

A detailed delineation of the four principal schools of Buddhism including resumés of their doctrines as far as they have been ascertained at present is the object of Book II. The study of either the Pāli or the Buddhist Sanskrit literature can give only a partial view of Buddhism, as such literature embodies the beliefs and doctrines of one or two schools of Buddhism which in time attained dominance in India over the other schools. The discovery and publication of a large number of works belonging to the Pāli and the Buddhist Sanskrit literature have brought so much into prominence the tenets and philosophy of one or two schools that one may be misled to think that they constitute the whole of Buddhism. But there were other schools which had their days of prosperity in India at some time or other in the past, and possessed literature, of which traces are available in the accounts of Chinese travellers, and in the Tibetan or Chinese translations of works of some of them. The Sāṃmitīya school, for instance, rose to be a dominant school in the sixth and seventh centuries A. C. in regard to the number of adherents and range of propagation. There are indications, again, showing that the sub-schools arising out of the Mahāsaṅghika school acquired at one time much influence in Southern India. The followers of each of the schools believed that they preserved more faithfully than the rest the words of Buddha and were acting up to their spirit more than others. Each of the schools professed to preserve intact, or make the nearest approximation to the words and thoughts of the Teacher in and through its literature and practices. Each of them is thus, as it were, a facet of a diamond contributing its mite to the totality of the brilliance, and cannot be left out of sight in a view of the entire diamond. Mr. Dutt in his sketches of the four principal schools has taken a stock of the information available at present, enabling a reader to acquaint himself without much labour with what is now known about the schools. The portions of the sketches bearing on the origin, development, and activities of the schools have been drawn by Mr. Dutt for the first time from the existing materials.

The importance of the knowledge of details about the schools of Indian Buddhism is also realized if we look at the fact that it enables us to understand clearly the forms of the religion that were transplanted from India to other countries. As I have stated elsewhere, when the missionary activities of the Buddhists were carried outside India, the school of Buddhism which happened to be the most prominent at a particular time sent its missionaries for propagating it in other countries. The people of the country where they went looked upon the form of Buddhism preached by them as the original form of the religion and adopted it, zealously preserving its literature and doctrines. As an illustration, I mention first the Sinhalese. At the time when the Sthaviravāda school reached the acme of its influence, Ceylon was converted, and as the result of this conversion, the literature of this school has been preserved in that country. Similarly, when under the patronage of Kaniṣka, the Sarvāstivāda school became the most powerful, the people of Khotan and Central Asia were converted to Buddhism ; for this reason, the fragments of manuscripts discovered in course of excavations in those places belong mostly to the Sarvāstivādins. The case of the Sāṃmitīyas is also similar ; though no manuscripts (or their fragments) of this school have yet been discovered, the people of Campā, so far as has been ascertained, were first converted to Buddhism by the missionary efforts of Sāṃmitīya preachers, when this school prevailed in India in the sixth or seventh century A. C.

I appreciate very much the point of view from which the author looks at Buddha and his activities. Though he is writing an historical account, in which the canons of historical criticism should be applied, he is at the same time not unmindful of the fact that he is handling a subject involving topics about which, in the absence of a better alternative, respectful silence is welcome instead of barren sceptical criticisms. In connection with the great personalities like Buddha, there may be many things which lie beyond the comprehension of people unacquainted with the ways of men in the higher or the highest stages of spiritual culture. A means of at least partially comprehending them is through an intimate knowledge of the actions, capabilities, and lines of thought of men actually advanced in spiritual culture, supplemented by the perusal of authoritative works garnering the past experiences of people on the subject, elucidating its obscure points, or furnishing corroboration of the known ones. Attempts are often made by authors to thrust into narrow moulds of their own making personalities like Christ and Muhammad, Buddha and Caitanya. The present work is free from a blemish of this kind. It is also free from another blemish which so often tarnishes historical monographs on particular religions viz. a dominating preconceived notion that the religion professed by the author is superior to the religion treated in the monograph. This blinds him to many of the excellences of the latter religion which only a deep sympathetic insight into it can make patent, and prompts him to institute comparisons between the two religions to exalt the one over the other. I hope that Mr. Dutt's work with its many attractive features, some of which have been pointed out above, has before it a career of usefulness, which will render it a welcome addition to the existing literature on Buddha and his activities.

April, 1925.

96, Amherst Street, CALCUTTA. NARENDRA NATH LAW

PREFACE

The perusal of Rev. Edkins' remarks in his Introduction to the *Chinese Buddhism* drew my attention to the subject-matter of the first book of this work. The remarks are : "If the beginnings of the world's religions are very interesting and important subjects of inquiry, their progress and development are not less so. The various causes which operated to aid the spread of Buddhism if carefully investigated will be a valuable contribution to the history of humanity." Rev. Edkins had in his mind the whole history of the spread of Buddhism in the different parts of the world. As the task is stupendous, I have confined myself only to India and, for the present, to the earliest portion of the history. The sources of my information have been naturally the *Vinaya* and the *Nikāyas* supplemented at times by other Buddhist works.

Though there is a great divergence of opinion as to the date of compilation of the Pāli *Nikāyas*, it is of little importance to me so far as the treatment of the subject-matter of this work is concerned, because the tradition contained in the *Nikāyas* is old and it is upon this tradition that my account has been based.

There are indications in the *Nikāyas* showing that the tradition recorded in them dates back as far as the time of Buddha, to whom are ascribed almost all the discourses embodied in the Collections.

The picture of the religious condition of Northern India furnished by the *Nikāyas* has in it a tinge of great antiquity. We find frequent delineations of the state of things that immediately preceded the advent of Buddha, or existed during his life-time. We see that Mahāvīra has established his influence, Makkhali Gosāla has placed his order of monks on a firm footing, a host of religious sects with their divergent beliefs and philosophical theories has been struggling with one another for recognition as the repositories of truths, while brāhmaṇism has reached a stage in which reaction has become a necessity.

The numerous parallels in the *Nikāyas* indicate that their subject-matter was drawn from an early common source. The differences among the *Nikāyas* are not so much in substance as in form. This is due to the fact that different groups of reciters called the *Dīgha-bhāṇakas, Majjhima-bhāṇakas,* etc. (*Sum. Vil.* p. 15) preserved the sacred words of Buddha in the form which was looked upon by each group as the most suitable for the purpose. The similarity in substance among the *Nikāyas* of the different groups would not have been so great as it actually is, if they had not been based upon a common foundation, viz., the words of Buddha as far as they could be preserved in oral tradition. In the existing works on the early history of Buddhism, chiefly the biographies of Buddha in Pāli, Sanskrit and other languages have been utilized. The *Nikāyas* have not been utilized to the full to yield the information they contain. It was for this reason that Prof. Kern following Oldenberg remarked that "after the narrative of the occurrences in the twentieth rainy season, there is in the history of the Master an almost complete blank. For a period of 23 years, a summary of Buddha's proceedings is wanting, although various incidents may be held to fall within that period" (*Manual*, p. 38). It is true that it is not possible to draw up an account of Buddha's activities for the last 23 years of his career, arranging the incidents year by year, but nevertheless the utilization of the information contained in the *Nikāyas* can make it possible to present a sketch which may be useful in various ways.

Book II of the present work has been devoted to the treatment of the four schools of

Buddhism that came into being within about four centuries after Buddha's *parinirvāṇa* and were alive up to the end of the mediæval period. The materials available for an account of the origin and development of these schools including their tenets and philosophical views do not enable one to satisfy his curiosity about all their details, but they can well be utilized for the drawing up of a sketch which can convey a clear idea of all the four schools with the distinguishing features of each of them. To make this sketch richer in details, it is necessary to have access to the store of information contained in the hitherto unused Chinese and Tibetan translations of the works of these schools.

It is a matter for regret that I could not complete this volume during the life-time of the great man Sir Asutosh Mukherji who initiated the study of Pāli in Bengal, infused into me as he did into so many others a desire for historical researches, and pointed out to me the importance of spade-work in the vast unworked field of Buddhism. My labour would have been amply repaid if this volume could have elicited from him a single word of appreciation. No less is my debt of gratitude to Dr. Narendra Nath Law a silent but nevertheless an ardent and untiring worker in the field of historical researches. It is from him that I have got the training for carrying on historical investigations on scientific lines, and it is he who has guided me most patiently, almost at every step, to keep me away from the quicksands that beset the onward course of students of history. He has laid me under a further obligation by writing a foreword to this book, and including it in his Calcutta Oriental Series, without which it could not have seen the light. My hearty thanks are due to Dr. B. M. Barua who has encouraged me in various ways in the course of my labours and has given me occasionally the benefit of his valuable suggestions. Lastly, I must thank my friend Mr. N. C. Paul, B. L., for his keen active interest in the progress of this work and Mr. Nirmal Chandra Barua, B. A., for his brother-like help in diverse ways. I also take this opportunity of expressing my gratitude to Mr. R. N. Seal, B. A., for piloting this book through the press with promptitude.

CONTENTS

Foreword

Preface

Book I—Early History of the Spread of Buddhism

		Page
I	Internal forces in the spread of Buddhism	1
II	External forces	27
	Spread of Buddhism in	
III	Magadha	82
IV	Kosala	129
V	Territories of the Democracies	155
VI	Other Eastern Countries ...	169
VII	Western and Northern Countries	182

Book II—Schools of Buddhism

I	Evolution of the Schools of Buddhism	197
II	Mahāsaṅghika School ...	225
III	Theravāda School ...	249
IV	Sarvāstivāda School ...	266
V	Sāṃmitīya School	297
	Index	303

BOOK I

Spread of Buddhism

(Mainly based on the Nikāyas)

I

The Internal Forces in the Spread of Buddhism

Rise of Buddhism in an epoch of religious awakening.

The rise of Buddhism took place at an epoch when not only India but also Greece, Persia and China were experiencing a stir in religious matters through the advent of Socrates with his distinguished pupils and contemporary philosophers in Greece, of Zoroaster in Persia, and of Lao-tse and Confucius in China. In India the elaboration of the brāhmaṇic sacrifices accompained with the killing of hundreds of victims had already run a long course in the beginning of the sixth century B.C., growing into a highly complex system of ritualism, the details of which failed to command the faith of many a Hindu who began to question whether, after all, the offerings to the gods, with their laborious construction of altars and collection of numberless requisites, recitations of *mantras*, chanting of hymns, expiation of errors in the rituals, really achieved the objects for which they were performed, and whether, after all, they were worth the time, energy, and expenses that were involvad in their performance? The sacrifices were believed, if rightly performed, as able to secure for them wealth, health, long life and strength, the good will and good grace of the gods in this world, and happiness in the other world. But the dubious among them began to question within themselves whether there was not the chance of this belief being wrongly based. Side by side with the elaborate sacrifices performed by the householders, there were prescribed shortened forms of them, or even mere cogitation of the Supreme, unaccompanied with any rituals for the *vānaprasthas* and the *yatis*. If these latter were right in the pursuit of the course prescribed for them, could not a similar course suited to the masses, but devoid of, or accompanied only with very simple rituals, be prescribed for the householders? Similar views, more or less developed and opposed to the *karmakāṇḍa* of the *Brāhmaṇas* and specially to the cruel slaying of animals in the sacrifices, were already in the air before Buddha arose to preach his doctrines.[1] Brāhmaṇism allowed various shades of philosophic and religious views to grow up within its fold

1 See Dr. B. M. Barua, *Pre-Buddhistic Indian Philosophy*, pp. 193, 194.

without taking objection to their existence within its limits. But the key to the reception of this toleration lay in the fact that the dissentient view, side by side with its opposition to one or more brāhmaṇic doctrines, showed its allegiance to one or more of the ultimate fundamental tenets of Brāhmaṇism such as the affiliation to the *Vedas*, belief in their authority, worship of any of the brāhmaṇic gods as such, recognition of the authority of the brāhmaṇas, or compliance with the caste-system. It is only when we keep this in view that we can understand how the sects like Cārvākas or Sāṅkhyas could hold to their doctrines and yet continue to to be recognized by the brāhmaṇas as orthodox. The elasticity of Brāhmaṇism was, no doubt, a source of its strength, and the existence of this toleration that admitted of the tether, by which a sect was tied to its peg, to be drawn and drawn away to long distance without severance, was the cause by which Brāhmaṇism could grow into a ramified religion, as wide as the Indian continent. But there was a limit to the degree to which the heresy of its views could be carried by a brāhmaṇic sect as such. This limit was crossed by Buddha, who stood up as a rock to stop the flow of the religion in order to direct the faiths of the people along channels of his own. He preached that religious truths lay, not in the sacrifices, not in the *Vedas* which prescribed these sacrifices, not in the worship of the many deities of the brāhmaṇic pantheon, not in the observance of the caste-rules, not in the magical practices of the *Atharva Veda*, not in the extreme forms of self-mortifications, and not, in short, in the many other pet beliefs and practices that came as corollaries to an allegiance to the bases of brāhmaṇic faiths, but in self-culture 'culminating in Arhatship' which constitutes the key-stone of Buddhism.[1]

Buddha's views against sacrifices:

Buddha's views against sacrifices and the rites or acts involved in them have been expressed in no uncertain terms throughout his sayings. Against the memorising of the Vedic *mantra* and their fruitless repetitions to retain them in memory, he tauntingly remarked that the brāhmaṇas were nothing but the repeaters of the hymns composed by the ancient sages such as Aṭṭhaka, Vāmaka, Vāmadeva,

1 Cf. "For the first time in the history of the world, it proclaimed a salvation which each man could gain for himself in this world, during this life, without any the least reference to God or to gods, either great or small." Dr. Rhys Davids, *Hibbert Lectures*, p. 29.

Vessāmitta, etc[1]. He also disparaged the sacrifices involving needless expenses and payments of heavy fees[2] to brāhmaṇas who, by dint of their craftiness, made them the means of procuring wealth for themselves[3]. The rituals were meaningless operations so minutely but mechanically complied with by the sacrificing brāhmaṇas[4], intending to keep their superstitious clients under a perpetual and unquestioning tutelage. In the *Pāyāsi Suttanta,*[5] Kumāra Kassapa an immediate disciple of Buddha instructs Prince Pāyāsi that the celebration of sacrifices without cruelty involved in the killing of victims is a degree better than the celebration thereof accompanied with the perpetration of that cruelty. A similar view is expressed by Buddha in the *Kūṭadanta Sutta*[6] where mention is made of sets of rituals to which toleration can be shewn in the ascending

1 *Majjh. Nik.*, II, p. 169; *Dīgh. Nik.*, I, *Tevijja Sutta*; Prof. Oldenberg's *Buddha*, pp. 172, 173.

2 *Dīgh. Nik.*, I, p. 138.

3 Dr. R. Fick, *Die Sociale Gliederung*, etc., transl. by Dr. S. K. Maitra.

4 Prof. E. W. Hopkins, *Religions of India*, p. 188 and fn.

5 *Dīgh. Nik.*, II, pp. 316ff.

6 *Ibid.*, I, pp. 127ff.

order in which they are arranged : sacrifice in which living creatures are slaughtered ; better than this is the one performed with only *ghee*, oil, butter, honey and sugar ; better still than this is charity, specially that extended to holy men ; better than this again is the building of monasteries ; and better than this is the observance of moral precepts ; and the best of all is the 'sacrifice' of the four-fold meditation[1]. In short, Buddha condemns the sacrifices in a general way by referring to them as but a 'low art' unworthy of whatever a brāhmaṇa should be according to his conception[2]. For the first time in the religious history of India appeared a dominating personality who, with his infinite sympathy for every living being from man to the lowliest crawling insect, felt intensely for the horrors that the brāhmaṇic sacrificial system kept daily in store for thousands of dumb victims who, though unable to resist effectively, or express their pain in an intelli-

1 Dr. Barua, *Pre-Buddhistic Indian Philosophy*, p. 193 fn.

2 *Dīgh. Nik.*, *Brahmajāla Sutta*, transl. by Dr. Rhys Davids in the *Dialogues of Buddha*, Part I, pp. 17, 25 ; cf. *Sutta Nipāta* (S. B. E.), pp. 48-50, *Majjh. Nik.*, I, p. 82 where Buddha expatiated on the inefficacy of sacrifice (*yañña*).

gible language, were as sentient as men and felt the pain as much as the slayers would have done if treated similarly; and for the first time in Indian history did a single individual venture to speak emphatically against all that was dear to the leaders of the then brāhmaṇic society with their numerous resources to help them and with the combined belief of almost the whole population of India to support them; and for the first time also did an Indian undertake to support his view by practically remoulding the existing social elements into an organization that could successfully stamp out or keep in abeyance the opposed ideas and practices in India for several centuries, and are even now materialising the wishes of the great Reformer to a great extent in a few localities in India and in a few countries outside India.

doctrine of *ahiṃsā.*

It was this doctrine of *ahiṃsā* that appealed so much to the hearts of the people and extorted even from the brāhmaṇas themselves the position of an Incarnation of the Deity for Buddha. Mahāvīra also launched upon the field of Indian thought before Buddha with his doctrine of *ahiṃsā* but his followers carried it to such an excess that it could not draw the admiration of the brāhmaṇas while the rational view of same taken by Buddha attracted the attention of every one, no matter, whatever creed he might profess. Everybody knows that owing to the radical doctrines that Buddha preached, there was no love lost between the Brāhmaṇas and the Buddhists, and yet the inclusion of Buddha as an *avatāra* is no doubt a clear testimony of the infinite kindness with which Buddha's heart was imbued,—to which even his enemies had to pay homage by including him in their pantheon.

and *mettā* feeling.

The doctrine of *ahiṃsā* was but an offshoot of the *mettā* feeling which embraced not merely the negative restraint upon causing pain to any living creatures but also positive acts of charity and love, removing or attempting to remove distress, wherever existing and whatever form they might assume. It was this spirit that brought into being the many works of public utility such as the construction of hospitals, the the digging of wells and tanks, etc., meant to alleviate human distress or supply positive convenience and comfort where they did not exist; and the growth of this spirit having its source no doubt in a religious motive but operating independently of any religious institution or religious endowment is a departure from the ways in which the acts of beneficence were used to be performed. Standing on this catholic view-point, the outlook of the Buddhists on caste-restrictions that introduced differences in degrees of high and low where in reality they did not exist and were accompanied in many instances with narrowness and hatred obstructing the exercise of *mettābhāva*, could not but be as it was enunciated by Buddha. Of this I would speak later on; suffice it to say for the present that Buddha has on many occasions asked his disciples to exercise the *mettā* feeling as one of the methods of attaining perfection in *samādhi* and along with it the kindred feelings of *karuṇā* (compassion), *muditā* (sympathy in others' joy), and *upekkhā* (equanimity).[1]

Views against the caste-system

Buddha has never laid out a complete scheme of social organization by which he wanted to remove the reprehensible features that he observed in the brāhmaṇic society of the time. He confined himself strictly to religious topics in his disquisitions and discussions, and

1 *Dīgh. Nik.*, III, pp. 49, 50, 223, 224 ; *Majjh. Nik.*, I, pp. 283, 284, 359ff.

it was in reply to questions put by others that he at times gave his views against the caste-restrictions of the brāhmaṇic society and the preferential treatment and other oddities that an application of pure reason, upon which he took his stand in this respect, could not but condemn. The brāhmaṇic standpoint had its basis in birth and in the cosmology by which the four castes were given the order of precedence of the limbs of the great *Puruṣa* supposed to have existed at the time of the creation of the Universe[1]. Buddha on the other hand took a rational view of the subject and wanted the individuals to be higher and lower according to their respective qualities and not according to the accident of birth[2] ; and instead of the cosmology looked upon by him as erroneous, he pointed to a cosmology of his own described in the *Aggañña Suttanta*[3] and representing according to him the real. state of things. In it he mentions in a descending scale beings begin-

1 See *Ṛg Veda, Puruṣa-sūkta.*

2 "The thought that a brāhmaṇa does not occupy a special place by reason of his birth but that virtue alone constitutes a true brāhmaṇa occurs also in the *Jātakas.*" —Dr. R. Fick, *Sociale Gliederung*, etc., transl., p. 20.

3 *Dīgh. Nik.*, III, pp. 80ff.

ning from the gods with their higher qualities and ending with men who possessed much inferior qualities, and among the latter were classes formed according to vocations ; and the members of these classes could easily transfer themselves from one to another by developing the qualities for the avocations of the class to which they transferred themselves. In connection with his replies to questions[1] and the discussions to which they led Buddha has given hints showing that the kṣatriyas could be superior to the brāhmaṇas, if by qualities the former were in reality superior to the latter; for the element of birth which was set out as the criterion of status by the brāhmaṇas was in fact a thing which reason cannot support. It could not be denied that there were brāhmaṇas who though claiming to be the highest in social status by their birth were inferior to many a member of the lowest caste by their habits and inferior qualities, and Buddha pointed this out as a very unreasonable disposition of social elements to put those higher who by nature were lower. Any strong comdemnation of this state of things cannot be expected

1 *Dīgh. Nik.*, I, *Ambaṭṭha Sutta ; Majjh. Nik.*, II, *Assalāyana Sutta*, pp. 147ff. ; *Madhura Sutta*, pp. 83ff.; *Ang. Nik.*, I, p. 162.

from the Incarnation of *mettā* feeling, for that might smack of ill-will and hatred but the passages bearing on this subject are numerous and show in the characteristic but mild and rational method of Buddha what he looked upon as a reasonable arrangement that should prevail among the laymen as opposed to the monks. As regards monastic life, there could never be any distinction excepting that brought about by stages of moral and spiritual progress on the path towards arhathood. As the rivers, says he, lose, each its individual distinctions after falling into the ocean, so the monks lose all their distinctions as regards social status after joining the monastic order.[1] It should be observed that Buddha's attitude in regard to castes is an expression of the feeling of brotherhood that he wanted to prevail among all sentient beings, and when we look at the matter from this standpoint, we see that this attitude was but a logical extension of his view of relations among human beings.

It was thus that Buddha held views subversive of the sacrifices and the caste-system,—the two main bases of the then existing brāhmaṇism. With such views of the two bases

1 *Vinaya Piṭaka*, Vol. II, p. 239.

of brāhmaṇism, he could not naturally keep terms with the brāhmaṇas in the acceptance of the authority of the *Vedas*, as such acceptance necessarily meant compliance with their injunctions in regard to the sacrifices and the caste-system which he condemned. From this logically followed his attitude towards the *Vedas*, the authority of which he denied point-blank.

Views against the authority of the *Vedas* and the worship of the deities.

In the *Sīlavīmaṃsa jātaka*[1] the Bodhisatta says, "*Of no value are the Vedas*, of no value is birth or kinsman for the future world ; only one's own pure virtue brings him happiness in the next world." Buddha disbelieves the revealed character of the *Vedas* by remarking that the ancient sages Aṭṭhaka, Vāmaka, Vāmadeva, Vessāmitta, etc., never saw Brahman from whom they state to have received the Vedic texts[2]. The denial of the revealed character of the *Vedas* and with it their authority led to his view of

1 *Jātakas*, III, 194ff.

2 *Dīgh. Nik.*, I, *Tevijja Suttanta*, p. 239 ; cf. Dr. Barua's *Pre-Buddhistic Indian Philosophy*, pp. 193, 243—"All the thinkers in the neo-vedic period agreed in estimating the four Vedas and Vedic sciences as the lower knowledge."

the gods as but beings reaching their divine nature in the course of evolution from human beings by dint of their virtue pursued by them strenuously. Worship of such divine beings was of no avail, for they were unable to raise men to a higher status by dint of their own powers ; for it was man's own virtue that could elevate him morally and spiritually, and not any external help from the gods. Of this import is the following passage from the *Brahmajāla Suttanta* : "Worship of Sun, worship of the Great One, invocation of Sīri the goddess of luck, the vowing of gifts to a god for the grant of benefit, the offering of sacrifices to the gods are low arts from which Gotama the recluse holds him aloof."[1] The attack of the *Mīmāṃsakas* upon the Buddhists on the ground that the latter themselves looked upon their texts as revealed proceeds upon the imputation of an idea to the original Buddhists they did not entertain[2].

Buddha discouraged the magical practices and the rites of the *Atharva Veda*, and even

1 Dr. Rhys Davids, *Dialogues of the Buddha*, I, p. 24.

2 Max Müller, *Ancient Sanskrit Literature*, pp. 43, 44.

the practice of other arts not excluding astrology, by which men were led to commit deviations from the right conduct. It is needless to say that many of these practices were of a puerile character such as performing rites for averting the supposed consequences of evil omens such as the sitting of a hawk on the roof of a house, etc. The magical rites are performed in the belief that the things desired by an individual can be procured by virtue of those rites as certainly as a particular effect follows a particular cause ; and moreover, the belief in the efficacy of these rites inspires one with the idea that abnormal powers can be acquired through them, so that right conduct which is believed to be productive of happiness or spiritual good might be discarded, and magical rites made to take its place. This idea is detrimental to the pursuit of virtue and this was perhaps one of the reasons why Buddha did not countenance these rites, apart from the question of superstitions underlying them.[1]

Views against the magical practices.

It is clear from the dissatisfaction expressed by Buddha at the fruitlessness of his own mortifications during his spiritual discipleship under

1 *Dīgh. Nik.*, *Brahmajāla* and *Kevaddha Suttantas.*

several preceptors in the first six years after his renunciation of the world that he lost his belief in the mortifications as means to salvation.[1] His enlightenment was preceded by the pursuit of the middle path in which the use of the necessaries of life as to food and raiment was not regarded as an obstacle in the attainment of spiritual success. Just as on the one hand the use of these necessaries must be combined with *moral conduct* and *meditation*, so on the other, the ascetic practices, if adopted in a moderate degree, must be associated with the same two essentials of spiritual life. Sanction was given by Buddha to a moderate use of ascetic practices as a concession[2] to the strong tendency of the Indian mind, imbued as it had been for a long time with the belief in the efficacy of such penances, to resort to the extreme forms of abstinence from comforts of life or even painful methods of positively inflicting pain upon the body as aids to the acquisition of spiritual merit in the direction of the mind towards the spiritual ideals.

Views against mortifications and other ascetic practices.

1 *Majjh. Nik.*, I, pp. 77ff., 242–246.

2 Dr. Rhys Davids, *Dialogues of the Buddha*, I, p. 219.

Buddha himself declared the hollowness of such extreme practices but left the moderate ones to be intertwined into the programme of life of the Buddhist monks who must in all cases look upon the observance of the moral precepts in the practice of meditation as forming essentially the basis of his religion. I need not dilate on what constituted the right conduct (*sīla*) according to Buddha, for it forms the subject-matter of a large section of Buddhist religious literature which is widely known. Suffice it to say that Buddha insisted on the moral purity in the use of speech, mind and body for all those who joined the Buddhist order, in and through which the salvation lies. He prescribes certain rules for observance by the laity but the means to salvation does not exist in their ways of life though conforming to the prescribed rules. The means are to be found in the monastic order which for this reason engaged principally his attention. This is a great departure from the doctrines of the brāhmaṇas whose *śāstras* declare that salvation is not the monopoly of monastic or ascetic life but is equally within the reach of students or householders provided they desire it keenly in and through the performance of their respective duties. As to the mode of meditation adopted by Buddha, it is evident from the Buddhist works or extracts on meditation such as the *Mahāsatipaṭṭhāna Suttanta*, the *Paṭisambhidamagga*, the *Visuddhimagga*, etc., that it was kept free from the practices belonging to *haṭha-yoga* as also from the several forms of *āsana* or *prāṇāyāma*. For instance, in the *Majjhima Nikāya*,[1] Buddha inculcates the avoidance of the mechanical process by which the tongue is pushed backwards towards the palate, a device that is so often resorted to in the Hindu system of *yoga*. Buddha has in short desired to keep his *yoga-mārga* free from anything that is fanciful, severe or unnecessary to the concentration of the mind.[2] Moreover, the abnormal devices tend to create a pride in the minds of the *sādhakas* and impress the uninstructed spectators, if any, with admira-

1 *Majjh. Nik.*, I, pp. 242–244.

2 Buddha's attitude towards the brāhmaṇic ascetic practices is set forth in many places in the *Nikāyas*, one of which is, for instance,—"An ascetic who has adopted the mode of taking food in the manner of a dog or cow (*kukkuravatika* or *govatika*) takes rebirth on account of his penance in this life either as a dog or a cow and if he longs to be reborn in the world of gods as a result of his penances in this life, he is doomed to perdition for the wrong view he holds." *Majjh. Nik.*, I, p. 239; II, pp. 387, 388.

tion which might tempt the former to utilize it for worldly purposes.[1] The Buddhist path of meditation is thus a simplified process in which the elements of the brāhmaṇic *yoga* exist sometimes with slight modifications but which has been kept clear of what was looked upon as either unnecessary, extraneous, or dangerous. It is suited to whoever joins the monastic order, provided by the exercise of the *sīlas*, he had succeeded in developing frames of body and mind in which he could launch himself on an attempt at concentration of mind leading to the ultimate wisdom. "The states (*samāpatti*) in the Buddhist system of meditation were of importance, not merely of importance for learners as a means for arriving at *Nirvāṇa*, but the temporal release they afforded from the sense-percepts and the concrete was so highly esteemed, that they were looked upon as luxuries and enjoyed as such by the saints and by the Buddha himself."[2] The ultimate object with which these meditations and forms af discipline were undertaken and towards which Buddha rose to lead the people in his easy but certain way was *Nirvāṇa*.

1 E. g. *Dīgh. Nik.*, III, pp. 42ff.

2 Prof. Warren's *Buddhism in Translations*, pp. 282, 283.

The signification of *Nirvāṇa* has assumed various complexions at the hands of interpreters, but this much is certain that the attainment of same meant for an individual a permanent escape from the whirlgig of *karma* and re-birth with their attendant miseries. It is futile for for us to try to define what is meant by this term ; the Vedāntists might identify it with union with the Brahman the indescribable substratum of the phenomenal universe, the votaries of any of the highest deities such as Śiva or Viṣṇu might call it *mukti*, or the Christians might think it to be nothing but salvation as conceived by them ; but the fact remains that Buddha is himself absolutely silent as to what he wanted the term to really mean. This attitude of Buddha is perhaps significant from one point of view, namely, his general unwillingness to enter into ultimate questions of metaphysics ; for a definition or a description of *Nirvāṇa* would certainly have led to the mention of things which would have proved a good ground for fruitless discussions among his followers as well as among the Buddhists and non-Buddhists. To those who are far away from the state in which *Nirvāṇa* is attained, the thing might be a subject of differences of opinion, but to those who attained

The signification of Nirvāṇa.

it, it was as clear as a perception, though the attendant conceptions and feelings may lie beyond the power of language to express. Indeed, disputes as to ontological questions often prove to be no better than quarrels over tweedledum and tweedledee. Buddha was perfectly aware of the worthlessness of such discussions and their evil consequences, and has for that reason been uniformly silent over questions which otherwise might have given rise to undesirable results.[1] Suffice it to say that Buddhism relies ultimately upon success in this *yoga* without which the life of a Buddhist cannot be complete. This is the fruition to which Buddhism leads and for the attainment of which it proposes to show the shortest way.

It will thus be seen that Buddhism struck out a path, of which easiness and simplicity were the characteristic features. These two features depended upon the fact that the undue importance attached by the Hindus to rites and practices that were difficult to undertake

1 Cf. *Sutta Nipāta* (S. B. E.), pp. 167-174,—"The different schools of philosophy contradict each other, they proclaim different truths, but the truth is only one. As long as the disputations are going on, so long will there be strife in the world."

on account of their elaborateness or expenses, and the arduousness involved in them, was absent in Buddhism. There were other reasons also for which Buddhism could attract the people so far as its tenets and practices were concerned :—

(1) The avoidance of metaphysical questions rendered it easily intelligible to the masses.

(2) The greater play of reason instead of belief that in the brāhmaṇic system is so peremptorily demanded by the sacred texts and in so wide a range of matters was an attractive feature to the people, who developed more than others the habit of reasoning for themselves the good and bad side of the religious questions.

(3) The doctrine of *ahiṃsā* and *mettā* feeling advocating the exercise of mercy to all creatures and the brotherhood of all human beings appealed very much to the hearts of all men, specially to those who were not staunch believers in the sacrifices but by independent reasoning looked upon the killing of hundreds of animal victims in the sacrifices as extremely cruel ; and also to those who though Hindus were feeling the exclusiveness of the brāhmaṇas in the treatment meted out to them.

(4) Buddhism did not rely so much upon appeals to the supernatural as brāhmaṇism did, always referring to their efficacy shown in unseen

ways by the utterance of *mantras*, the performance of sacrifices, and in fact, compliance with the many rituals prescribed in the *śāstras*. The reference to this unseen and supernatural element in brāhmaṇism became so much exaggerated that an error in the smallest detail of a ritual, or a mistake in the utterance of a single syllable of a *mantra* had to be expiated by proper ceremonies or rectified by going through the same things again, and the belief of the clients of the priests appears to have approved of such demands upon their credence. There are many other directions in which exaggerated demands upon the belief of the laity in general were made by the brāhmaṇas. But Buddhism was shorn to a very great extent of such utilizations of the supernatural element that often mystified the vision of the laity in regard to having a clear idea of what the religion was and what they were actually doing. This gave Buddhism a practical turn making it include rites and ceremonies with their accompanying formulas that the masses could understand and the reason of which was generally patent to their understanding.

(5) The language in which it was preached and its ceremonies conducted was the dialect of the people concerned and therefore their

reason could obtain greater scope for exercise in the intelligent following of the discourse or the rituals to which they attended, while Sanskrit used by the brāhmaṇas in connection with all religious matters could not satisfy them in these respects.

(6) The great stress laid by Buddhism upon right conduct, so much so that it became one of its most prominent features, was also an attractive factor. Buddhism is often described as an ethical religion on the ground of the prominence of this feature as against several others that are emphasized in other systems of religion. From the very time when a convert enters into the monastic order up to the time when he attains to arhathood, the keynote of his life is right conduct. Ordinarily the unsophisticated conscience of even an untutored man approves very greatly the intrinsic rightness of a scheme of conduct that proposes to deal out goodwill and charity to all, and demands strict continence, and silent forbearance that sees an error in an act where others would have seen offence and ill-will. Upon this view of man that has its root in his inborn conscience rests the strength of the tables of the rules of conduct for general guidance like the ten commandments of the Bible and it was to this

element in man's mental constitution that this side of Buddhism appealed so much, and appeals even now.

(7) The prevalence of the practice of *yoga* had become widely spread for a long time previous to the advent of Buddha and carried with it the general belief among the Hindus that it was one of the most potent instruments for effecting the highest spiritual progress. Buddha was also an advocate of *yoga* and, as already stated, laid the greatest stress on it with its preliminaries, right conduct, etc., which might be regarded as making an individual fit for the exercises of mind and body that it involved, while he discouraged the mortifications which he regarded as useless. It was rendered simpler and more popular, while to this method of spiritual culture he made a contribution of his own in which the realization of impermanence of the world, the absence of soul as an indestructible and permanent entity, and the existence of suffering in all worldly affairs, led to a habitual practice of the *aṣṭāṅgika mārga* and the attainment of bliss by the dispersal of ignorance (*avidyā*) the root-cause of misery.

From the facts stated above it will be manifest that the way of life that Buddha looked upon as the path to *Nirvāṇa* was a good deal similar to the life of the *vānaprasthas* and *yatis.* The wanderings of the *yatis* combined with the comparatively stationary life of the *vānaprasthas* with an absolute non-attachment to the worldly matters were engrafted into a monkish organization with right conduct and simplified *yoga* as their methods of *sādhana,* the radical difference lying in the fact that while the *vānaprasthas* and the *yatis* recognized the authority of the *Vedas* and the former performed simplified forms of sacrifices and rituals, the Buddhist monks cut off absolutely their connection with the *Vedas* the authority of which they discarded outright.

II

The External Forces in the Spread of Buddhism

We are now in a position to enumerate the external causes and circumstances that helped the wide-spread propagation of Buddhism during the period from the first preachings of Buddhism by its Founder to the reign of the emperor Asoka when the religion spread over a very large portion of the continent of India and even over parts of countries lying outside India.

The commanding personality of Buddha, his self-sacrifice, the strength of his character, his

i. Personality of the founder of the religion

spiritual attainments, his super-sensual vision, and the occasional manifestations of miraculous powers[1] served in a great degree to convince the people of his spiritual greatness and made them attach importance to his words. Prof. Keith attributes the vast success of Buddhism not so much to the merits of the religion as to the personality of the founder.

[1] See, for instance, *Vinaya*, I, pp. 16, 25ff.

He says that "the founder of Buddhism must rank as one of the most commanding personalities ever produced by the eastern world"[1].

ii. Character and personality of Buddha's immediate disciples.

The character and personality of Buddha's immediate disciples such as Sāriputta, Moggalāna, Mahākassapa, Mahākaccāyana, Puṇṇa Mantāniputta, Ānanda were also a powerful factor in the propagation of Buddhism. Their excellences are mentioned sometimes by Buddha himself and sometimes by their brother monks. Sāriputta is described as excelling all in wisdom, self-control, and virtue, well-composed in his inner self, dwelling on the highest planes of thought, expert in the knowledge of the doctrines and possessing capacity for preaching persuasively[2]. Moggalāna was valiant, self-controlled and possessed of supernormal powers and able to raise the disciples to the highest stages of moral and spiritual progress[3]; Mahākassapa was foremost in the ascetic ways which Buddha permitted as a concession to the tendencies of the age, self-sacrificing, and loving

1 Prof. A. B. Keith's *Buddhist Philosophy*, p. 147.

2 Mrs. Rhys Davids, *Psalms of the Brethren*, pp.69, 388, 402 & 390 f. n.

3 Ibid., p. 390 f. n.

to dwell remote from men; Mahākaccāyana was a great expositor of *dhamma*[1]; Puṇṇa Mantāniputta was an appealing preacher; and Ānanda was the foremost bhikkhu in erudition, morally watchful, steadfast, versed in the sacred lore, and eloquent[2]. The qualities mentioned are no doubt but hints that they were present in more than ordinary degree in the character of the monks, though it should not be supposed that the requisite qualities required for a monk but not mentioned above were absent in them. The monks were all at one in their zeal for the propagation of the religion, in the strength of which they had unswerving belief, and to the founder of which they all bore the highest reverence. This was the bond that combined them and their followers into a closely compact body to march on in the path of duty prescribed by Buddha and to materialize his wishes by propagating his doctrines. The earnestness with which the first generation of Buddha's disciples performed their duties can be best described by comparing it to the zeal with which the Christian apostles did their share of work by practising and spreading the doctrines promulgated by Christ.

1 Mrs. Rhys Davids, *op. cit.*, pp. 386, 387.

2 Ibid., pp. 352, 353.

iii. Personality of the subsequent Buddhist leaders up to the reign of Asoka.

The Buddhist leaders in the generation following the immediate disciples of Buddha up to the reign of Asoka included likewise prominent characters who might well take their place by the side of his immediate disciples. The names of monks who took a prominent part in the deliberations of the church organization and maintained discipline, moral or otherwise, are many, but the biographical details of only a few of them are found in the Buddhist literature. Among these few may be mentioned Siggava whose presseverance in the cause of the conversion of non-Buddhists to Buddhism is found in the description where he is said to have daily visited, with ultimate success, the house of a brāhmaṇa for so long as seven years to pursuade his son with teachings and arguments to embrace the religion[1] ; Sambhūta Sānavāsika whose zeal in the work of conversion carried him so far as Kashmir and Kandahar to preach and secure converts in those places[2] ; Revata vastly learned and free from *āsavas* (moral impurities) ; Yasa extremely energetic in the work of

1 *Mahāvaṃsa*, ch. v.

2 Edkins' *Chinese Buddhism*, p. 67.

consolidating the Buddhist doctrines for which the second council was convened, and also in eliminating the evils that the Vajjians were trying to introduce into the church organization by modifying its rules[1]; Udena who was able to convert Ghoṭamukha brāhmaṇa after the death of Buddha and have an upaṭṭhānasālā built at Pātaliputta by him[2]; Upagupta of the time of Asoka who was highly intelligent and eloquent and was a pillar of strength to the Buddhist church. It was the charm of his character and personality that made Asoka accept him as his spiritual preceptor and help the Buddhist organization by building monasteries and stūpas in numberless places and give donations for the maintenance of the monks and the spread of Buddhism. Materials are yet lacking for drawing up a list of energetic and religious workers like those already mentioned showing the period in which they worked, the prominent qualities by which they were distinguished, and the share of burden borne by them in regard to preaching and conversion. Such a list is sure to be very useful in giving a picture of the personnel upon whom rested the arduous task of extending the limits of conver-

1 *Mahāvaṃsa*, ch. iv.

2 *Majjh. Nik.*, II, p. 163.

sion, and in drawing a sketch of the gradual spread of Buddhism.

iv. Internal strength of the organization.

It is supposed that Buddhism while in its full bloom lacked an organization possessing a central power that could co-ordinate and bring into a line the local units scattered throughout the length and breadth of the region over which Bnddhism had spread. This supposition, I think, is not supported by full reasons and evidences because the very fact of the rapid and extensive spread of Buddhism as well as the maintenance of its hold upon the country for such a long time gives the lie direct to such an inference. Though there was no central authority of the kind that we generally find in the organization with which we meet ordinarily, the central authority in the Buddhist organization was derived from a source of a different sort. It did not comprise praticular men, composing a central body, whose dictates were predominant and who could check and control the smaller bodies in the various parts of the country, but it was the invisible body of rules, prescribed by Buddha and very minute in their injuctions, that regulated the smallest details of monastic life and commanded the common respect and obedience from all the monks whatever might be the position occupied by them in the organization or in whichever locality they might be stationed[1]. The one or two instances of difference of opinion or quarrel or disobedience that are found in the Buddhist works are generally interpreted as signs of the weakness of the organization lacking a central authority, but when we remember that the central authority as pointed out above was of a different kind and was obeyed with great respect by all the monks on account of their living faith in the words of Buddha, we are led to look upon that interpretation as wrong. Observers of the development of the Buddhist religion might fall easily into the error of thinking that the defect which afterwards grew into a source of weakness lay in the constitution which was left without a governing body. But it should be remembered that the founder of the Buddhist religion ought to be credited with the knowledge claimed

1 *Dīgh. Nik.*, II, p. 154. *Yo vo Ānanda mayā Dhammo ca Vinayo ca desito paññatto so vo mama accayena satthā* ; *Majjh. Nik.*, III, p. 10. Ānanda explains to Gopaka Moggalāna about the headship of the church: "*Na kho mayaṃ, brāhmaṇa, appaṭisaraṇā* ; *sappaṭisaraṇā mayaṃ, brāhmaṇa, dhammapaṭisaraṇā 'ti vadesi*".

as a matter of course by the present day writers of the story of the development of Buddhism. The fallacy that is often committed by writers in tracing the causes of the decline of a social or religious institution or organism lies in the fact that they find fault with a particular limb of the organization or a particular practice which was really a source of strength when the institution or the organism was in its healthy state. If in old age a finger of a man is attacked by gangrene, are we justified in laying the blame and in finding fault with the existence of the very finger itself and tracing the cause of the decline to the possession of that limb by the man when he was young and healthy. Similarly, to say that the cause of the decline of Buddhism is to be found in the want of check upon the local *saṅghas* while the whole Buddhist organization with the mutual co-operation of the local *saṅghas* was able to keep Buddhism in a flourishing state for so many centuries is to take as a cause of decline a thing which was a cause of its prosperity or at its worst but a neutral something upon which the real cause operated its ruin. In the question before us, the invisible but yet forceful authority to which I have referred was existent though it was intangible, and it was the gradual deterioration of the living faiths of the monks and the introduction of elements that chilled the warmth of their faiths that are really responsible for bringing about weakness in that very organization which in the heydey of the prosperity of Buddhism worked so well, strengthened by the devoted attachment of the believing monks to the invisible central authority of Buddha's words constituting the life of the whole organization. What I want to point out is that the strength of the Buddhist religion with its organizations lay in the living faith and devotion of its followers and not so much in the structure through which the faith and devotion were ordained by Buddha to be given a material shape. Buddha gave his best consideration to the details of the structure of the organization and even changed them or added to their number as soon as the suggestion made by his followers met with his approval. No mundane organization can be perfect and it is enough if the common neccessities pertaining to the object for which it is founded are provided for. Buddha went much further than this and prescribed a *Vinaya* which was meant to meet even the probable or minute exigencies of monastic life ; and to find fault with this organization while the real defect lies in the gradual decline cf faith is to misread and misunderstand the real story of the Buddhist religion. So long as the faith was warm, Buddhism was alive ; and as soon as it began to cool, the pulsation slowed down until the death of Buddhism in India synchronised with the full disappearance of the warmth of faith.

V. The unorthodoxy of the people in the area in and around Magadha.

One of the reasons why Buddhism could spread more rapidly in the Magadhan area than it could perhaps have done had it been started in regions like the North-western area of Kuru-pañcāla was the fact that the people of that area were not so strictly orthodox in their adherence to the brāhmaṇic faith, and the doctrines and rules, of which it was the basis. It is the inference of scholars such as Grierson, Oldenberg, that the Aryans entered into India in two groups, the later being separated from the earlier by a pretty long distance of time. The group represented by the Kuru tribe settled in the mid-land comprising the country near the modern Delhi and its immediate north, while the other group settled in the outland encircling the mid-land on the east, south and west. Brāhmaṇic orthodoxy had its home in the mid-land while the outland represented unorthodoxy roughly in proportion to the distance from the said centre of orthodoxy, because distance hindered the process of keeping on the same level the orthodoxy of the people of the remote districts ; while it is also recognised that between the two groups of the Aryans, there were differences of ideas, manners, customs and even perhaps of language. The diluted orthodoxy of the people of the eastern outland favoured the growth of systems of thought that did not care to be in correspondence with those prevailing in the Kuru-pañcāla country. The eastern mid-land comprised the Magadhan area as one of its components and the favourable circumstances offered by it for the growth of heterodox ideas were one of the causes why Buddha's preachings could be received by the people more rapidly than they could have been done, had they taken place in the stronghold of brāhmaṇism in the mid-land[1]. Moreover, there are evidences in the Piṭakas that the organization of the brāhmaṇical orders in Magadha and Videha was not so strong and well-knit as to resist effectively the progress of Buddhism. The members belonging to the

1 See *Encyclopaedia of Religion and Ethics*, II, p. 540 and Oldenberg's *Buddha*, appendix I.

community were not also so strong in dialectics as to defeat in argument Buddha or the more eminent of the Buddhist monks and several cases are recorded of debates between the brāhmaṇas and Buddhists in which the former could not defeat the latter by showing the hollowness of the logic underlying the arguments. The brāhmaṇas of this part of the country are found in the Buddhist works to be tracing their descent from brāhmaṇas of the northern portions of India (*udīcca*) which shows that the source of nobility and brāhmaṇic purity was looked upon as existing there and not in the region where Buddhism flourished at first[1]. The well-known reference of the *Śatapatha Brāhmaṇa* states the river Sadānīrā as the limit beyond which lay areas of land which were made fit for habitation for brāhmaṇas only in so far as the sacrificial fire was lit up by them for the performance of sacrifices. This sacrificial fire had stopped on the Sadānīrā in its migration towards the east which pointed to that river as the boundary of the area that had some time before been considered as the sacred land. It therefore stands out that the tract

1 Dr. R. Fick, *Sociale Gliederung* etc., transl., pp. 34, 40. 213.

of country east of the river was inferior to lands in the west from the view-point of brāhmaṇic orthodoxy. One more noticeable feature is the predominance of the kṣattriyas in the eastern lands by virtue of wealth and acquisition of learning which made them powerful enough to carry on reactionary movements as against the existing conditions of things as settled or desired by the brāhmaṇas. It is very difficult to say how far the kṣattriya origin of Śākya Siṃha brought strength to his religious propaganda by virtue of this mere affinity of origin between him and the kṣattriyas of the place. To assert that this element was altogether absent in the forces which made them cluster under his religious flag would be perhaps going too far. But it should always be borne in in mind that the innate strength and attraction of Buddha's personality and the doctrines preached by him were so great as to put into shade the force of this element, specially when entrance into the Buddhist order meant a cleavage between the family origin and the new life that was brought into being.

Predominance of the kṣattriyas in the prācya-deśa.

The rapid spread of Buddhism within a few centuries after its foundation is due to the fact that conversion of non-Buddhists to Buddhism was regarded as a part of the duty of the monks at the highest stage of their spiritual development. The attainment of *Nirvāṇa* by a Buddhist may be the goal of a monk, but to attain it without at the same time giving others the opportunity of realizing its importance and taking to the right course for reaching it has about it a taint of selfishness however slight. The means by which the highest can be known and tasted ought not to be the secret of the select few or of an individual. It should be given a wide publicity in order that all men from the highest to the meanest may have the opportunity of exercising his judgment and take to the way that leads to the highest goal of manhood. The miseries of this world are countless, and they weigh down the hearts of men constantly with their heavy weights. If the truths found by Buddha, the means discovered by him can lessen them even temporarily it is certainly a blessing ; and the truths in fact profess to bring within reach of mortals permanent blessings. Those who have realized this truth in their lives cannot sit idle and look upon their fellow human beings with unconcern while the remedy is within their reach. It was this

vi. Buddhism, a proselytizing religion. Why so ?

feeling of love and compassion that animated Buddha and the Buddhists to preach broadcast the truths of their religion in order that the groping humanity may know that there are saving truths which can be attained by particular ways of regulating life and thought. It was from this point of view of looking at proselytizing that the Buddhists drew their stimulus for activities in this direction, and we find the Hīnayānists and, in a greater measure, the Mahāyānists exercising their best energies for the propagation of their faith for the diffusion of general well-being and the alleviation of miseries incidental to human existence. The sacred books of the Buddhists from the *Nikāyas* downwards contain passages extolling the merits of preaching and conversion. The verse of the *Dhammapada* (354) "*dhammadānaṃ sabbadānaṃ jināti*" testifies to the high esteem in which the duty of conversion was held by the Hīnayānists. The scriptures of the Mahāyānists look at the propagation of the faith in the same light. In the *Saundarānanda Kāvya*, Nanda's duty is not finished by the attainment of his own *nirvāṇa*. He wanders about with the object of bringing salvation to the distressed beings. The same work describes Buddha as making the remark that all beings are under delusion, and it is

Nanda's supreme duty to preach to them the *dhamma*, for he will be a lesson to those who are steeped in worldly passions[1]. The *Śikṣāsamuccaya* quotes passages from the *Prajñāpāramitā*, *Saddharmapuṇḍarīka*, *Candrapradīpa-Sūtra*, and *Sāgaramati Sūtra* on the merit of preaching and doing it with discrimination[2].

Missionary work, a departure from the traditional ways for the spread of religion.

Conversion by the evangelical method marks out Buddhism as making a radical departure from the traditionary lines on which the Indian religions brought new adherents into their fold. The ways in which Hinduism extended the boundaries of its domain are peculiar to itself. Its methods of enlisting new recruits are in consonance with the caste-system, its spirit of exclusiveness specially in religious matters and its power of slowly adapting itself to the changes effected by forces from within or without. The process followed by it consisted in absorbing the new recruits into the Hindu society by attracting them slowly and imperceptibly to adopt

1 *Saundarānanda Kāvya*, sarga 18, ślks. 54-58.

2 *Śikṣāsamuccaya* (Bendall's translation), pp. 310, 311.

more or less the social customs and practices of the Hindus and thus occupy a place within an existing caste or sub-caste, or form a new sub-caste, as the case may be. The alteration of the religious views is left to follow the social absorption that gradually sets in. The early Jainas, discarding as they did the caste-system, were in a position to follow a course different from the traditional method of the Hindus, but the Buddhists struck out a radically different path. The conversion of a new adherent was done deliberately, and his embrace of the new faith was effected in a way that could be well marked as a change that was being made with a deliberate object. With the Buddhists these features were more prominent ; but among the Hindus, the change was slow and imperceptible. It was no doubt the zeal of the founders of religions and their best disciples to share with others the blessings of the state they attained and the truths they realized that impelled them to take to missionary activities. The radical departure made by the Buddhists from the traditional method was responsible for the rapid way in which Buddhism spread not only in India but also in the countries outside. The very first resolution made by Buddha after the attainment of the *summum bonum* was to become a religious preacher and save mankind from worldly cares and miseries.

Buddha's zeal in preaching.

He went to Sārnāth to convert the five brāhmaṇas, after whom he made many more converts. He formed them into a band of missionaries, of whom he was the leader. In the *Vinaya*[1] we find Buddha speaking thus to his followers who then numbered only sixty one : "Go, ye now, O Bhikkhus, and wander, for the gain of the many, for the welfare of the many, out of compassion for the world. Let not two of you go the same way. Preach the doctrine which is glorious in the beginning, middle, and end, in the spirit and in the letter ; proclaim a consummate, perfect, and pure life of holiness. There are beings whose mental eyes are covered by scarcely any dust, but if the doctrine is not preached to them, they cannot attain salvation. They will understand the doctrine. And I will go also, O Bhikkhus, to Uruvela-senānigāma in order to preach the doctrine". Buddha passed from one country to another preaching *dhamma*

Buddha exhorts his disciples to propagate the doctrine.

1 *Mahāvagga*, I, pp. 20, 11 (translated in the S. B. E., Vol. XIII, pp. 112, 113 ; *Saṃ. Nik.*, I, pp. 105-6 ; Bhadrakalpāvadāna in Dr. R. L. Mitra's *Nepalese Buddhist Literature*, p. 43.

which is heard by house-holders or their sons who being convinced of its excellence retired from the world leaving their possessions great or small[1]. This example was followed ardently by many of his disciples. Sāriputta was considered the fittest person after him to roll the wheel of Law[2]; Moggaliputta, to preach the religion to the denizens of hell, gods and spirits of heaven; Puṇṇa Mantāniputta, to carry on the work among the rough people of Sunāparantaka[3]; Piṇḍola-Bharadvāja, the chief of the *sīhanādikānam* (lion-roarers), to remove doubts regarding Buddhistic path or fruit[4]. This shows how the disciples fulfilled their Master's desire. The Master was satisfied with their activities as indicated by his departure from the mortal world, which, as said by him to Māra, was conditional on his seeing that his disciples had been sufficiently large in number and able to refute the doctrines of their adversaries, and that his religion well and widely

Propagation of Buddhism by Buddha's disciples.

1 *Majjh. Nik.*, I, p. 179. This is one of the many passages which constantly recur in the *Nikāyas.*

2 *Aṅg. Nik.*, I, 13, 7; *Milindapañha*, p. 362.

3 *Majjh. Nik.*, III, p. 268.

4 *Psalms of the Brethren*, p. 111.

preached[1]. A passage in the *Saddharma-puṇḍarīka*[2] is an evidence of the earnestness which animated the disciples long after Buddha's death for propagating the religion: "When the Tathāgata has become wholly extinct, we, O Lord, want to go in ten directions and make all beings write, read, think over, and proclaim this *dharmaparyāya* by the power of the Lord". The history of Buddhist faith both in its earlier and later phases reveals the fact that the Buddhist monks gave their best energies for the propagation of the religion and thus acted up to the wishes of the founder of the religion. The despatch of missionaries to various countries both within and abroad during the reign of Asoka, the successful attempt of the Buddhist monks to colonise Central Asia during the reign of Kaniṣka, and the perilous journey and voyages undertaken to China, Tibet, Cambodia, Java and the Malay Archipelago by the monks in the later history of Buddhism amply show to what a great extent the Master's bidding was carried out.

The success of the methods employed by

1 *Digh. Nik.*, II, p. 106; Mr. Rockhill's *Life of the Buddha*, p. 34.

2 Dr. Hoernle's *Manuscript Remains etc.*, p. 155.

the Buddhists for spreading their religion depended upon the following factors :—

VI. Methods employed for making converts.

(a) The easiness with which the religion could be followed ;

(b) The tolerant spirit shown to converts ;

(c) The tenacity of the preachers in persuasion ;

(d) Power of disputation ; and

(e) Appealing way of preaching.

Graudal course of training in Buddhism.

(a) The tenets and practices of Buddhism are simple and can be made perfectly clear to a layman without much difficulty if only its exoteric side be put before him. Again, to those who intend to follow it, their course can be made easy by asking them to follow at first the tenets and practices that are suitable to their yet undisciplined and undeveloped powers, and take to the gradually difficult ones by stages[1]. To a householder, a Buddhist monk can preach at first the *dānakathaṃ, sīlakathaṃ, saggakathaṃ, kāmānaṃ ādīnavaṃ okāraṃ saṃkilesaṃ nekkhamme ānisaṃsaṃ* (the discourse

1 For the gradual course of training in Buddhism (*imasmiṃ dhammavinaye anupubbasikkhā anupubbakiriyā anupubbapatipadā*) see *Majjh. Nik.*, III, pp. 2-4.

on alms-giving, moral precepts, the heavens, the danger, corruption and impurity of desires, and the blessings of retirement) and when he perceives that his mind has been sufficiently prepared by hearing the discourses, he can preach the excellent teachings of Buddha, viz. *dukkhaṃ samudayaṃ nirodhaṃ maggaṃ* (suffering, the origin of suffering, the removal of suffering, the way to the removal of suffering)[1]. These discourses have an appealing force which moves the hearts of the people irrespective of their creeds. The higher and deeper truths of Buddhism were gradually imparted and explained to the initiated or rather to the *sotāpannas*. Thus the Buddhists from the lowest grade to the highest did not feel embarrassed by the weight of doctrines and practices too difficult for their yet limited understanding or their undeveloped powers of fortitude and devotion.

(b) Buddhism had in it a large element of catholic spirit[2] which appealed to even the

1 *Digh. Nik.*, I, p. 148 ; *Vinaya*, I, 7, 5-6 ; VI, 36, 5; Oldenberg's *Buddha* (Hoey's translation), p. 186.

2 *Majjh. Nik.*, I, p. 523-'*na ca saddhamma okkasanā na paradhamma vambhanā* (one should neither extol

members of other religions. To attack another religion as a whole was never sanctioned by Buddhism. Buddha had to recruit his converts from other religions; he never disparaged any particular religion to which any of them might have belonged, though, of course, he showed at times that particular doctrines or practices of that religion were wrong, erroneous, or unworthy of being followed. Buddha, again, held the view that gifts should be made by the Buddhists to the deserving members of all other religious orders and not to the Buddhists alone[2]. He permitted a Jaina householder after his conversion to Buddhism to continue his charity to the Jaina monks winning thereby the admiration of the members of other sects[3]. In the *Majjhima Nikāya*[4], he is recorded to have said that a particular Ājīvaka was reborn in heaven by virtue of his being a *kammavādin* (i.e. a believer in the law of Karma), indicating that the claim of a non-Buddhist to heaven was not denied by

Catholicity of the religion.

his own religion nor disparage other religions); *Aṅg. Nik.*, I, p. 27.

2 *Aṅg. Nik.*, III, 57, I.

3 *Vinaya*, VI, 32; *Aṅg. Nik.*, IV, p. 185.

4 *Majjh. Nik.*, I, p. 483.

Buddha merely because he was not a Buddhist. He held in high respect the brāhmaṇas who led truly moral life[1]. The spirit of toleration is no doubt a prevailing feature of the religious life of India but yet it should be said to the credit of Buddhism that it was practised by the religion in a more thorough-going manner than perhaps any other contemporary religion of India.

Perseverance of the preachers.

(c) The Buddhist scriptures do not furnish us with very many instances in which the Buddhist preachers had to be tenacious in the prosecution of their works of conversion in regard to particular individuals who were hard to be convinced; for the general trend of the instances is rather the other way, viz. the followers of other persuasions were eager to embrace Buddhism and therefore presented little difficulty to the Buddhist missionaries in their conversion. The examples in point are few and far between but yet they show clearly the zeal which animated some of the Buddhist preachers in propagating their faith. It is mentioned in the *Divyāvadāna*[2] that Pūrṇa resolved

1 *Sutta Nipāta*, *Brāhmaṇa-dhammika Sutta.*

2 *Divyāvadāna*, p. 39; *Mahāvastu*, I, p. 245.

to carry on his missionary work among the ruffians of Śroṇāparāntaka even at the risk of his life. This elicited the admiration of Buddha who spoke to him in the following terms, "Pūrṇa, you are endowed with patience (*kṣānti-saurabhena*) and a fit and proper person to live among the Śroṇāparāntakas. Go Pūrṇa, free those who wish to be freed, rescue those to be rescued, console those to be consoled, and emancipate those to be emancipated." The *Milindapañha*[1] relates the account of Rohana visiting the house of Nāgasena's father continually for seven years and ten months with the object of converting Nāgasena. The visits were made from a time before the birth of Nāgasena in the midst of taunts and insults hurled at him. The visits inspite of the unfavourable circumstances ultimately served to conciliate the parents of Nāgasena who was then converted to Buddhism. The *Mahāvaṃsa*[2] has a similar account but the persons mentioned in it are different. It is difficult to state how far the narratives are based on actual incidents, but the fact that the narratives themselves did not appear as uncouth to the writers of the two

1 *Milindapañha*, pp. 8ff.
2 *Mahāvaṃsa*, pp. 41-43.

aforesaid books is itself a proof that such perseverance of the Buddhist preachers in the work of conversion was not quite an unusual thing in those days.

(d) Many are of opinion that Buddha himself avoided entering into discussions with others, and discouraged those of his disciples who entered into discussions on religious matters in the course of their preaching and wandering. Such opinion is not wholly correct. There are passages in the Buddhist scriptures which lend colour to the aforesaid view but we have to go deeper to get at the true state of things. To cite one or two such passages: He is said to have declared that his dhamma is not to be grasped by mere logic (*atakkāvacara*)[1] and he condemned the śramaṇas and brāhmaṇas who took to hair-splitting disputations saying, 'Issue has been joined against you, you are defeated, set to work to clear your views, disentangle yourself if you can' (*āropito te vādo, niggahīto 'si. Cara vādappamokkhāya, nibbeṭhehi vā sace pahosīti*).[2] From such passages, it is not right to jump to the conclusion that Buddha condemned or prohibited the holding of all disputations on reli-

1 *Dīgh. Nik.*, I, p. 12 (*Dial. of Buddha* Vol. II, p. 26).
2 *Dīgh.-Nik.*, I, p. 8 (*Ibid.*, p. 15).

gious matters. In fact, the *Dīgha Nikāya*[1] has a passage which may mislead one into the opinion that all disputations were discouraged by Buddha but in fact only such discussions as those pointed out above were meant to be avoided. The correct construction should therefore be this that the disputants should have the elicitation of truth as their object and not the obscuration of same by the use and counter-use of words which serve only to mystify. The bhikkhus should have love of truth and nothing but the truth. The defeat of the opponent in a wordy fight is but a way of self-assertion which contributes to self-conceit and lowers thereby the inner man from the spiritual standpoint. It was disputation of such a character that Buddha condemned. Such verbal passages at arms often took place regarding points which can never be decided by disputation. Such subjects are the indeterminable problems which cannot be solved by disputation but may, if at all, be realized in the highest stages of *dhyāna*. The feelings and realizations during the prosecution of *dhyāna* cannot be felt or realized by those who have not

Disputation indispensable in the spread of a religion; Buddhism was no exception to it.

1 *Dīgh. Nik.*, I, *Brahmajāla Sutta.*

had the experiences personally and hence the wide gulf that has always existed between the two classes of men. Words intended to describe the experiences appear meaningless or untrue to the lay people who think that argumentation on the lines approved by logic can take them to the highest truths. It was in view of this gulf between the two classes of men that the Hindu *ṛṣis* asked their lay followers to follow the Hindu scriptures without questioning them, allowing, of course, the conflict between two or more passages on a point to be removed by the methods prescribed therefor. Hence it would, I think, be apparent that Buddha was not unreasonable in what he said, and it is wide of the truth to suppose that he enjoined the bhikkhus to avoid all vain disputations.

It should also be kept in mind that the state of the country at the time of Buddha was not such as could permit a missionary to keep clear of disputation. One of the essential works of a missionary is to convince his audience, and this is hardly possible if argumentation is given a wide berth. At the time of Buddha, accounts are available of brāhmaṇa and non-brāhmaṇa heads of religions, wandering about over the whole of eastern India, sometimes with their numerous disciples, and holding disputations with the heads of the rival sects to assert their influence and increase their following. There were the *paribbājakas* who wandered about with their minds open for the reception of religious light wherever available. The lay people also liked to hear disputations as indicated by their setting up of *kutūhala-sālās* (halls for people in quest of truths) or *paribbājakārāmas* in different places where the wandering teachers may reside and hold controversies with convenience and sometimes in the midst of a large gathering composed of men flocking to the place from the neighbouring localities. The people felt proud if a good many religious teachers visited their *kutūhala-sālās* or *paribbājakārāmas.*[1] References are available in plenty in the Buddhist works showing that it was often stated at the disputations that the defeated teacher with his followers would relinquish his own doctrines and embrace those of the winner. These defects in disputations were a fruitful source for the enlisting of converts to the many doctrines and religions that prevailed in the country at the time and the teachers vied and struggled with one another for getting the largest following for leading

1 *Saṃ. Nik.*, II, p. 32; V, p. 115; *Majjh. Nik.*, II, pp. 1, 2, 99; *Divyāvadāna*, p. 143.

them to the highest spiritual goal. The discussions among the teachers of the rival sects indicate that they had to be well-grounded not only in the rules by which the disputation was guided and the argumentation was rendered free from fallacies, but also in the doctrines of the various opponents who had to be faced, over and above their own school of tenets and practices with their philosophical bases, if any. In view of these facts, it is incorrect to hold that Buddha laid down a prohibition for entering into religious controversies. He himself has been described in several places in the Buddhist works as a master of the tenets and practices of the heretical sects. A large number of his disciples was recruited either as the result of defeats suffered by the opponents or from among the followers of the brāhmaṇic and the heretical teachers convinced of the superiority of the doctrines propounded to them. His discussions with Soṇadaṇḍa, Kūṭadanta, Upāli, Sakuludāyi, Vekhanassa, Assalāyana and a host of others are instances in which he argued out his own views and convinced his adversaries at the end. The victories thus gained in large numbers in disputations elicited the remark from Dīghatapassi, a Jaina monk to the effect that Gautama was a sorcerer who by the force of his art drew the people of other sects into his own net[1]. The list of his disciples who were convinced and won over to Buddhism from their own beliefs and practices is a large one, from which the names of the following may be given here by way of illustration. Those named here are among the foremost of Buddha's followers and were well-versed in the doctrines and practices of the sects to which they belonged before conversion : Mahākoṭṭhita, Piṇḍola Bharadvāja, Mahākaccāyana, for instance, were masters of the three Vedas and perfect in all the accomplishments of a brāhmaṇa ; Sāriputta and Moggalāna were the chief disciples of Sañjaya with whose teachings they could not be satisfied ; the Kassapas were the leaders of the Jaṭilas ; Abhayarājakumāra was a distinguished disciple of Nigaṇṭha Nātaputta who deputed him for his intellectual acumen and mastery over the Jaina doctrines and philosophy to hold a controversy with Buddha.

It was Buddha's practice to deliver his dis-

1 *Majjh.Nik.*, I, p. 375 ; *Aṅg. Nik.*, II, p. 190. (*Gotamo māyāvī, āvaṭṭanim māyaṃ jānāti yāya aññatitthiyānaṃ sāvakā āvaṭṭetīti.*)

courses through dialogues in the following four ways :—

Four ways of delivering discourses through dialogues.

(1) *Paṭipucchāvyākaraṇīya* ;
(2) *Ekaṃsavyākaraṇīya* ;
(3) *Vibhajjavyākaraṇīya* ; and
(4) *Ṭhapanīya*[1].

In the first method, the doubts of the interlocutor are ascertained by suitable questionings and removed by suitable replies ; in the second, a direct reply is given to an enquirer without entering into a discussion with him ; in the third, answers are made piecemeal i.e. taking one aspect of the question first and then another and so forth[2] ; in the fourth, the indeterminate nature of the problems put to him for solution is pointed out to avoid discussions on same, as they lead to no finality. It was for this as also for other reasons stated already that he wanted the bhikkhus to avoid these topics in their discussions[3]. Even if these subjects be set aside, those on which discussions were allowed left room enough for the play of keen intelligence and subtle arguments.

1 *Dīgh. Nik.*, III, p. 229.

2 For an illustration of this method, see *Majjh. Nik.*, II, p. 197.

3 *Dīgh. Nik.*, I, pp. 187ff.

To be a successful disputant, one has to be equipped with all the outfit of specious arguments (*kūṭatarka*) to meet those opponents who make a free use of them whenever needed. It is clear from Buddha's injunctions to the bhikkhus, that he wanted them to use their power of argumentation in the service of truth and truth alone, and not to take to sophistry of their own accord. But a preacher ignorant of the wiles of a specious arguer and unable to use counter-wiles for self-defence would certainly be a weak disputant. It was for this reason perhaps that we see Buddha applying such a method with men who came to argue with crooked intention, or took to crooked ways of disputation. This is seen in the *Ambaṭṭha Sutta*[1] where Buddha, in order to silence Ambaṭṭha, who claimed the superiority of brāhmaṇas over all by birth and stated that the Sākyas were of servile origin, relates the fictitious account of the origin of the Sākyas and Kaṇhāyanas showing that the latter were the descendants of a *dāsīputta* (son of a slave-girl) of the former. The object of the use of the story was to put it as a stunner to Ambaṭṭha exposing his really low origin.

1 *Digh. Nik.*, I, pp. 92, 95.

This, however, could not achieve the desired end. Ultimately Ambaṭṭha was made to admit his low parentage by a miracle. The *sutta* makes it clear that as the use of logic pure and simple would have been inefficacious in a debate with a conceited person like Ambaṭṭha, Buddha took to the right means of correcting him.

Detailed accounts of disputations with Buddha are rare in the Buddhist literature. Such an account is found in the *Culasaccaka Sutta* of the *Majjhima Nikāya*[1], in which a disputation took place between Buddha and Saccaka Nigaṇṭhaputta, a great disputant of the time. A summary of the account will give the reader an idea of the ways in which the Buddhists had to meet and parry the attacks of their opponents in such a contest: When Bhagavā was dwelling at Vesāli, Saccaka Nigaṇṭhaputta proclaimed that he did not find any person who would not quake in fear to enter into a debate with him. He had heard of the teaching of Buddha to the effect that each of the five skandhas is *anicca* (impermanent) and *anatta* (devoid of a permanent entity). He denounced it as a wrong view and was anxious to meet

Majjh. Nik., I, pp. 227ff.

Buddha for a discussion. He went to Buddha at the *Kūṭagārasālā* with 500 Licchavis to witness the latter's defeat in the disputation. After taking his seat, Saccaka said, "I wish to put a proposition (*desam*) to you, if you permit me to do so." On obtaining assent, he put questions.

Saccaka. What instructions are generally imparted by you to your disciples ?

Buddha. (I teach) Body is impermanent, Sensation is impermanent, Perception is impermanent, the Mentations are impermanent, Consciousness is impermanent. Body is insubstantial, Sensation is insubstantial, and so on. All compounded things are impermanent and void of substance.

S. An illustration presents itself to my mind.

B. Say as it appears to your mind.

S. Just as whatsoever seeds and plants grow and expand and come to maturity do so all in dependence upon the earth, and, firm-based upon the earth, and, thus come to maturity, and just as whatsoever deeds that require strength are all done in dependence upon the earth, and firm-based upon the earth, thus these deeds are done, in the self-same way, by Body is this individual man and, firm-based upon Body, does he bring forth deeds good or evil. By Sensation etc. etc.

B. Thou sayest, 'Body is my self, sensation is my self, etc.'

S. I say, 'Body, Sensation etc. each of these is my self.'

B. What thinkest thou, Aggivessana, does a reigning khattiya king, such as King Pasenadi of Kosala, possess the power of pronouncing and causing to be carried out sentences of death, outlawry and banishment ?

S. Yes.

B. Inasmuch as thou hast but now said, 'Body is my self,' doest thou possess this power over body 'Let my body be thus, let not my body be so ?' Thus questioned, Saccaka sat silent. Buddha repeats his question to which Saccaka replies.

S. That I have not.

B. Consider, and then give answer, for thy last does not tally with thy first nor thy first with thy last. Body, Sensation, etc. are permanent or impermanent ?

S. They are impermanent.

B. Is that painful or is it pleasurable ?

S. It is painful.

B. But that which is impermanent, painful, subject to all vicissitudes—is it possible thus to regard it, 'This is mine ; this am I ; this is my Self ?'

S. That is not possible.

B. Can such a one who holds the view, 'This is mine ; this am I ; this is my Self,' comprehend suffering or keep clear of the suffering that encompasses him ?

S. He cannot.

B. Just as a wood-cutter seeking solid (*sāra*) wood, goes to forest and cuts the root of a Banana tree and then chops off the head, leaves etc., but fails to get at the pith, so also you by entering into disputation with me have found your doctrine vain and useless[1].

1 The portion in smaller types has been abridged

How the *paribbāja-kas* and the various religious orders helped the spread of Buddhism.

The *paribbājakas* and the members of the various contemporary religious orders offered a very fruitful field for the recruitment of converts to Buddhism. The embracing of the religion of the victor by the vanquished in a debate was a general practice and this proved an effective means of spreading Buddhism, because Buddha himself as well as many Buddhist preachers were powerful disputants. It is a peculiar feature of the time that members of many of the religious orders attached more importance to belief based on reasoning than to blind faith, and pursuant to this state of things, the vanquished in a disputation left his religious belief as soon as it was brought home to him in a public debate that there was a flaw in the chain of reasoning upon which his belief was based, while no such flaw could be pointed out in the reasoning upon which the belief of the victor was founded. No stigma attached to the relinquishment of a religious belief by reason of defeat in a controversy or by a change in faith brought about in other ways. It was not so in

from Bhikkhu Śilācāra's *First Fifty Discourses*, Vol. II, pp. 84-88.

later times when the ceremonial and social exterior of religion almost ceased to have a living connection with the inner conviction of an individual. At the time of which we are speaking, many students after finishing their education used to wander about in the various parts of India as *paribbājakas* in order to learn the various religious doctrines and gain mastery over the art of disputation[1]. They were at liberty to embrace any religion that appealed to them most as the vehicle of ultimate truths. In spite of the parents' objection, we read of many instances of young brāhmaṇas and kṣattriyas joining the Buddhist order. It was this state of things that helped Buddha and his band of preachers a good deal in the spread of the religion. The conversion of the followers of Sañjaya counting among them Sāriputta and Moggalāna, the Jaṭilas, Pokkharasāḍi, Sakuludāyī, Mahākassapa the Acela, Cañki, Esukāri, Ghoṭamukha, Vekha-

1 *Majjh. Nik.*, II, p. 148. Assalāyana, a master of brāhmaṇical lore, was asked whether he had wandered about as a *paribbājaka* (to complete his education) "*Caritaṃ kho pana bhotā Assalāyanena paribbājakaṃ; ma bhavaṃ Assalāyano ayuddhaparājitaṃ parājayīti.*" See also Dr. Barua's *Pre-Buddhistic Indian Philosophy*, p. 192.

nassa, Saccaka, and a host of others signifies a good record of Buddha's success in conversion among the *paribbājakas* and the religious orders both brāhmaṇical and non-brāhmaṇical. Dhammika upāsaka in the *Sutta-Nipāta* was right in saying that the disputing *titthiyas*, Ājīvakas, Nigaṇṭhas, many of whom were aged, submitted to the captivating power of Buddha's exposition of his religion[1]. The influx of converts from the aforesaid classes was so great that Buddha had to introduce a bar to a ready ingress of undesirable men into the order by laying down that those who belonged to a religious order must pass a period of probation for four months[2].

Ways of preaching.

(e) The dialectic method of preaching was adopted by Buddha very frequently. This method had a great resemblance to Socratic dialogues. At the beginning of his discourse, he tried to have an idea of the leanings of the persons by putting to them questions on religious matters or answering the questions that he allowed them to put to himself. In this way he used to select a subject most suited to the occasion and agreeable

1 *Sutta Nipāta*, p. 67.

2 *Majjh. Nik.*, I, p. 391 ; *Vinaya*, I, p. 69.

to the persons composing the audience and delivered a discourse on same. He preferred to use the popular dialect as the medium of his discourse. Similes, parables, fables very often drawn from experiences of every day life were interspersed with his speeches along with pithy verses to make his arguments sweet and effective[1]. He attached great importance to the art of preaching and tried to impress upon the minds of his disciples the sense of its importance. The particular features by which his speeches were rendered so very impressive were, first because he utilized his higher knowledge *abhiññā*, by which he could find out the persons who would benefit by his discourses on a particular day ; secondly because the selection of the subjects of his discourses was the result of a correct diagnosis (*sanidāna*) of the mentality of the listeners[2] ; and thirdly because he utilized his occult powers (*pāṭihāriya*) in three ways, viz. *iddhis* (the *ṛddhis* of the Hindu Yogaśāstras) which impressed his audience with awe at the sight of manifestation of powers ostensibly in transgression of the physical laws ;

1 Dr. Oldenberg's *Buddha* (Hoey's trans.) pp. 185-193.

2 *Divyāvadāna*, pp. 96, 124: "*Āśayānuśayaṃ viditvā dhātuṃ prakṛtiṃ ca jñātvā tādṛśi dharmadeśanā kṛtā*".

ādesanā or the exhibition of his power of thought-reading; and *anusāsani* or the warning to a person to give up his discursive or evil thoughts revealed to Buddha through thought-reading[1].

Buddha foresaw the abuses incidental to the cultivation and use of such powers by his disciples, for many of them might be in a lower plane of spiritual culture and utilize them for selfish ends. To avoid such abuses, he strictly enjoined his disciples not to display such powers before the householders[2]. In the opinion of Buddha, a good preacher should conform to the following rules :—

(a) He should in ordinary discourses before householders make them gradual i. e. commence with *dānakathaṃ*, *sīlakathaṃ*, etc[3].

(b) Observe sequence (*pariyāyadassāvī*) in the details composing a theme;

(c) Use words of compassion (*anuddayataṃ paṭicca kathaṃ*).

(d) Avoid irrelevant matters (*nāmisantara kathaṃ*) and

1 *Aṅg. Nik.*, I, p. 276; *Dīgh. Nik.*, I, pp. 212-214.

2 *Vinaya*, II, p. 112; *na bhikkhave gihinaṃ uttarimanussadhammaṃ iddhipāṭihāriyaṃ dassetabbaṃ.*

3 See *ante*, pp. 47, 48.

(e) Make his speeches free from caustic remarks against others[1].

VIII. Patronage of kings, clans and others.

In the 5th century B. C. there was no paramount sovereingnty in Northern India which was divided into a large number of independent states. Of these, the four monarchies of Magadha, Kosala, Vatsa, and Avanti rose into importance and fought with one another for the conquest of places in the possession of the smaller states[2]. The number of preachers of various religions, working in all these domains, was large and the more prominent among them vied with one another for gaining the support of one or other of the several kings. There are passages in the Buddhist scriptures hinting that Buddha was anxious to enlist the sympathy and patronage of kings, clans, and noblemen in support of his religion. The story of the conversion of Malla Roja, a nobleman, shows explicitly the anxiety felt by Buddha on this score. When Buddha was entering the city of the Mallas, Malla Roja went to welcome him, not out of reverence but for avoiding the liability of paying a fine laid down by the

1 *Ang. Nik.*, III, pp. 184, 196.

2 Dr. Rhys Davids' *Buddhist India*, p. 3.

Mallas for those who refused to welcome Buddha. When he came near Buddha, he spoke out to Ānanda his real feeling at which the latter became sorrowful and requested Buddha to work upon the mind of Malla Roja in such a way as to make him one of his ardent adherents, because he was a distinguished nobleman whose influence and example would go a great way towards making Buddhism popular in the locality. Buddha agreed and overcame the indifferent attitude of Malla Roja by exercising the feeling of love (*mettā*), whereby he was won over to the doctrine[1]. Though we do not come across any express passage in the *Sutta Piṭaka* showing that Buddha is acting with a similar motive to any of the royal personages, his direction to his disciples in the *Vinaya Piṭaka* to fix the day of commencement of the *vassāvāsa* in compliance with the wishes of Bimbisāra on a particular occasion points to the same inference[2].

The first king met by Buddha after his enlightenment was the Magadhan king Bimbisāra who accorded him a very warm welcome, placed at Buddha's disposal his pleasure-garden and asked the headmen of the villages in his

1 *Vinaya*, Mahāvagga, VI, 36, 1-4.

2 *Ibid.*, III, 4.

domain to listen to Buddha's discourses. It was most probably for Bimbisāra that Buddha gained a very wide popularity in Magadha[1]. The king was bent so much upon the welfare of the *saṅgha* that he issued the decree that none must do any harm to the Sākyaputtiya samanas[2] and on many occasions he advised Buddha to frame rules for the welfare of the *saṅgha.* Some of these rules are, for example, not to give ordination to those who were in royal service, as the kings who were not in favour of the faith might harass the *saṅgha* on that ground[3]; to hold religious assemblies on the 8th, 14th and 15th day of each month like the other religious orders for the benefit of the *upāsakas*[4].

Bimbisāra of Magadha.

Pasenadi was also a great benefactor of Buddha and his *saṅgha*, but he does not seem to have given his unqualified support like Bimbisāra. Though he supported many brāhmaṇa teachers, yet his attention to the welfare of Buddha and his *saṅgha* was not less than that shown to those

Pasenadi of Kosala.

1 *Mahāvastu*, III, p. 449.
2 *Vinaya*, MV., I, 42, 1.
3 *Ibid.*, I, 40, 4.
4 *Ibid.*, II, 1-4 ; see *infra.*

teachers. His anxiety to make a suitable gift to Ananda[1], his joy at the conversion of the robber Aṅgulimāla who was given immunity for his past misdeeds and was promised a supply of the requisites for a monk[2]; his earnest desire to marry a Sākya princess and his ultimate marriage with Vāsabhakhattiyā to regain the confidence of the monks lost through inattentions to them[3] ; his expression of pride at the fact that he was of the same age with Buddha and belonged to the same caste and province with him[4] amply show his love for the religion and his desire to be counted as one of its well-wishers and supporters. In the *Nikāyas* it is stated that he became a lay-devotee and an ardent admirer of Buddha.[5] The bas-relief depicting him as proceeding to meet Buddha shows that he was respected by the Buddhists of the 2nd or 3rd century B. C. as a patron of the religion.

It is doubtful how far Buddha was successful

1 *Majjh. Nik.*, II, p. 116.

2 *Ibid*, II, p. 101.

3 Burlingame's *Buddhist Legends*, I, p. 91.

4 *Majjh. Nik.*, II, p. 124.

5 *Sam. Nik.*, I, p. 70; *Aṅg. Nik.*, V, p p. 65 ff; see also *Divyāvaadāna*, p. 154.

in winning over the other two monarchs, Pajjota of Avanti and Udena of Kosambī. The references to these kings in the Buddhist scriptures are few and far between. It is said that king Pajjota once sent Mahākaccāyana to welcome Buddha to his dominion, but Buddha, thinking his purpose would be better served by Mahākaccāyana himself preaching the doctrine, did not accede to the king's request. The king was satisfied with Mahākaccāyana's exposition of the Law and became an ardent follower of the religion[1]. The *Saṃyutta Nikāya*[2] and the Tibetan translation of the *Vinaya*[3] state that king Udena of Kosambī became a convert to Buddhism. The *Dhammapadaṭṭhakathā* gives in detail the occasion of king Udena's conversion. He was much impressed by the piety of one of his queens Sāmāvatī who had been an upāsikā of Buddha and at whose request the king became a convert to the religion and made generous gifts[4]. Evidence is not strong that these two kings actively aided the spread of

Caṇḍa Pajjota of Avanti aud Udena of Kosambī.

1 *Psalms of the Brethren*, pp. 238-9.

2 *Saṃ. Nik.*, IV, p. 113.

3 Rockhill's *Life of the Buddha*, p. 74.

4 Burlingame's *Buddhist Legends*, I, p. 84.

Buddhism but yet it is a great gain that they did not actively oppose its propagation. The mere tolerance of the activities of the Buddhist preachers within their kingdoms should be taken as a favourable circumstance in the spread of the religion.

Support from influential men.

Buddha was successful in making a large number of converts from among the nobles, ministers, bankers and wealthy citizens. That the enlistment of the supports of Anāthapiṇḍika, Visākhā, Sīha, Abhayarājakumāra, Jīvaka, Yasa, Ambapālī, Nandaka, etc., furthered the cause of Buddhism to a very great extent needs hardly any comment.

Last but not the least was the support obtained by Buddha from the various clans of the period[1]. Inspite of the fact that Mahāvīra had already been in the field and obtained a footing among the clans, Buddha was fairly successful in his missionary activities. It was not very difficult for Buddha to win over the Sākyas because he himself was of the clan. Anuruddha, Kimbila, Bhagu, Ānanda, Devadatta, Nanda, Upāli and many other Sākyas joined the order at Buddha's request. Under the leadership of

1 For detailed treatment, see infra. V.

Mahāpajāpati Gotamī[1], many Sākyan ladies also followed the example of the Sākyan youths and joined the order leading to the growth of the order of nuns.

The Licchavis and the Mallas.

Next to the Sākyas, the Licchavis and the Mallas came under the influence of Buddha's teaching. Buddha paid three visits to Vesāli, the city of the Licchavis, and by his preachings brought home to them the charm of Buddhism. He converted many distinguished members of the clan and obtained from them gifts of *cetiyas.*[2] His work among the Mallas was also successful. It was perhaps as a token of favour to the faithful Mallas that Buddha selected Kusinārā, a *upavana* within their country, as a suitable place for his *mahāparinibbāna.*[3]

The Bhaggas and the Koliyas.

Buddha's missionary activity among the Bhaggas and the Koliyas was not perhaps so successful as among the previously stated clans. Buddha visited three nigamas of the Koliyas, and Ānanda one, but there is a remarkable paucity in the number of the converts mentioned

1 *Majjh. Nik.*, I, p. 462; *S.B.E.*, XIX, pp. 226-227.
2 *Dīgh. Nik.,* II, p. 102.
3 *Ibid.,* II, p. 169.

as hailing from those places.[1] Still less successful was Buddha's religious mission to the Bhaggas. The only place that was visited by Buddha was the Bhesakalāvana deer-park near Suṃsumāragiri and the persons won over were Nakula's parents and Bodhirājakumāra[2].

We do not hear of other clans coming under the influence of Buddhism except in the statement of the *Mahāparinibbāna Suttanta* that the Bulis of Allakappa and the Moriyas of Pipphalivana along with the clans already mentioned claimed Buddha's relics for erecting stūpas in their respective countries.

Thus we see that Buddhism owed much of its expansion to Buddha's ability in securing sympathy and patronage of kings, nobles, and clans, who in many cases had already been supporting other religions. Though later in the field, Buddhism could supplant at times the other religions, ultimately monopolising the sympathy and support of some of the magnates.

The part played by women[3] in the spread

1 Kakkarapaṭṭaṃ, Haliddavāsanaṃ, Uttaraṃ, and Sāpugaṃ.

2 *Majjh. Nik.*, II, p. 91.

3 I am indebted to Dr. B. M. Barua for suggesting this point.

of Buddhism cannot be ignored or brushed aside as of little importance. On many occasions it was through their influence that whole families were converted to Buddhism. Visākhā and Ambapālī, for instance, rendered signal services to the *saṅgha* by their munificent gifts and the former's work was more valuable because she became the means of conversion of all the members of her father-in-law's family from Jainism to Buddhism. Anāthapiṇḍika's daughter made it possible through her exertions to establish a centre of Buddhism in Aṅga through the conversion of the whole of her father-in-law's family[1]. The conversion of king Udena was effected through one of her queens named Sāmāvatī[2]. It was with the help of the brāhmaṇa girls of Sākya family married at Bhadramukha that Buddha could convert Meṇḍaka gahapati[3]. Instances like this can be multiplied to show that ladies helped a good deal in the propagation of Buddhism.

ix. Part played by ladies in the spread of Buddhism.

The formation of the order of nuns was highly appreciated by the womenfolk generally, while at

1 Kern's *Manual of Indian Buddhism*, pp. 37-38.
2 See *ante*, pp. 72-3.
3 *Divyāvadāna*, p. 128.

the same time it furthered the cause of Buddhism to a great extent. Not only did it afford relief to many a woman in her knawing miseries but it also recognised the dignified position in which the women had claim to be placed along with the men through the implication that they were as much eligible to the making of efforts for spiritual emancipation as the males. Those of the nuns who could enter into the mysteries of the religion naturally felt an inclination to initiate others into the same mysteries and offer them a permanent solace in their lives. They like the bhikkhus visited the householders and through their easy access to the ladies of the houses had greater opportunities of working upon their impressionable minds and enlisting them either as lay-devotees or nuns. Conversions of this nature were frequent and there are examples in the *Therigāthā* of women becoming nuns through the exertions of the advanced bhikkhunīs. The bhikkhunīs thus carried the light of the new religion from house to house and helped the spread of Buddhism far and wide.

The last factor but not the least was the resort to occult powers to bring conviction home to the minds of the unconvinced and make them converts. In writing of the spread of a religion, or the life of a founder of a religion, scholars, as a rule, leave this factor out of account, as it is not looked upon as in keeping with the standpoint of the present-day material sciences. It may be said that if once the possession and use of the occult powers be admitted and believed, there will be no criterion by which to sift out the actual expression of the occult powers from the fiction with which the credulous writers would in course of time mix them up, and in consequence, the grossest absurdities will have credence. But apart from the question as to which of the exhibitions of such powers are to be believed and which to be disbelieved, the point that has to be settled is whether it is reasonable to leave altogether out of account a factor without which there would certainly be left a gap in the aggregate of causes that are responsible for the degree and range of influence of a particular religion at a particular time. We often notice in the account of the life of the founder of a religion or its branch that mere disputations, mere appeals to the intellect and reason often fail to convince a person of the truth of a statement or the power of the arguer to lead to the path that takes one to the *summum bonum* of human life. Argumentators, however powerful, are often found to cause bitterness of

X. Resort to occult powers.

feeling unless they are aided by other factors including the one under discussion. An exemplary character, a persuasive tongue, acuteness of intellignece, self-abnegation and other elements that make a strong and imposing personality are not sufficient to produce the results that were actually achieved by the founders of religions like Christ, Buddha, Muhammad, and others. A single leper healed by the mere touch of Christ, the power of vision restored to a single blind man are more effective in the spread of a religion than numberless victories in disputations. But such powers are disbelieved by us of this material age, the age of the predominance of the physical sciences and the general ignorance of the spiritual. In the life of Buddha, we meet with many cases where mere arguments failed to achieve the desired ends, and ultimately, resort was had to occult powers. It should not be supposed that I am advocating belief in the existence of such powers as the result of my credulity. I have not, on the other hand, the least objection to making the rules of criticism for keeping facts apart from fiction as stringent as possible. What I want to contend for is that a most powerful factor in the spread of a religion should not be left out of account, and the rest of the factors put forward as sufficient to produce the results achieved by its founder and his disciples within a particular period. The influence of the mere fact that occult powers are possessed and used by a certain preacher high in spiritual culture goes a great way in disarming opposition to him. I do not speak of the details in which such powers may be manifested, for the descriptions of such details offer opportunities for mixing fiction with facts. I am only speaking of the fact of mere possession of such powers and their use within the limits natural to the laws governing their use; for the powers obtained as special gifts of nature, or acquired by *sādhana* (spiritual devotion and discipline) have to work through the human frame, which by its own limitations naturally obstructs and limits the expression of the powers. India has been noted for ages as the land of those who are adepts in spiritual matters. *Yoga* and *sādhana* have nowhere been so much cultured as in this country. The treatises on these methods of *sādhana* from Patañjali downwards speak of certain occult powers as naturally acquired by the true *sādhakas*. The assertions of these works are put aside by scholars trained in the western methods of criticism and acquainted merely with the laws of the material world laid down in the works on the physical sciences. But utterly ignorant as they are of these matters, they do not hesitate to speak as authorities on spiritual matters, and as ignorance of these things is the order of the day, they naturally have a large following. So long as the West does not see eye to eye with the East in this respect and researches do not settle it definitely how far to believe and how far to disbelieve, it is certainly risky to try to sift the truth from fiction in the details furnished by the scriptures; but the position may yet be thus far clear to some intimate with the life of any of the few Indian *sādhakas* of the true stamp that the possession and use of the occult powers are not an unreality and their influence as a factor in the spread of religion is not less if not greater than any other.

III

Magadha

It will be evident from what has been said in the previous section[1] that Magadha was a suitable place for the origin and development of non-brāhmaṇic religions like Buddhism. If we look back to the remote period when it was known as Kīkaṭa, it was even then considered by the orthodox brāhmaṇas as wanting in sanctity and unsuitable for the performance of sacrifices. It shows that it was for a long time disliked by the orthodox brāhmaṇas as a place of habitation and therefore its inhabitants lived in comparative freedom from brāhmaṇic orthodoxy. Hence it is that we find in the *Majjhima Nikāya*[2] that Sakuludāyi paribbājaka is telling Buddha that in ancient times Magadha 'seethed with sophistic discussions. That this country was a centre of intellectual activity is evident from the *Sāmaññaphala* account of king Ajātasattu's interview with six sophistic

1 See *ante*, pp. 36-38.
2 *Majjh. Nik.*, II p. 2.

teachers"[1]. The attraction of the country for non-brāhmaṇic religious teachers was heightened by reason of the fact that it was not only suitable for free expression of religious views but also for the advantages offered by it for the propagation of those views among a large number of people who naturally went there on account of its political importance. The *Brahmajālasutta* which was delivered by Buddha at Rājagaha gives us a panoramic view of the various doctrines prevailing at the time. Many of the doctrines might be classed as brāhmaṇic while the rest were non-brāhmaṇic. I mention below the names of a few adherents of brāhmaṇic and non-brāhmaṇic doctrines, having their abodes at Rājagaha. The brāhmaṇic religious teacher Rudraka Rāmaputra had his āśrama at the place. Prince Siddhārtha became one of his disciples at the commencement of his renunciation, and practised under his guidance self-mortifications along with the disciples of Rudraka[2]. Sañjaya Belaṭṭhaputta, a teacher of

Existence of a number of both brāhmaṇic and non-brāhmaṇic religious views in Magadha.

1 Dr. Barua's *Pre-Buddhistic Indian Philosophy*, p. 281.

2 *Mahāvastu*, II, p. 207; Watters, *Yuan Chwang*, II, p. 142.

non-brāhmaṇic doctrines, had also his āśrama there with Sāriputta and Moggalāna as his chief disciples[1]. There was again the brāhmaṇical teacher Kūṭadanta maintained by grants of villages from Bimbisāra[2]. He used to perform sacrifices on grand scales, killing hundreds of animal victims on the occasions. There was no lack of teachers believing that supernatural powers and heavenly happiness could be obtained through rigorous ascetic practices[3]. The *Sāmaññaphala* and other *suttas*[4] make it clear that the distinguished teachers of non-brāhmaṇic doctrines viz. Purāṇa Kassapa, Ajita Kesakambalin, Makkhali Gosāla, Pakudha Kaccāyana, and Nigaṇṭha Nātaputta with their disciples dwelt in different parts of Magadha from time to time. The noteworthy fact, not of course peculiar to Magadha, is that the monarch viz. Bimbisāra and Ajātasattu were tolerant to both brāhmaṇic and non-brāhmaṇic cults, and extended their patronage to the brāhmaṇa teachers quite as much as to the Buddhist and Jaina monks,

1 *Vinaya*, I, pp. 39ff.

2 *Dīgh. Nik.*, I, pp. 127ff.

3 For details, see *Buddhist India*, pp. 140-146; Dr. Barua's *Pre-Buddhistic Indian Philosophy*, pp. 188ff.

4 *Dīgh. Nik.*, I, pp. 47ff; *Majjh. Nik.*, II, 2ff.

by virtue of which they all claimed the sovereigns as their devoted followers[1].

Thus we see that Buddha had to encounter the opposition of a large number of sects but fortunately he had this advantage that there were several sects whose views were far from the brāhmaṇic standpoint. This was however but as a few rays of light in the gloom of opposition that darkened the path of progress and hindered him in his onward march. He had phenomenal success in the brāhmaṇa villages of Khānumata and Ekānālā where he could win over to his side two renowned brāhmaṇas Kūṭadanta and Kasibharadvāja[2]. The piṭakas, though silent on Buddha's failure, mention as an example of Buddha's triumph over Māra, that in the brāhmaṇa village Pañcasālā, he could not obtain a single spoonful of rice in his begging round[3]. From this we get a glimpse into the volume of opposition that Buddha had to encounter on certain occasions. There are also in

Buddha and the brāhmaṇas.

1 *Ind. Ant.*, XLV, p. 12; *Dīgh. Nik*, I, pp. 114, 127.

2 *Dīgh. Nik.*, I, pp. 117ff.; *Saṃ. Nik.*, I, pp. 172, 173; *Sutta Nipāta*, p. 13.

3 *Saṃ. Nik.*, I, p. 114.

the *Nikāyas* passing allusions to the frivolous grounds on which his opponents wanted to make his path thorny. Some brāhmaṇas, for instance, tried to rouse oppositions to him by saying that Buddha was wanting in reverence towards the aged brāhmaṇas and claimed superiority over them[1]. Buddha had also to meet with opposition from the influential brāhmaṇas e.g. the minister of Ajātasattu who instigated other members of his caste to alienate the people from Buddha by saying broadcast that all the blessings that man desired could be had from them and they need not seek Buddha's help in the matter[2]. It was through his personality, his appealing way of preaching a rational *dhamma*, his ability in disputations with the brāhmaṇas and laying bare their weak points, and his firm stand against the abuses of belief and religion prevailing at the time that he could win over people including many brāhmaṇas to his side.

The resistance, offered by the non-brāhmaṇical sects, many of whose objects and methods of spiritual training were akin to those of Buddhism, was in no way less than that of the brāhmaṇas. I have, of course, in mind the intensity of the

1 *Sutta Nipāta*, p. 50.
2 *Avadāna Śataka*, pp. 83, 84.

feeling of opposition that the members of the different sects entertained towards the new rival sect. But as the followers of brāhmaṇic religion were far too many in comparison with those of the non-brāhmaṇic sects, the chances of Buddha and his disciples coming into collision with them were much greater than with those of the aforesaid sects. The episodes of Buddha meeting with opposition from the members of the other religious sects have this peculiar feature about them that the opposition from the non-brāhmaṇic sects exceeds in many cases the limits of mere verbal disputations rising up to resorts to practical make-shifts for blackening Buddha's character, while the opposition from the members of brāhmaṇic sects did not, as a rule, cross the said limits.

Buddha and Sañjaya Belaṭṭhaputta.

Sañjaya Belaṭṭhaputta, the centre of whose activities was at Rājagaha, was the first non-brāhmaṇic religious teacher to feel the power of the religion preached by Buddha for within a very short time he saw that half of his following had been won over to Buddha's side. It was Assaji, a disciple of Buddha, who commenced the onslaught by converting Sāriputta, the principal follower of Sañjaya to Buddhism, and Sāriputta in his turn followed him up until half of his quondam fellow disciples embraced Buddhism. This event together with the previous conversions made by Buddha and his followers created in Magadha a sensation which served as the basis of the remark found in the *Vinaya* that Buddha took into his order 1000 Jaṭilas, 250 followers of Sañjaya, and the sons of distinguished Magadhan families, thereby making the families sonless and the wives husbandless, and there was no knowing who might be taken in next[1].

Buddha and Nigaṇṭha-Nātaputta.

Nigaṇṭha Nātaputta was a formidable rival of Buddha, and as he was at work earlier than Buddha, he made a fair progress in the spread of his religion in Magadha and the neighbouring states. It appears from the accounts of conversions to Buddhism that Buddha could not convert the followers of Nātaputta in large numbers, as he did the followers of other cults. But he stole a march upon Nātaputta by being able to enlist among his *upāsakas* Bimbisāra and Ajātasattu who had been lay-supporters of Nātaputta[2]. Though a religion

1 *Vinaya*, I, pp. 39-44.

2 The Jaina *āgamas* claim Bimbisāra and Ajātasattu as Jainas while the Buddhist *piṭakas* declare them as Buddhists. Neither the Jaina nor the Buddhist litera-

spreads irrespective of the social or political position of the people, the spread of religion is facilitated by the conversion of influential people, because, after all, the masses at times follow in such matters the example of leaders held by them in high esteem, for they lack in many cases the capacity to judge the merit of two rival religions which agitate the country. The importance of the conversion of Bimbisāra to Buddhism will appear from what he did for it. He continued to be its warm supporter and allowed one of his queens

ture admits that they were supporters of the religions at different times or at the same time in different degrees. The facts of the lives of the two emperors, however, point to the inference that Bimbisāra supported Jainism when it appeared on the field but inclined decidedly towards Buddhism when it asserted itself as a rival of Jainism. Ajātasattu was a supporter of Devadatta who initiated a sect holding views similar to Jainism so far as its discipline was concerned. Abhayarājakumara, a Jaina, expostulated with Buddha for condemning Devadatta. This shows that Devadatta had Jaina sympathies and Ajātasattu by supporting him shows the nature of his religious views. He, however, was converted to Buddhism a year before Buddha's parinibbāṇa (Mr. V. A. Smith's *Early History of India*, p. 33).

not only to be an upāsikā but also later on a nun[1]. He persuaded his subjects to become lay-devotees of Buddha, paved the way for the conversion of Rudrāyaṇa, king of Roruka[2], made a gift of the Veluvana garden to the Buddhist order for use as a resort of bhikkhus and gave advice to Buddha in regard to the framing of some of the *Vinaya* rules. So great was his confidence in Buddha that he did not allow a competition of miraculous powers between Buddha and some of the teachers of non-brāhmaṇical sects who requested him to arrange for it. These teachers were afterwards defeated by Buddha at a competition which was arranged by Pasenadi, king of Kosala, at their request[3]. Buddha had occasions to enter into discussion with four distinguished disciples of Nātaputta at Nālandā which was a stronghold of Jainism. These four disciples were Abhayarājakumāra[4], Asibandhakaputta gāmaṇī, Upāli, and Dīgha-

1 *Psalms of the Sisters*, pp. 81, 82; *Manorathapūraṇī*, I, p. 345.

2 *Divyāvadāna*, pp. 550ff.

3 Ibid., pp. 143ff; Prof. Kern's *Manual*, p. 33.

4 *Majjh. Nik.*, I, p. 392.: Prince Abhaya was one of the chief patrons of Nigaṇṭha Nātaputta's order (Dr. Barua, *op. cit.*, p. 375).

tapassī[1]. With the exception of the last named ascetic, the rest were, as the result of the disputations, converted to Buddhism[2]. So far as Buddha's missionary work among the Jainas is concerned, the above account records the very limited success that he was able to achieve.

Buddha and the remaining four non-brāhmaṇical teachers.

Instances of conversion to Buddhism as a result of Buddha's activity among the followers of the remaining four non-brāhmaṇical teachers are wanting in the *Nikāyas*, but that Buddha was not inattentive to recruiting his followers from among the disciples of these teachers appears from the fact that the religious doctrines held by them were criticised in detail by Buddha. Many of the *suttas* contain such criticisms, which show that there was a movement set afloat by Buddha against the activity of the four teachers viz. Pakudha Kaccāyana, Makkhali Gosāla, Ajitakesakambalī and Purāṇa Kassapa[3]. These criticisms are often found as side-issues on Buddha's discussions

1 *Saṃ. Nik.*, IV, p. 317.

2 *Majjh. Nik.*, I, p. 371.

3 For a detailed treatment of the doctrines of the four teachers, see Dr. Barua's *Pre-Buddhistic Indian Philosophy*, chs. XVIII, XIX, XX, XXI.

with his own disciples, and with men who used to come to him with the object of getting religious light from him or defeating him in disputation. Abhayarājakumāra, for instance, defined Purāṇa Kassapa's doctrines in course of his conversation with Buddha who had thus an occasion to criticise them[1]. Similarly Ānanda once referred to the classification of beings made by Makkhali Gosāla but Buddha convinced him of the hollowness of such classification[2].

Buddha's missionary activities in Magadha.

We have so far dealt with the volume and nature of opposition met with by Buddha in the different places in Magadha. I am now delineating Buddha's activities in Magadha in connection with the propagation of his religion as recorded in the Buddhist scriptures. The places which have been recorded as the scenes of his religious propaganda in Magadha are Gayā, Uruvela, Rājagaha and its suburbs Nālandā, Pāṭaliputta, Dakkhiṇāgiri, Andhakavinda, and Kallavālamuttagāma.

Bodh-Gaya is in the eye of a Buddhist

1 *Saṃ. Nik.*, V, p. 128.

2 *Aṅg. Nik.*, III, pp. 383ff; see Dr. Barua, *op. cit.* p. 278.

the most sacred place on the earth, as it was the birth-place of the religion which became almost pan-Asiatic in later times. Buddha's missionary work proper was started at Benares a sketch of which has been given elsewhere. It was when he visited Gayā after finishing his first activities at Benares that we find Buddha carrying on his missionary work at this place. Uruvela, a village in the suburb of Gayā, was the stronghold of the Jaṭilas, an order of brāhmaṇical ascetics. As these ascetics were very difficult to be weaned from the cults in which they had placed implicit faith, it is said that Buddha was put to the necessity of exhibiting miraculous powers to soften their minds in his favour, though he was extremely reluctant to make use of these powers if it could be helped. After preparing his ground in this way, he tried to explain to them the efficacy of following the truth that he had discovered. This explanation shook the foundation of their beliefs to a great extent, though of course, their minds required to be worked up a little further before they could be fully converted[1]. They accompanied Buddha to Gayāsīsa where he delivered

Gayā.

1 *Vinaya*, I, pp. 34, 35.

the discourse *Adittapariyāyaṃ* (Fire Sermon) intended to explain to the Jaṭilas that the *summum bonum* which they wanted to attain through fire-worship could be had not through the worship of fire but through the extinction of fires of *rāga, dosa,* and *moha* kindled by the action of the sense-organs on the objects of those senses. The Jaṭilas after hearing this discourse gave up their cults and joined the order initiated by Buddha as bhikkhus. It was with these bhikkhus and the sixty one converts recruited at Benares and its neighbourhood that Buddha created a sensation at Rājagaha where he went next.

Rājagaha.

On the occasion of Buddha's first visit to Rājagaha in the second year after Enlightenment, he stayed at Laṭṭhivana, five miles from the town. It was here that Bimbisāra with his ministers, courtiers, and village-headmen came to meet him. Buddha's youthful appearance led them to think that he was a disciple of the hoary-headed Uruvelakassapa who had been the leader of the Jaṭilas, and accompanied Buddha to Laṭṭhivana. But Uruvelakassapa's homage to Buddha in their presence belied their impression. The youthful Buddha with his sonorous voice explained the first principles of Buddhism, the *anicca* (transitoriness) and *anattā* (absence of permanent essence) of the five *skandhas* (constituents of being), and brought home to the mind of the Emperor and his attendants that the religion preached by Buddha had excellences, by virtue of which it could lay claim of superiority to other religions of the time[1].

The importance of Rājagaha from the point of view of missionary work was very great. It was a great resort of religious teachers and wanderers (*paribbājakas*) who used to come to the city usually in the company of the traders who supplied them with food and raiment in their journey from distant places. The city was moreover situated at the junction of several trade-routes facilitating communication and transit of messages to and from distant places. This made it extremely important for the propagation of the truths that Buddha wanted to preach broadcast. Over and above these, the city provided other advantages, valuable for a religious organizer, viz. of entering into disputations with the religieaux and asserting the superiority of the religion by defeating them ; of setting on a sound footing the organization by

1 *Mahāvastu*, III, p 441 ; *Vinaya*, I, 22, 1-2 ; Watters' *Yuan Chwang*, II, p. 146 ; Rockhill's *Life of the Buddha*, pp. 42, 43.

which the bhikkhus could pursue the ideals, secure from cares for the bare needs of their lives ; and of establishing suitable hermitages for the monks in the caves of the surrounding hills so convenient for deep thinking and the pursuit of *yoga*. The description of the hills with their hermitages requires a little elaboration in view of their importance in the history of the spread of Buddhism. The highest of the hills called the Vultures' Peak (*Gijjhakūṭa-pabbata*)[1] was a favourite resort of Buddha. In the first few years after Enlightenment, he spent his time frequently at this place with some of his distinguished disciples, viz. Sāriputta, Moggalāna, Mahākassapa, Anuruddha, Puṇṇa Mantāniputta, Upāli, Ānanda, and Devadatta, delivering discourses and imparting them necessary training for their spiritual progress and missionary works. To facilitate communication with Buddha and his disciples, Bimbisāra made a road from the foot to the top of the hill[2]. The peak was the scene of the nefarious attempts of Devadatta supported by Ajātasattu to kill Buddha for not putting

1 For its identification, see *Arch. Surv. Report*, 1905-6 ; Mr. Cunningham identifies it with Śailagiri (*Anc. Geo.* p. 466).

2 Watters' *Yuan Chwang*, II, p. 151.

him in charge of a body of monks, as he did in regard to Sāriputta and Moggalāna.

Cave-dwellings.

Besides the hermitages on the Vultures' Peak, there were ten other abodes of bhikkhus on the hills surrounding Rājagaha[1] viz.,

(1) Corapapāta (the precipice whence robbers were flung to death);

(2) Isigilipasse Kālasilā (the black rock[2] by the side of the Ṛṣi-giri)[3];

(3) Vebhārapasse Sattapaṇṇiguhā (where the first Buddhist Synod was held);

(4) Sītavana Sappasoṇḍikapabbhāra (the cave situated in a hill infested with snakes

1 *Dīgh. Nik.*, II, pp. 116, 263; *Vinaya*, II, p. 76; see D. N. Sen's *Rājagṛha in the Buddhist Scriptures* in the *Report of the Second Oriental Conference*, pp. 613-624 and *Sites in Rajgir* in the *J. B. O. R. S.*, Vol. IV.

2 Watters' *Yuan Chwang*, II, p. 155. The Chinese pilgrims refer to the cases of religious suicide commited here, said to have been approved by Buddha. Cf. *Sam. Nik.*, III, pp. 119-124; IV, pp. 55-60; V, p 320.

3 The name Ṛsi-giri was transformed into Isi-gili which was supposed to have been derived from the fact that the hill devoured (*gila* = to devour) the ascetics i. e. those ascetics who entered it never returned, so congenial the place was to them (*Majjh. Nik.*, III, pp. 68ff.)

and near the crematorium called Sītavana which Buddha used to visit with his disciples for passing some time at the place as part of the spiritual training of his disciples[1]. From the nature of this hermitage it would appear that it was specially suited to those monks who took up the *sosānika-dhutaṅga* i. e. practising *samādhi* on a cremation-ground for their spiritual uplift;

(5) Gomata-kandara;

(6) Tinduka (the cave deriving its name from the Tinduka trees '*Diospyrus Embryopetris*');

(7) Tapoda-kandara (*Tapoda* = hot spring);

(8) Tapodārāma[2];

(9) Indasālaguhā[3] where Buddha delivered the Sakkapañha-sutta (No. 21) of the *Dīgha Nikāya*;

(10) Pipphali-guhā named after Pipphali mānava, the former name of Mahākassapa who used to stay here[4].

1 *Divyāvadāna*, p. 268.

2 Hot springs still exist there, see *Arch. Sur. Rep.* 1904-5.

3 Watters' *Yuan Chwang*, II, p. 173.

4 *Manorathapūraṇī*, I, p. 175; *Psalms of the Brethren*, p. 363.

These hill hermitages could not provide sufficient accommodation for all the monks staying at Rājagaha. For this reason as also out of love for solitude, many monks dwelt in *araññа-kūṭikas* (leaf-sheds) in the jungles on the hills[1]. Dabba Mallaputta was entrusted with the charge of grouping the monks according to their subjects of study or methods of spiritual discipline, and of allotting to them suitable residences.

Araññа-kūṭikas.

Though Buddha accepted the Veluvana Kalandakanivāpa[2] from Bimbisāra and resided there very often, the Vinaya rules did not yet allow the monks to have any residences specially made for them by the laity. A seṭṭhi of Rājagaha felt for this inconvenience of the Buddhist monks and enquired whether it would be objectionable to them if he built monasteries (*vihāras*) for their use. He was told that up till now the monks had not been permitted by Buddha to have such *vihāras*. They had to dwell in "the woods, at the foot of trees, on hill-sides in grottoes, in mountain caves, in cemetries,

1 *Majjh. Nik.*, III, p. 217; *Jātakas*, III, pp. 33, 71; V. p. 176.

2 For a description of the Veluvana monastery, see Mr. D. N. Sen, *op. cit.*

in forests, in open plains, and in heaps of straw" (*arañña, rukkhamūla, pabbata, kandara, giriguhā susāna, vanapattha, ajjhokāsa, and palālapuñja*)[1]. This question raised by the query of the seṭṭhi was put up before Buddha, who thenceforward permitted the monks to use with some restrictions five sorts of residences viz. *vihāra, aḍḍhayoga, pāsāda, hammiya, guhā* (monastery, cottage, storied dwelling, attics, cave)[2]. When Buddha allowed the monks to live in *vihāras* given by the lay-devotees, the latter commenced building them in large numbers.

Notable vihāras given by the laity.

Three such *vihāras* in the suburbs of Rājagaha are often mentioned in the Buddhist scriptures viz., Veluvana, Jīvaka-ambavana, and Maddakucchi migadāya. The first *vihāra* was presented by Bimbisāra on the occasion of Buddha's first entrance into Rājagaha, the second by Jīvaka in the twentieth *vassa* of Buddha's ministry, and the third very probably by a Madda prince when Mahākappina was ordained as a monk[3].

1 *S. B. E.*, XX, p. 157; *Vinaya*, II, p. 146.

2 *S. B. E.*, XIII, pp. 173, 174 and fn.; *Vinaya*, II, p. 146.

3 Mahākappina's wife was a Madda princess,

Buddha's followers at the time of his visit to Rājagaha were the five brāhmaṇa ascetics converted at Sārnāth, Yasa with his fifty four companions, the thirty Bhaddavaggiya youths and three Kassapa brothers with their band of Jaṭilas. After enlisting Bimbisāra and his gāmaṇīs and courtiers as lay-devotees and fixing Veluvana for his own residence, Buddha made attempts to carry on further his misionary work.

Buddh's attempts at conversion of paribbājakas and the members of the religious orders.

Sāriputta and Moggalāna were the first to be converted at Rājagaha with their companions the two hundred and fifty disciples of Sañjaya. Sāriputta had already made a good deal of progress in spiritual culture and took only a fortnight to reach arahathood. This stage was attained at the time when Buddha was delivering a discourse at Sukarakhatalena in Gijjhakūṭa on the three *vedanās*, their origin, and destruction for the benefit of Dīghanakha paribbājaka, a relative of Sāriputta, who was fanning Buddha on the occasion[1]. Moggalāna who went to Kallavāla-

see *Vinaya*, I, p. 105 ; Burlingame's *Buddhist Legends*, II, pp. 169-176.

1 The sutta is named '*Dīghanakha Suttantam*' in the *Majjh. Nik.*, I, p. 501 and '*Vedanāpariggaha*

muttagāma for practising meditation of the elements (*dhātukammaṭṭhānaṃ*) fell into sloth and torpor on the seventh day after his ordination; but admonished by Buddha, he became diligent and attained the perfection of knowledge[1]. After the conversion of Sañjaya's followers, Buddha frequently visited the various halls (*kutūhalasālās*) and the abodes of Wanderers (*paribbājakārāmas*) and non-brāhmaṇical teachers of Rājagaha with a view to convince them of the efficacy of his religion by discussions. The discourses that were delivered at Rājagaha dealt mainly with the various doctrines of the paribbājakas and religious teachers, because Buddha had at this time to lay bare the weak points of their faiths and vindicate the strength of his own doctrines. He succeeded on many occasions to win over to his side as lay-disciples many followers of other sects but he could not add much to the number of his bhikkhus. As for instance, the paribbājakas Vacchagotta, Dīghanakha, Sakulūdāyi, and Acela

Suttantam' in the commentary of Buddhaghosa (Burlingame's *Buddhist Legends*, I, p. 203) because the first part treats of the tenets of Dīghanakha and the last part of the *Vedanās*.

1 *Manorathapūraṇī*, I, p. 161; *Aṅg, Nik.*, IV, p. 85.

Kassapa took life-long *saraṇa* in Buddha, Dhamma, and Saṅgha but did not become bhikkhus.

Buddha utilized the opportunity of meeting the large number of emissaries sent to him in batches by his father Suddhodana for taking him to Kapilavatthu by converting them to Buddhism. Sakulūdāyi, a playmate of Buddha was the head of the last batch of the emissaries. After conversion he was able to persuade Buddha to pay a visit to Kapilavatthu. The story of what Buddha did at this place forms the subject-matter of the next section. This much I should mention here that some of the converts, joining his order now, played shortly after an important part in the work of propagation of Buddhism and became in later times very prominent figures in the history of the religion. They were Anuruddha, Ānanda, Upāli, and Rāhula. Less prominent were Buddha's cousin Nanda, Bhaddiya, Bhagu, and Kimbila. Devadatta who joined the order along with others became prominent by his opposition to Buddhism rather than by helping it.

Buddha's flying visit to Kapilavastu and the converts made.

During the periods of Buddha's residence at Rājagaha throughout his career, Buddha used to keep himself busy with the training of the bhikkhus. He constantly watched their conduct and their mode of performance of spiritual practices ; inclucating upon them at the same time the essential principles of Buddhism. The discourses in the *Nikāyas* show clearly how Buddha studied their character and predilections, and corrected their weaknesses by suitable advice, admonitions and courses of disciplinary practices. In the *Rāhulovādasutta,* for instance, Buddha instructed Rāhula how *kāyakamma,* (deed), *vacīkamma* (word), and *manokamma* (thought) could be kept pure by *paccāvekkhana* (examination and introspection) because he had seen that Rāhula was not sufficiently self-controlled. When, however, the disciple made some progress in self-control, he led him up to realise gradually the *anicca* (want of permanent essence) and *dukkha-bhāva* (miseries inherent in the nature) of all worldly things and that the four *dhātus* or five *skandhas* collectively or separately do not constitute the *attā* (ego)[1]. Nanda, another of his disciples, could not check his anxieties for food and raiment, for which he used

Buddha's industry for training up his disciples.

1 *Aṅg Nik.,* II, pp. 164-5; *Saṃ. Nik.,* III, p. 136; IV, pp. 105-7 ; *Majjh. Nik.,* I, pp. 414ff; III, pp. 277-80.

to be taken to task by the Teacher. In due course the check put upon him helped him to control his senses so much that he has been praised in the *Aṅguttara Nikāya* as the chief of those who have control over their senses (*indriyesu guttadvārānaṃ aggo*)[1]. To cite another instance, Anuruddha could not, owing to slackness of exertion, attain *cittavimutti* (emancipation) though he had advanced much through his diligence in the path of meditation whereby he attained *dibbacakkhu* (the divine eye). This slackness which was clogging his way was removed by Buddha's guidance supplemented by the personal care taken of Anuruddha by Sāriputta[2].

Buddha's cousin Nanda.

Anuruddha.

The weakness of Kimbila lay similarly in his inability to muster up sufficient mental concentration through in-breathing and out-breathing. This was detected by Buddha and removed by his advice with special reference to the processes which he could not practise in a perfect way[3].

Kimbila.

1 *Saṃ. Nik.*, II, p. 281 ; *Aṅg. Nik.*, I, p. 25 ; IV, p. 166.

2 *Aṅg. Nik.*, I, p. 282 ; IV, pp. 228ff.

3 *Saṃ. Nik.*, V, pp. 322-325.

Ānanda.

The case of Ānanda is interesting. In spite of his insatiable love of knowledge by which he rose to be the chief of the *bahussutas* (the learned), and in spite of the great care that was bestowed upon him by Buddha for his spiritual culture, he could not attain arahathood until after the death of Buddha, the reason being that he could not divest himself of his great attachment to Buddha, not as the founder of a religion but as a master to whom he was related as a servitor. This attachment had the element which proved a clog to his practice of the doctrine of detachment from the world, the corner-stone of Buddha's teachings. Buddha used to admonish Ānanda for his inability to get rid of this attachment because therein lay the cause of his failure to attain the state of mind required for arahathood; and in the *Mahāparinibbāna Sutta* we find Buddha expostulating with the disciple for shedding tears when Buddha expressed his desire to leave this world[1]. So long as Buddha lived, Ānanda could not rise above the stage of *bahussuta* with his inordinate desire for knowledge as evidenced by the frequent questions that are recorded to have been put by him to Buddha about

1 *Dīgh. Nik.*, II, pp. 142-144.

the correctness of Purāṇa Kassapa's divisions of mankind, Sāriputta's exposition of the origin of *dukkha* (suffering) from *phassa* (contact), the theory of causation (*paṭicca-samuppāda*), the sense of the terms *nirodha, loka, suñña, vedanā, iddhi, ānāpānasati* and so forth[1]. The training imparted to Devadatta by Buddha was on lines that were calculated as suitable

Devadatta.

to his peculiar mental tendencies. This disciple made some progress in *yoga* attaining ability to perform some miracles. Buddha detected his predilection for gain and fame through the exercise of his power to perform miracles by which he had won over Ajātasattu to become his patron; and with the view of removing this love of gain and fame, he gave him advice and delivered to him discourses calculated to remove this weakness; but so deep-rooted had been this tendency that he continued on his way to ruin, turning deaf ear to his master's warnings[2]. The instances can be multiplied but those that have been cited are enough to show how the great teacher used to see through the mental composition

1 *Aṅg. Nik.*, III, pp. 383ff; *Saṃ. Nik.*, II, pp. 34-37; VI, p. 167.

2 *Majjh. Nik.*, I, pp. 192ff.; *Vinaya.* MV, VII. 2ff.

of the disciples whom he had occasion to train personally, reading their tendencies and mental weaknesses as clearly as if they were reflected on a mirror. This accounts for his great success as a spiritual trainer. His superhuman insight enabled him to spot the deficiency of his followers, and to suggest the remedy that could remove it. He was a master of this art and could play on the mental gamut of his disciples perfectly, creating spiritual symphony by striking on the right chords of their minds and enchanting them by the music thus produced.

Buddha felt the necessity of framing Vinaya rules.

Shortly after his arrival at Rājagaha, Buddha felt the necessity of framing rules by which the conduct of the bhikkhus could be directed on right lines and the organization constituted by them worked smoothly but vigorously for the fulfilment of the ideals that the new religion held before the bhikkhus. Though at the outset he himself was watching and guiding the conduct of his disciples, he saw that as the number of bhikkhus was growing gradually and was not confined to a particular locality, it was necessary that he should frame a body of rules that would gradually dispense with his personal watch and ward. Moreover, as he was founding a religious organization which was intended to work long after his own span of life on the earth, it ought to be made in such a way that it might be self-sufficing, meeting its own exigencies in addition to making full provision for the performance of the daily duties that are required of its members. But though he felt the necessity of framing rules that could meet completely the requirements of his religious organization with its branches, he saw that it was not possible to frame them all at once, because the whole set of rules could not be evolved without having experience of the deficiencies of the organization and the faults of commission and omission committed by the bhikkhus. The factor that accelerated the framing of the rules was the fact that his disciples were at times deviating from the line of conduct that the popular opinion of the time generally laid down for the monks e.g. want of moderation in eating, impropriety in dressing, and the like. Any case for which no rule was in existence had to be handled on its merits and a rule had to be framed. The existence of the rules could prove to be a check upon the monks' conduct, as otherwise they enjoyed absolute latitude in the fields of action that were without any restraint. The Vinaya rules evolved gradually by the occurrence of new incidents or the commission of new offences. Many of the rules, of course, were laid down on the model of those already current in the religious orders of the day, e.g. the holding of *uposathas.* There are others also that were framed, pursuant to the mentality of the people at large, while there were others again prescribed in compliance with the requirements of the state. As an instance of the former may be cited the prohibition of a prolonged stay of a bhikkhu at a particular place[1] and the prescription of the rule for passing *vassa* and holding *pavāraṇā* at a particular locality[2], while examples of the latter will be found in the rule that soldiers and convicts must not be allowed to join the order. It took a long time, of course, for the set of rules to be evolved in its completeness. A good deal of care was taken to make the code of conduct as perfect as possible, and that Buddha succeeded in achieving this object is apparent from the smooth working of the code for centuries. The basal frame-work of the code which was made at Rājagaha served to check the delinquencies on the part of the bhikkhus against which Buddha on many occa-

1 *Vinaya.*, MV., I, 53,
2 *Ibid.*, MV., III, 4, 3.

sions gave this warning: "These will not conduce, O Bhikkhus, to the conversion of the unconverted and to the augmentation of the number of the converted ; but they will result, O Bhikkhus, in the unconverted being repulsed from the faith, and in many of the converted becoming estranged[1]." I mention below the Vinaya rules framed at Rājagaha along with references to the circumstances which necessitated or suggested the framing of the rules[2] :—

(*A*) *Re. Initiation.*—Difficulties arose by the delegation of the power of initiation to the disciples, as there took place cases of either indiscriminate initiation or refusal to initiate deserving persons. To avoid these difficulties, the power was vested in a panel of ten monks (I. 31), and the procedure for ordaining a person was as far as possible laid down in details. The rules are in the main the following,—

(1) The practice of giving ordination by the *trisaraṇa* formula was abrogated and the form of *ñatti catutthena kammena upasampādetabbaṃ* (conferring ordination by three proclamations) was introduced (I. 28).

1 *S. B. E.*, XVII, pp. 18, 19.

2 The references that have henceforth been put in the body are from *Vinaya*, Mahāvagga.

(2) No one should be ordained unless he seeks it (I. 19); and if a heretic excepting a Jaṭila or a Śākyan seeks ordination, he should pass through a probationary (*parivāsa*) period of four months (I. 38), as there had been cases of heretics joining the order but giving it up shortly after. They used to speak ill of the *dhamma* as they were ignorant of its essence.

(3) Ordination should not be given to persons suffering from five kinds of diseases (I. 39), to men in royal service, criminals proclaimed or punished, debtors, and slaves (I. 40).

(4) The person to be ordained must have a *upajjhāya* and an *ācariya*. The reason for laying down this rule was that the untrained, though ordained, bhikkhus incurred the displeasure of the laity by their shabby clothing, want of moderation in their meals, want of refinement in manners etc. The initiated bhikkhu had to undergo a period of training under the *upajjhāya* or *ācariya*,[1] who should be a bhikkhu

1 Regarding the distinction between *upajjhāya* and *ācariya*, see *S.B.E.*, XIII, pp. 178, 179 fn.; Mr. S.K. Dutt in his *Early Buddhist Monachism*, pp. 180, 181 says "the Ācariya was the actual instructor and the Upajjhāya, who was formally elected at the upasampadā, was instructor only in name. The latter, however,

of ten years' standing. Elaborate rules were made regarding the mutual duties and obligations of the student and the teacher, and the checks for non-compliance with them, the qualifications of a teacher, the period for which the student should live with the teacher, the reasons for the cessation of the relationship between the the student and the teacher and so forth (I. 25; I. 31 ; I. 32 ; I. 35-37 ; I. 53).

(5) Restriction of age. Ordination was once given to some boys of tender age who had not the capacity to know what the life of a bhikkhu means. Hence the rule was made that persons below twenty years should not be given *upasampadā* (higher ordination) while those below fifteen should not be given *pabbajjā* (I. 49, 50).

(6) The system of telling the four *nissayas* at the time of the ordination. Though the bhikkhus took the vow of poverty, some of them took advantage of the devotion and charity of the laity to pass an easy life. This led to the laying down of the rule that every person when admitted into the order should be told that he must live on the morsels of food

enjoyed a higher status. There was, however, absolutely no difference between the duties and obligations of an Ācariya and those of a Upajjhāya"

received by begging, clothe himself in robes made of sewn rags, dwell at *arañña*, *rukkhamūla*, *vanapattha*, etc. and take (*gomutra*) decomposing urine of cows as medicine[1]. The severity of the rule scared away intending converts ; therefore a relaxation of the rule had to be introduced. The bhikkhus were permitted to accept invitations to the houses of the laity and receive food and raiment offered by them. Through the efforts of Jīvaka, the bhikkhus were allowed to use robes of six kinds of stuff besides the *paṃsukūla* (VIII. 3). Five other kinds of residences were sanctioned in addition to those mentioned above to diminish the hardships endured by the bhikkhus. These five were *vihāra*, *aḍḍhayoga*, *hammiya*, *guhā*, and *pāsāda*. The acceptance of the *vihāras* constructed by the seṭṭhis of Rājagaha was sanctioned by Buddha at the earnest request of the seṭṭhis. This however led to some abuses, as the undisciplined of the bhikkhus gave themselves up to luxuries and teased the people by asking them for contributions for constructing the *ārāmas* or supplying their luxuries. A large number of restrictions had therefore to be appended to the rule e. g. prohibiting the bhikkhus to ask the people for *vihāras* and dimini-

Vinaya, MV., I, 30.

shing the size of the buildings to limited dimensions[1] etc. The rule regarding medicine was also relaxed to some extent, allowing bhikkhus to use ghee, butter, oil, honey, molasses etc. as medicines. (VI. 15, 17, 26).

(*B*). *Re. Uposatha and Pātimokkha assemblies*[1].—It was Bimbisāra who brought to Buddha's notice that the institution of holding *uposathas* (i. e. assemblies for religious discussions held thrice fortnightly), prevalent in some of the religious orders of the time, was very useful and requested Buddha to incorporate it in the Buddhist code of *Vinaya*. These assemblies developed in course of time an offshoot in the *Pātimokkha* gatherings where the monks confessed their offences of omission or commission as expiation for them. The *Pātimokkha* assemblies gave rise to some serious difficulties which were obviated by the framing of rules under the following heads :—

(1) Defining (*sīmā*) the limits of jurisdiction of parishes (II, 5-6 ; II, 12. 7).

(2) Selection of the President of the *Pātimokkha* assembly (*uposathapamukha*).

1 See *Saṅghādisesa* VI, in *Vinaya*, III, pp. 144ff. and *Cullavagga*, VI for detailed rules re. dwellings and furniture.

(3) Selection of a person to answer questions on *Dhamma* and *Vinaya* (II, 15, 5-6; 16).

(4) Uposatha Hall and its requisites (II, 20).

(5) Persons not allowed to attend the *Pātimokkha* assemblies (II, 36).

(6) Confessions by sick and absentee bhikkhus (II, 22, 24).

(7) Procedure for convening a *Pātimokkha* assembly (II, 3, 19).

(*C*). *Re. Vassavāsa.* The practice of spending the rainy season at a particular place was current among the ascetics of various religious orders. This was adopted by Buddha. Either the day after the full-moon of Āṣāḍha or the day after a month from it was fixed as the day of commencing *vassavāsa* (III, 1-2).

(*D*). *Re. Use of Foot-wear.* Buddha per mitted the use of foot-wear in view of the great hardship suffered by the bhikkhu Soṇa Kolivisa on account of the delicate skin of his feet, by a few monks who had boils in their feet, and by a few other bhikkhus for having had to walk with bare feet on soil full of gravels in places like Avanti. The use of foot-wear generally by all monks was allowed later on to remove the inconvenience in walking long distances, though many restrictions as to the nature of the foot-wear had to be laid down (v, 1ff.).

Lastly, at Rājagaha a few rules for settling disputes (cv., iv, 4-10) and elaborate rules for the guidance of monks in their daily life (cv., v) were laid down. Of the *Pātimokkha* rules, twenty one were framed at Rājagaha, viz. under *Pārājikā* one, *Saṅghādisesa* six, *Nissaggiya Pācittiya* three, *Pācittiya* ten and *Pāṭidesanīya* one[1].

Preparation at Rājagaha for missionary work at Vesālī and Sāvatthi.

In the fifth *vassa*, Buddha was invited by the people of Vesāli to visit the place for removing the pestilence ravaging the city. Buddha in response to the invitation visited the place and stayed there for a short time. The end of the pestilence synchronized with his stay there and was believed to have been due to the beneficent power of the Teacher who made efforts to drive away the epidemic by uttering the *Ratana Sutta*. The incident went far to prepare the minds of the people to follow the lead of the wonder-worker in the religion. Buddha visited Vesāli in the fifth *vassa* and many times subse-

1 Paṇḍit Vidhuśekhara Śāstrī's *Pātimokkha*, pp. 378ff; *Vinaya*, V, pp. 144ff.

quently and succeeded in having a large number of converts.

During the second *vassa* when Buddha was residing at Sītavana at Rājagaha, Anāthapiṇḍika, the Lord High Treasurer of Kosala came to see Buddha, and was converted to Buddhism. He invited the teacher to Sāvatthi to spend there his *vassa*; this marked the commencement of the spread of Buddhism in Kosala, details of which will be given in the following section.

Lay-devotees indispensable for a religious order. Buddha's attention to same.

In the early years of Buddha's career he was not so attentive to the formation of a society of lay-devotees, as to the order of monks, but he soon realized that a religious organization composed of bhikkhus needed a lay-society for its upkeep. The simple formula of *tri-saraṇa* which he had originally prescribed for utterance by his lay-devotees as a mark of their devotion to Buddhism was not regarded by them as adequate to bind them up closely with the Buddhist order; hence Buddha in course of time prescribed that every lay-devotee of his should observe the five precepts, and the more advanced among them the eight precepts on the six *uposatha* days and hear the religious discussions and discourses held at the assemblies of the saṅghas. The topics that formed the subject-matter of his discourses meant for the lay-devotees were the merits of *dāna* and *saddhā*, the four truths, mental discipline etc. The growth of the lay-Buddhist society was imperceptible in its first stages but gradually became sufficiently noticeable not only by the number but also by the distinguishing marks of the members of the lay society[1]. The first remarkable enlistment of lay-devotees took place at the time when the chiefs of the eighteen śreṇīs and other officials of Bimbisāra paid their homage to Buddha and became his followers in the second year of Buddha's career. Before this, of course, the conversions of Trapusa and Bhallika at Gayā, and Yasa's father at Benares as lay-devotees had been effected; but then the mere utterance of the formula indicating the taking of refuge in Buddha, Dhamma, and Saṅgha was the mark of their belonging to the Buddhist lay-society. The lay-society of Rājagaha gradually attained larger dimensions, so much so that the Buddhist bhikkhus swelling in number could be easily maintained by the supply of the bare necessaries of life by the lay-society. A few names of lay-devotees preserved to us in connec-

1 See Dr. N. Law's *Historical Miscellany*, pp. 95ff.

tion with the discourses in the *Nikāyas* may be given here to show the classes of people who joined the Buddhist order as lay-devotees during the periods of Buddha's missionary work at Rājagaha:

1. The gāmaṇīs—Talapuṭa naṭagāmaṇī (*Saṃ.* iv, p. 306)[1] ; Yodhājīvagāmaṇī (*Saṃ.* iv, p. 308) ; Assāroha gāmaṇi (*Saṃ.* iv, p. 310) ; Maṇicūlaka gāmaṇi (*Saṃ.* iv, p. 325) ; Rāsiya gāmaṇi (*Saṃ.* iv, p. 340) ; etc.

2. The gahapatis—Jotikā (*Saṃ.* v. p. 344) ; Mānadinna (*Saṃ.* v, p. 178.) Sirivaḍḍha (*Sam.* v, pp. 176-7), Soṇa gahapatiputta (*Saṃ.* IV, p. 113) ; Dārukammika gahapati of Nādika (*Aṅg.* iii, p. 391) ; Belaṭṭha Kaccāna, a sugar merchant of Andhakavinda (*Vin.* I, p. 224) ; Pukkusāti kulaputta (*Majjh.* iii, p. 237) ; Dighāvu upāsaka (*Saṃ.* v. p. 344) ; Jīvaka ; Anāthapiṇḍika and his seṭṭhi friend ; etc.

3. Jaina disciples of Nālandā—Asibandhakaputta gāmaṇī, Upāli, Abhayarājakumāra (see *ante*, p. 90.).

4. Brāhmaṇas—Kasibharadvāja brāhmaṇa of Ekanālā ; Dhanañjana brāhmaṇa (*Sam.* I, p. 160) ; etc.

5. Ladies—Sāri brāhmaṇī and paribbājikā, mother of Sāriputta of Nālakagāma ; Dhanañjanī a brāhmaṇī (*Saṃ.* i, p. 160) ; Velukaṇṭakī Nandamātā of Dakkhiṇāgirī (*Aṅg.* iv, p. 63) ; Cundī rājakumārī (*Aṅg.* iii, p. 35) ; etc.

6. Kings—Bimbisāra, Ajātasattu.

1 Later on he became a bhikkhu (see *Psalms of the Brethren*, p. 369)

7. Paribbājakas—Vacchagotta (*Majjh.* I, p. 489); Sakuludāyi (*Majjh.* II, p. 1); etc.

Of course no inference can be drawn from the above list as to the number of people who became lay-devotees of Buddha, because the list is only fragmentary and far from being exhaustive. The largest amount of support came from the rich seṭṭhis, some of whom have been mentioned above. So far as Rājagaha was concerned, I do not think it would be erroneous to state that the largest number of converts was supplied by the vaiśya community. This inference draws its support from the fact that eighteen śreṇīs visiting Buddha with Bimbisāra were all of the vaiśya community, each of the śreṇīs consisting of a large number of individuals. The list of the eighteen śreṇīs is found in the *Mahāvastu*[1], from which it appears that the crafts and industries constituting the professions of the śreṇīs covered a large range, showing that they fairly represented the various branches of the vaiśya community. The *Nikāyas* bristle with instances of seṭṭhis lending their whole-hearted support by men and money to the Buddhist saṅgha. We shall have occasion to mention them as we deal with the various localities to which they belonged.

1. *Mahāvastu*, III, p. 44.

The interview between Buddha and Anātha piṇḍika was brought about by a rich seṭṭhi relation of the latter a resident of Rājagaha[1] ; and it was through this relation of Anāthapiṇḍika that the other rich seṭṭhis of Rājagaha became disciples of Buddha.[2] A great emporium as Rājagaha was, it was natural that Buddha should have a large number of followers from among the local merchants. They could on account of their wealth make munificent gifts to the Buddhist saṅgha providing the bhikkhus with boarding and lodging ; for instance, it was at the offer of an ārāma by a seṭṭhi, who was moved by the hardships of the monks as to shelter, that Buddha allowed the monks to live in the ārāmas ; and at the offer of a sugar-merchant to supply the monks with sugar that Buddha permitted the use of sugar by the bhikkhus. It was on account of the active interest taken by them in the progress of Buddhism that names of many of them have been recorded in the Buddhist scriptures.

In the closing years of Buddha's life in took place two notable conver-

Vinaya, II, pp. 154-5.

Hardy's *Manual of Buddhism*. p. 216.

sions viz., of Ajātasattu and Jīvaka. Ajātasattu became king in the 72nd year of Buddha's life and continued his patronage to Devadatta who with Kokālika, Kaṭamoratissaka, Khaṇḍadeviyāputta Samuddadatta and Thullanandā bhikkhuni[1] as the foremost disciples started a sect intended to be a rival to Buddhism. The cause of his influence with a few people is attributed to his power of working miracles attained through *jhāna* under the direction of Buddha at Sukarakhata in Gijjhakuṭa[2]. He collected about 500 disciples and established a centre at Gayāsīsa where a monastery was built for him by Ajātasattu[3]. A point of difference between the religious doctrines preached by him and those by Buddha lay in the bias to rigorous life that appealed so much to the people at large, but which Buddha left to the option of his disciples for adopting or rejecting it. Ajātasattu, who was used as a tool by Devadatta for the execution of his purposes, felt remorse when he was advanced

Buddha's activities in Magadha towards the end of his career.

1 *Vinaya*, III, p. 171; IV, pp. 66, 335.

2 Watters' *Yuan Chwang*, II, p. 10 refers to it as 'Devadatta Samādhi cave.'

3 *Jātaka*, I, pp. 67, 319.

in age for helping Devadatta in his evil designs as he gradually became impressed with the decided superiority of Buddha to Devadatta in all directions. Jīvaka, who about this time returned to Rājagaha after completing his medical education at Takkhasīlā and became so eminent a phycian that his services were eagerly requisitioned by the ruling princes, volunteered his services for the medical treatment of Buddha and his dissiciples and professed his firm faith in Buddhism. He was a medical adviser of Ajātasattu and thereby got opportunities of bringing home to his mind the greatness of Buddha and his teachings. The introduction to the *Sāmaññaphala Sutta* relates how he brought about the interview between Buddha and the king, on which occasion the latter was converted by Buddha by means of a discourse on the secular and spiritual merits acquired by a bhikkhu by his joining the order. This conversion took place in the 79th year of Buddha's life i. e. just a year before his *parinibbāna.*

Other countries in Magadha.

While staying at Rājagaha, Buddha used to visit other places within Magadha with his bands of disciples. Only the places which rose into prominence by reason of establishment of monasteries and large number of adherents there have been recorded in the *Nikāyas.* They are :—

1. Nālandā—It was then a small but a prosperous village situated at a distance of a *yojana* from Rājagaha[1]. The usual residence of the monks was at the monastery *Pāvārika-ambavana*. There was another monastery midway between Rājagaha and Nālandā called Ambalaṭṭhikā where Rāhula stayed at times.[2] From the nature of the discourses delivered there and from the particulars of the persons with whom Buddha entered into disputations, it appears that Nigaṇṭha Nātaputta had there a firm footing[3]. Most of the discourses were intended to refute the doctrines of the Jaina faith, while the learned disputants, viz, Dīghatapassī, Upāli, Abhayrāja-kumāra, and Asibandhakaputta gāmaṇī were the followers of Nigaṇṭha Nātaputta, all of whom were converted by Buddha except the one named first. From the *Bhagavatī Sūtra* also, we learn that Nālandā was the meeting place of Mahāvīra with Gosāla.

1 *Sum. Vil.*, p. 35 ; *Majjh. Nik.*, I, p. 377 ; *Dīgh. Nik.*, I, *Sutta* 11. It is stated in Yuan Chwang's *Records* and *Mahāvastu* that Nālandā was the birth-place of Sāriputta, but in fact his birth-place was Nālaka which was an unimportant village near Nālandā.

2 *Majjh. Nik.*, I, p. 414.

3 *Majjh. Nik.*, I, pp. 379, 392ff ; *Saṃ. Nik.*, IV, pp. 110, 317, 323 ; *Mahāvastu*, III, p. 56.

2. Pāṭaliputta—During Buddha's life-time, it was only a village called Pāṭaligāma which Buddha visited with his disciples in the last days of his life. The laity of the place invited Buddha and his disciples who on their arrival at the place were accommodated in a rest house probably known later on as the Kukkuṭa-ārāma. It was at this time that Sunīdha and Vassakāra two ministers of Ajātasattu were fortifying Pāṭaligāma as a defence against the Vajjians. This fortified village afterwards rose to be Pāṭaliputta, the capital of Magadha and a great emporium[1]. Out of respect for Buddha, the two ministers named the gate through which Buddha passed and the ferry ghat whence he departed as Gotama-dvāra and Gotama-tittha. Near Pāṭaliputta, there were two villages called Koṭigāma and Nādika where Buddha stopped in his last journey. It was at Koṭigāma that Ambapāli came to invite Buddha to Vesāli[2]. Buddha passed from Koṭigāma to Nādika where he had many faithful monks and nuns and male and female lay-devotees, some of whom died before his visit to the place[3], hence the

1 *Vinaya*, MV., VI, p. 28; *Dīgh. Nik.*, II, p. 85.
2 *Vinaya*, I, p. 231.
3 *Dīgh. Nik.*, II, pp. 91-92.

discourses that he delivered here were all concerning the *Maraṇa-sati*[1].

3. Dakkhiṇāgiri—In the 11th year of Buddha's ministration, he visited the brāhmaṇa village Ekanālā and converted the two brāhmaṇas Kasi-Bharadvāja[2] and Sampūrṇa[3]. A distinguished female lay-devotee Velukaṇṭakī Nandamātā lived here[4]. It was at this place that Buddha formed his idea of the way in which the *cīvaras* (robes of the bhikkhus) should be made out of pieces of cloth stitched together like the rectangular pieces of land tilled by different persons in the rice-fields near the village.

4. & 5. Andhakavinda and Kallavālamuttagāma, two other villages near Rājagaha, though not so well-known had monasteries where Buddha stayed at times. At Andhakavinda we find him instructing some newly ordained bhikkhus and converting Belaṭṭha Kaccāna, a sugar-merchant of the place. Mahākassapa while here had once to ford a stream to attend a Pātimokkha assembly at Rājagaha. After this incident the Vinaya rule was ins-

1 *Aṅg. Nik.*, III, pp. 303ff; 391.
2 *Sutta Nipāta.*, pp. 12ff; *Saṃ. Nik.*, I, pp. 172-3.
3 R. L. Mitra's *Nepalese Buddhist Literature.* p. 18.
4 *Aṅg. Nik.*, IV, pp. 63ff.

tituted that a bhikkhu need not cross a stream, as wherever it exists, it should be made a boundary of the jurisdiction of a monastery. Kallavālamutta-gāma is important on account of its association with Moggalāna who underwent there his first course of training.

IV
Kosala

The kingdom of Kosala is next in importance to Magadha in the history of the spread of Buddhism. It was at Sāvatthi, the capital of Kosala, that Buddha spent almost the half of his career as a teacher[1], delivered the largest number of discourses and framed the largest number of *Pātimokkha* rules[2]; and it was here that the religion, which had passed its infancy in Magadha, developed into its full stature as found in the *Nikāyas*. Though according to Dr. Oldenberg[3], Kosala was outside the limits within which orthodox brāhmaṇism prevailed, the territory was in fact within the said limits containing, as mentioned in the *Nikāyas*, many brāhmaṇa settlements. Dr. Oldenberg bases his opinion on two passages, one of the *Cullavagga* (XII. 2, 3) viz., "Buddhas are born in the *puratthima* janapadas", and the other of the *Majjhima*

Importance of Kosala.

1 *J.R.A.S.*, 1891, p. 339; Hardy's *Manual*, p. 356.

2 *Vinaya*, V, pp. 144-5.

3 Oldenberg's *Buddha*, Appendix, :

Nikāya (II, p 124) refering to Buddha as a Kosalaka. The word *puratthima* however does not imply prācya-deśa. The passage contemplates only Kapilavatthu lying on the northern extremity of Kosala and not the whole of the territory ; and moreover both the town and the territory lay on the west of Sadānīrā, an early limit of Aryan colonization as mentioned in the *Śatapatha-Brāhmaṇa*[1]. Hence, as a citizen of Kapilavatthu, Buddha could well be called a Kosalaka, though for the matter of that he was not an inhabitant of prācya-deśa. We therefore find that at the time of the rise of Buddhism, Kosala was a brāhmaṇical country, where the progress of the religion was not without its difficulties. The tracing of progress in the propagation of the faith in the kingdom is interesting in view of the above fact as well as for its inclusion of the home of the Sākya clan, to which the Teacher had belonged. Though Kosala was a brāhmaṇical territory, it did not deter Buddha from making attempts to spread his religion there from the very commencement of his career as a preacher. The *first attempt* was made

Introduction of Buddhism in Kosala.

1 *Śatapatha Brāhmaṇa*, I, 4. 1 quoted also in Oldenberg's *Buddha*, pp. 398, 399.

at the time of his stay at Benares through the first band of Buddhist missionaries, among whom figured the five inhabitants of Kapilavatthu and its precincts, namely the first five brāhmaṇa converts of the Teacher[1]. The *second attempt* was made by Buddha personally. While at Rājagaha, he was repeatedly invited by Suddhodana and at last induced by Buddha's play-mate Udāyi to go to the place. During his short stay at the town on this occasion, he succeeded in converting some of the Sākyan youths to his faith. The *third and the most successful attempt* was made at the time when he visited Sāvatthi at the request of Anāthapiṇḍika, who presented to the Teacher the Jetavana-ārāma distinguished in later times as a great resort of bhikkhus, and placed at his disposal all the influence that he could command for the propagation of Buddhism in Kosala.

1 *Mahāvastu*, III, p. 420; *Psalms of the Brethren*, p. 284. According to the Buddhist legends, the thirty Bhaddavaggiya youths, converted by Buddha on his way from Benares to Uruvela, also belonged to Kosala (Hardy's *Manual of Buddhism*, p. 188). Buddhaghosa says that the Bhaddavaggiya youths were brothers of the king of Kosala. They after their ordination lived at Pāṭheyya, a country situated to the west of Kosala (*S. B. E.* XVII, p. 146fn.)

Opposition encountered by Buddhism in Kosala.

Inspite of the efforts of Anāthapiṇḍika to give Buddhism a footing at Sāvatthi, the heads of the local sects resented the intrusion of a new religion into the field which they considered as their monopoly. Buddha expected to meet a stubborn opposition from the leaders of the sects, and to ward it off, he had sent to Sāvatthi his ablest lieutenant Sāriputta entrusted with the ostensible work of supervising the construction of the Jetavana vihāra. Sāriputta was a past master in the art of disputation and had deep knowledge of the brāhmaṇic lore as well as that of the non-brāhmaṇic sects. He had to enter into disputation with many teachers, all of whom he was able to silence by dint of his able exposition of the Dhamma[1]. A ground was thus prepared for the advent of Buddhism at the time of Buddha's arrival at the place. In addition to the opposition from the local teachers the disciples of the six non-brāhmaṇic teachers were also at Sāvatthi to render thorny the path of Buddha's progress in his mission. These people as also king Pasenadi were great admirers of these teachers and used to speak of them as distinguished teachers of schools and heads of

1 Watters' *Yuan Chwang*, I, pp. 384; 394.

orders, and revered by the wise (*sanghino ganino ganācariyā ñātā yasassino titthakarā sādhu-sammatā*) while of Buddha as young in age and fresh as a recluse (*daharo ceva jātiyā navo ca pabbajjāyāti*)[1]. Sāvatthi, according to the *Uvāsagadasao*, was the head-quarters of the Ājīvika sect which held its founder Makkhali Gosāla in very high respect[2]. The influence established by this as well as the other five teachers was long standing, and honours and largesses used to be heaped upon them by the local people. These teachers were not agreeable to give in an inch of ground to the new preacher who in their eyes was but a callow youth, yet a long way off from the winning of his laurels. They therefore tried every means to dissuade the people from listening to his preachings. All his teachings, they said, were but reflexions of what they taught[3]. They made a combined effort to oust him from Kosala by persuading Pasenadi to hold a competition in the exhibition of their miraculous powers. Buddha defeated them all in this competition and thereby

1 *Saṃ. Nik.*, I, p. 68; *Majjh. Nik.*, I, pp. 205, 400, 426.

2 Dr. Barua, *op. cit.*, pp. 298, 299, 300.

3 *Majjh. Nik.*, I, p. 84.

established his reputation as a great religious seer. The name and influence of the six teachers began to wane after this event, while those of Buddha increased. Out of envy, they, it is said, went to the length of making the futile attempt of blackening Buddha's character by setting on him two courtezans Ciñcā and Sundarī[1]. Buddha laid bare before the public the weak points in their doctrines and thus gradually sapped the foundation of their influence in the place. During this period, Buddha at times instructed his disciples in the ways in which to meet the arguments advanced by their opponents of the six non-brāhmaṇical sects and trained them to make clear expositions of the rational principles on which Buddhism is based[2].

Buddha and the brāhmaṇas of Kosala.

The opposition put forth by the six teachers and their disciples to the progress of Buddha's mission was not so strong as that of the orthodox brāhmaṇas and brāhmaṇical teachers. They could not look with favour upon persons having no sympathy with their faiths and discouraging the observance of the

1 Kern, *op. cit.*, pp. 33, 37; Watters' *Yuan Chwang*, I, pp. 389, 392.

2 *Majjh. Nik.*, I, pp. 64ff.

forms and practices of their religion, not to speak of one who had raised the standard of revolt against same[1]. To some of the orthodox brāhmaṇas, even the sight of the shaven-headed Buddha at the time of performance of sacrifices was considered ominous. The sight of Buddha at some distance was a cause for consternation to Aggika-Bharadvāja who exclaimed as follows to stop the further progress of the Preacher towards the place where he was performing a sacrifice : "*Tatr'eva muṇḍaka tatr'eva samaṇaka, tatr'eva vasalaka tiṭṭhāhi*" [(Stay) there, O Shaveling, (stay) there, O Samaṇaka (wretched *samaṇa*) (stay) there, O Vasalaka (outcast)][2]. The adverse opinions held by the brāhmaṇas generally about him have found expression in many places in the *Nikāyas* in passages like the following,—"Who are these shavelings, sham friars, menial black fellows, the offscouring of our kinsmen's heels."[3] They even sneered at the idea of Buddha coming 'to converse with brāhmaṇas versed in the threefold Vedic lore'[4]. We find

1 *Sutta Nipāta*, pp. 50ff.

2 *Ibid.*, p. 21 ; (translated in *S. B. E.* vol. X., 20)

3 *Dīgh. Nik.*, I, p. 103.

4 *Ibid.*, I, pp. 81ff.

it mentioned that a brāhmaṇa was offended with a brāhmaṇa lady with buddhistic leanings for uttering in his presence the formula of salutation to Buddha and cursed her for doing so[1]. Evidences of hatred of Buddhism like those mentioned above can be multiplied but those that have been adduced are enough to show the antipathy felt by the brāhmaṇas of Kosala towards Buddha and his disciples. The nature of the opposition encountered by Buddha in the place accounts for many of the topics on which discourses were delivered by him or discussions were carried on with the local brāhmaṇas e.g. the origin of the caste-system and the purpose it serves ; inefficacy of sacrifices ; absurdity of solving the indeterminable problems like the existence or non-existence of soul ; permanence and impermanence of the world etc ; the falling off of the brāhmaṇas from the ancient brāhmaṇic ideal ; the truth underlying the belief in spiritual sanctification by bathing in the rivers ; the dependence of the gods of the brāhmaṇic pantheon on the law of *karma*, and so forth[2].

The brāhmaṇas of Kosala had strong attachment to their religion and were lovers of truth,

1 *Majjh. Nik.*, II, p. 210.

2 For references, see *ante*, I.

in whichever form it might be found. Buddha achieved success in his mission in a great measure by appealing to this love of truth. He explained to them that the religion which they were following had in it a large measure of alloy which had diminished the value of the religion. The rites and ceremonies and false beliefs that grew round the modicum of truth imbedded in the religion served but to cover it with a thick coating of untruth. Buddha by his power of disputation and knowledge of the brāhmaṇic lore brought home to the brāhmaṇas the truths that he was preaching. As soon as they saw the hollowness of their beliefs or the unsoundness of their philosophy, they with their characteristic love of truth embraced the religion which was placed before their eyes with all its charm. Some of them continued as laymen declaring their faith in Buddha, Dhamma, and Saṅgha while others went further and became bhikkhus. Rich and influential brāhmaṇa householders like Jānussoṇi[1], Aggika-Bharadvāja[2], and Dhanañjani[3]

Extent of success of Buddha's mission among the brāhmaṇas of Kosala.

1 *Majjh. Nik.*, I, p. 175.
2 *Sutta Nipāta*, p. 21.
3 *Majjh. Nik.*, II, p. 209.

professed themselves as life-long upāsakas of of Buddha, Dhamma, and Saṅgha. Intelligent and learned as they were, they naturally presented difficulty to Buddha in having them converted but once convinced of the truth of Buddha's doctrines, they proved to be his staunch adherents. When Buddha commenced his missionary work in Kosala, he was not so hopeful, but judging by the results of his missionary work here, it would not, I think, be wide of the mark to state that the difficulty of the task added to the glory of the success achieved, and the number of brāhmaṇas converted at this place was larger than those converted by him at any other. The distinct achievement of Buddha in this brāhmaṇic country is the conversion of some of the distinguished brāhmaṇa teachers (*mahāsālas*) who lived on grants of villages made by kings and were held in high respect by the people of the locality. In spite of their high positions as orthodox brāhmaṇa teachers, and regardless of the advice and importunities of their disciples and admirers, the renowned *mahāsālas* Pokkharasādi of Ukkaṭṭha[1], Lohicca of Sālavatikā[2], and Cañki of Opasāda

1 *Dīgh. Nik.*, I, p. 87.

2 *Ibid.*, I, p. 224.

took refuge in Buddha and promised to be his followers up to the end of their lives (*ajjatagge pāṇupetaṃ saraṇaṃ gataṃ*). So great became Buddha's fame in Kosala that the sixteen disciples of Bāvari came from as far a place as the bank of the Godāvarī to join the order[1]. It is not expressly stated in the *Piṭakas* how far the social status of the brāhmaṇas was affected by their becoming *upāsakas* (lay-devotees). Dr. Law suggests on the basis of a few statements in the *Nikāyas* that these *upāsakas* by their declaration of attachment to Buddhism, however slight it might be, made themselves marked in the eyes of the people belonging to the Hindu society, and the thin end of the gulf that intervened at this stage became wider in proportion to the greater degrees of devotion to Buddhism developed in them in course of time. This gradually gave rise to a Buddhist lay-society[2]. The *Nikāyas* mention only those names of brāhmaṇa converts with whom Buddha or his disciples had con-

1 *Sutta Nipāta.*, pp. 192ff—Bāvari was once the *purohita* of King Mahākosala and his son Pasenadi. He retired to the bank of the Godāvarī where a hermitage was built for him by Pasenadi.

2 Dr. N. Law, *op. cit.*

versation or disputation. The names when scrutinized show that a pretty large number of brāhmaṇas of various ranks in life were converted. To give a clear idea, a few of these names with the names of the places to which the brāhmaṇas belonged are given below :—

Brāhmaṇagahapatis of	Sālā,	*Upāsaka,*	(*Majjh.* I, 285)
Kapaṭhika mānava of	Opasāda,	,,	(*Majjh.*, II, 164)
Brāhmaṇas of	Nagaravinda,	,,	(*Majjh.*, III, 290)
,, ,,	Manasākaṭa,	,,	(*Dīgh.*, I, 235)
,, ,,	Venāgapura,	,,	(*Aṅg.*, III, 30)
,, ,,	Icchānaṅgala,	,,	(*Aṅg.*, III, 30)
,, ,,	Daṇḍakappakaṃ,	,,	(*Aṅg.*, III, 402)

Also Jānussoṇi, Sundarīkabharadvāja, Piṅgalakoccha, Assalāyana, Esukāri, Subha, Saṅgara and a host of brāhmaṇas of Sāvatthi who became *Upāsakas.* (See *Majjh.*, I. pp. 39, 175, 205 ; II, pp. 147, 177, 208, 209 ; *Dīgh.*, III, p. 81 ; *Saṃ.*, I, pp. 177ff).

Like other countries, Kosala had also many *paribbājakārāmas*[1] the most frequented of which was the one provided by Queen Mallikā at Sāvatthi[2]. Buddha and his disciples, and even, sometimes, his lay-disciples[3] visited these ārāmas,

1 *Aṅg. Nik.*, IV, p. 378 ; V, p. 48 "*aññatitthiyānaṃ paribbājakānaṃ ārāma*"

2 *Majjh. Nik.*, II, p. 22 "*Samayappavadako tindukācīro ekasālako Mallikāya ārāmo*"

3 *Ibid.*, II, p. 23.

eagerly heard the views of these paribbājakas, and expressed their disapproval of those views if they thought it necessary to do so. There were also occasions when the *paribbājakas* approached Buddha for removing their doubts. As the result of these interviews we hear of paribbājakas like Vekhanassa[1] and Poṭṭhāpada[2] becoming lay-devotees of Buddha. The high estimation in which Buddha was held by some of the paribbājakas is evident from the reply given by Pilotika to Jānussoṇi's query about Buddha's erudition, "Who am I to judge of the knowledge of Samaṇa Gotama, who am I to be able to praise him ; he is the praised of the praiseworthy, the best of gods, of men ; whoever approaches him for disputation whether he be a brāhmaṇa, khattiya, gahapati or samaṇa-paṇḍita, he comes back satisfied with the exposition of his dhamma"[3]. From these remarks it need not be supposed that Buddha had an unqualified success among the *paribbājakas* as there were many members of the

Buddha and the paribbā jakas of Kosala.

1 *Majjh. Nik.*, II, p, 40. He was the founder of a brāhmaṇical paribbājaka order.

2 *Dīgh. Nik.*, I, p. 178.

3 *Majjh. Nik.*, I, p. 175.

class who would never recognise the excellences of the religion.

The greatest part of Buddha's missionary career was spent at Jetavanārāma in Sāvatthi. He resided here for twenty one *vassas* in addition to many visits paid to it at other times. In this way king Pasenadi got many opportunities of meeting him and holding with him conversation on religious topics.

Buddha converts Pasenadi of Kosala.

From the references to Pasenadi in the *Majjhima* and *Aṅguttara Nikāyas* and in the *Kosala-saṃyutta* of the *Saṃyutta Nikāya*, it is evident that the king was a follower of the brāhmaṇic religion, had the brāhmaṇa Bāvari as his first *purohita,* and celebrated sacrifices involving slaughter of hundreds of animal victims.[1] One of his queens Mallikā, and his two sisters Somā and Sakulā, were lay-devotees of Buddha[2]. It was probably through the influence of these ladies combined with the occasional instructions from Buddha that the mind of the king was gradually softened towards Buddhism. Later on he declared himself a lay-devotee of Buddha and

1 *Saṃ. Nik.,* I, pp. 75-6; *Sutta Nipāta.* p. 192.

2 *Majjh. Nik.,* II, pp. 108, 125-6.

showed signs of his devotion by occasional gifts to the members of the Order[1].

Though the infant religion could not at first secure patronage from the king, it did from

Anātha-piṇḍika.

Anāthapiṇḍika, a great magnate of Sāvatthi and the High Treasurer of the realm. His valuable advice combined with pecuniary help made it possible for the religion to strike its root deep into the soil of Kosala. It was he who organised the delivery of a few discourses by Buddha to lay-people regarding the duties of house-holders and the place occupied by them under his religion. It was these discourses that served as the guide of the house-holders in the performance of their duties as lay-Buddhists[2]. Thus it was Anāthapiṇḍika through whose efforts a place was assigned by Buddha to the lay-Buddhists in the framework of his religion. The postponement of a due recognition of their relation to Buddhism, important as it was, would not have been conducive to the speedy development of the organisation, in and through which the religion expanded itself.

The lay-devotee, who as a supporter of

1 For details, see *supra*, pp. 70, 71.

2 *Aṅg. Nik.*, V, p. 1.

Buddhism ranked next to Anāthapiṇḍika in importance, was Visākhā, the daughter of a seṭṭhi of Sāketa, and wife of the son of a rich seṭṭhi of Sāvatthi. She persuaded her father-in-law Migāra and other members of the family to give up their faith in the doctrines of Nigaṇṭha Nātaputta and adopt those of Buddha. Her anxiety for the comforts of the monks and nuns has become proverbial[1]. She built the Pubbārāma monastery where Buddha resided for six *vassas*. It was at her instance that many of the *Vinaya* rules for both the *bhikkhus* and *bhikkhunīs* were framed. Three other note-worthy lay-converts of Kosala whose names may be mentioned in this connection are Gaṇaka Moggalāna,[2] Pañcakaṅga thapati and Isidatta-purāṇa thapati who were all high state-officials.

Visākhā and others.

A notable incident connected with Buddha's missionary work in Kosala is the radical change brought about in the life of Aṅgulimāla who was so turbulent that even the king of the realm could not restrain him. He turned a bhikkhu and ultimately reached *arahatship.* This conversion made a great impression upon the

1 *Vinaya*, MV., VIII, 15, 7.
2 *Majjh. Nik.*, III, p. 1.

minds of the people of Kosala as also of the king[1], and helped greatly the propagation of the religion.

I have confined myself up to now to the relation of incidents that took place at Sāvatthi and its neighbourhood in course of Buddha's missionary work there. The events connected with the Sākyas in the Sākya territory will now engage our attention. Though the kingdom of the Sākyas falls within the limits of Kosala, the Sākyas were politically independent and formed a separate entity from the social standpoint with customs and practices peculiar to itself. They were followers of the brāhmaṇic religion and did not at first look with favour upon the idea of Buddha launching a new religion in direct opposition to the time-honoured ones. If we examine carefully the account of the reception accorded by the Sākyas to Buddha at the time of his visit to the land of his birth after Enlightenment, it will be evident that there was a rift in the lute welcoming his arrival. The people forgot to provide food for the Teacher and his disciples on the first day, refused to give them alms on the following day

Buddha among the Sākyas.

1 *Majjh. Nik.*, II, p. 23.

when they went out for collection of alms, deputed only those Sākyas who were junior to Buddha to receive him. These acts reveal the feeling entertained by them at the time towards Buddha and his religion[1]. The situation was so dismal that Buddha had to have recourse to miracles for bringing the Sākyas under control. Ultimately he made a few converts from among the Sākyas, some of whom came to be counted among the leading disciples of Buddha[2].

Nigaṇṭha Nātaputta among the Sākyas.

Nigaṇṭha Nātaputta had been among the Sākyas some time before Buddha and secured some followers. Mahānāma, a relation of Buddha, had Jaina leanings. To bring him round, Buddha delivered to him a discourse on the uselessness of the severe forms of self-mortification practised by the Jaina ascetics[3]. The result of this discourse upon Mahānāma's mind has not been mentioned anywhere. He, however, appears as an interlocutor[4]

1 Hardy's *Manual of Buddhism*, pp. 198ff.; Burlingame's *Buddhist Legends*, III, pp. 2ff.

2 See *supra*, pp. 103-8.

3 *Majjh. Nik.*, I, pp. 91-95.

4 *Aṅg. Nik.*, I, p. 219; III, p. 286; IV, p. 220.; *Majjh. Nik.*, I, pp. 91, 354 etc.

in many discourses, but nowhere does he appear as giving up his faith to adopt Buddhism. The nature of the topics dealt with in the discourses delivered by Buddha at Devadaha near Kapilavatthu suggests the inference that there were at the place a few followers of Nigaṇṭha Nātaputta. There is no reference to the conversion of any of these Jainas to Buddhism. Moggalāna who was with Buddha at the time succeeded however, in converting Vappa, a Sākyan Jaina to Buddhism[1]. The discourses delivered by Buddha at Nigrodhārāma in Kapilavatthu speak of many lay-devotees coming to hear them[2]. This as well as the fact that the Sākyans requested the Teacher to celebrate the inaugural ceremony of a new santhāgāra at Kapilavatthu testify to the fact that by his preaching he succeeded in making his religion popular among the local Sākyas[3]. He could not however make any headway in the brāhmaṇa village in the Sākyan territory, such as Sīlavati, Sakkara, Sāmāgama, Cātumā, Medalumpa[4] with the

1 *Aṅg. Nik.*, II, 196ff.

2 *Ibid*, V, p. 83.

3 *Majjh. Nik.*, I, pp. 358ff. *Saṃ. Nik.*, IV, pp. 182ff; *Buddhist India*, pp. 19-20.

4 *Buddhist India*, p. 18; *Saṃ. Nik.*, I, p. 119; II,

exception of the village Khomadussa where all the brāhmaṇas seated in an assembly embraced Buddhism after hearing the preaching of the Teacher[1].

As stated above the essential portion of the Buddhist disciplinary code was made at Rājagaha, where the organisation of the Buddhist monastic order was first set on foot. The disciplinary rules framed at Sāvatthi and Kapilavatthu were therefore of a more or less supplementary character, though in point of number they were the largest. As new cases arose, the rules framed at the primary stage of the Saṅgha had to be added to or modified at Sāvatthi. During his long stay at the place Buddha thought out the minute details of many of the Vinaya rules and tried to make the code as comprehensive as possible. The rules framed in Kosala are :—

(*A*). *Re. Initiation.*—(1) Rāhula having been ordained without the knowledge of his mother and grandfather, the latter requested the Teacher to introduce the rule that no one should be ordained without the permission of his parents (I. 54. 6.).

p. 243, III, p. 5, IV, p. 14, V, p. 2; *Majjh. Nik.*, I, p. 456, II, p. 118.

1 *Saṃ. Nik.*, I, p. 184.

(2) The following were declared ineligible for admission into the order in addition to those already named in the rules framed at Rājagaha, viz., a maimed person, an eunuch, a false *titthiya*, a parricide, an arhanticide, a *saṅghabhedaka* etc. It was further enjoined that if any ineligible person be ordained by mistake, he should be turned out of the order (I. 6). To stop the ordination of undesirable or disqualified persons, an elaborate procedure for ordination was also formulated. (I. 76, 77, 78).

(3). A slight relaxation of the rule for initiation was made by allowing a bhikkhu who reverted to the life of a house-holder to have ordination again if he repented for his action. (I. 79).

(*B*). *Re. Upajjhāya and Ācariya.*—Hitherto the rule was that a bhikkhu could have one sāmaṇera only, but at Sāvatthi, the rule was modified permitting intelligent bhikkhus to have more than one sāmaṇera. Additional checks were also laid down on the mutual duties of the student and the teacher (I. 55, 57, 58, 60).

(*C*). *Re. Ten Precepts.*—During the first few years of Buddha's career he did not specify the number of precepts that the bhikkhus should observe, though in a general way they were taught through discourses the necessity of establishing control over *kāyakamma*, *vacīkamma* and *manokamma*. The sāmaṇeras became naturally inquisitive as to the number of the precepts, and requested Buddha to enumerate and define them. Buddha complied with their request, thereby framing the rule as to the number of precepts to be practised by the bhikkhus.

(*D*). *Re. Vassavāsa.*—Though the idea of introducing the system of remaining at a fixed place (*vassavāsa*) during the rains first struck the Teacher when he was at Rājagaha, the detailed rules for the guidance of monks as to their duties and functions during the period of *vassa* as well as at its close were worked out at Sāvatthi. The mentionable among them are :—

(1) *Sattāhakaraṇīya* or the rule of breaking the continuity of *vassavāsa* for seven days on account of unavoidable circumstances connected with the welfare of the Saṅgha. (III. 5-8).

(2) The detailing of the adverse circumstances under which *vassavāsa* may be discontinued.

(3) The rules for holding the *Pavāraṇā* ceremony at the end of *vassa* when the bhikkhus had to confess their sins committed during the period ; also rules prescribing punishments to be inflicted on them for non-confession, or for maliciously bringing a false charge against any bhikkhu.

(4) The rules regarding the *Kaṭhina* ceremony of the offering of robes to the bhikkhus by the laity at the close of a *vassavāsa* Many difficulties arose regarding the proper preservation and distribution of the robes. Elaborate rules had therefore to be laid down.

(*E*). *Re. Medicaments.*—Originally, the bhikkhus could use cow's urine only as medicine. But in course of time the rule regarding the use of medicines was much relaxed, permitting the bhikkhus to use all kinds of medicines. Permission was also given to the invalid bhikkhus to use, for their conveyance vehicles, sedan-chairs, etc. (VIII. 26).

Though the order of nuns was instituted at Vesāli in the *fifth* year of Buddha's ministry, the necessity for a bhikkhuṇī-code was not felt till a year or two later. Sāvatthi provided a large number of abodes for the nuns. This accounted for the existence of a large number of nuns in the town. This fact suggested to Buddha the urgency of disciplinary code for the nuns. Buddha thus set himself to framing the code and as the result of his labours, almost the whole of the *Pātimokkha* for the bhikkhuṇīs was completed. According to the *Parivārapāṭha,* 294 rules of the bhikkhu and bhikkhuṇī-*Pātimokkha* were laid down at Sāvatthi, but on actual calculation, we find the number to be 286. They comprise *Pārājikā* 4, *Saṅghādisesa* 15, *Aniyatā* 2, *Nissaggiyā* 34, *Khuddakāni* 148, *Gārayha* 10, *Sekhiya* 73[1].

It was at this place that a very important part of the *Vinaya* came into existence. Though Buddha had framed a good many rules for the guidance of the monks he mentioned in general terms the punishments for the breaches of the rules. In regard to many offences Buddha only referred to the class of the punishment that should be visited upon the offender. This gave rise to uncertainty as to the gravity or length of term of the punishment. To remove this difficulty as also to put on a sound footing the procedure for proving the guilt of an alleged offender before a panel of monks, he formulated elaborate rules governing the details of the various cases.

This sketch of the spread of Buddhism in Kosala would not be complete without a reference to at least some of the various centres established within the territory for facilitating the propagation of the religion and the pursuit of spiritual exercises by the bhikkhus. The name of Jetavana rises first in our mind.

1 *Vinaya*, V, p. 145.

As it is too well-known to need a description here, I pass on to the next important centre, Pubbārāma, a great monastery, built by Visākhā six to seven miles to the north-east of the Jetavana Vihāra. It could accommodate a large number of monks and nuns in its numerous chambers while it afforded facilities for deep meditation in its secluded cells. On account of the amenities of monk-life available here, it was a favourite resort of Buddha and his disciples, the former passing there so many as six *vassas*[1]. The existence of the hermitages of Kālākārāma, Kaṇṭakivana and Añjanavana[2] at Sāketa is responsible for the name of the place as a resort of bhikkhus. It was very probably Visākhā's father Dhanañjaya, who by taking a leading part in the movement, made it a Buddhist centre. Andhavana, situated at a short distance to the north-west of Jetavana Vihāra, ranks next to Pubbārāma in the provision of facilities to monks and nuns for meditation and spiritual exercises. It has been specially mentioned in the *Saṃyutta Nikāya*[3]

1 Hardy's *Manual*, p. 356

2 *Aṅg. Nik.*, II, p. 24; III, p. 169; IV, p 427; *Saṃ. Nik.*, V, pp. 73, 174, 217.

3 *Saṃ. Nik.*, I, p. 128, *Alavikā bhikkhuṇī yena Andhavanaṃ ten' upasaṇkami vivekatthikinī.* See also Watters' *Yuan Chwang*. I, p. 398.

that nuns of Ālavi (a suburb of Sāvatthi) seeking solitude used to come to this monastery. There were at Ālavi the hermitages Aggālava and Gomagga Siṃsāpavana which were also resorted to by the nuns. Midway between Sāvatthi and Setavyā stood Ukkaṭṭha containing an ārāma where two discourses of Buddha relating to the position of Brahmā were delivered[1].

[1] *Majjh. Nik.*, I, pp. 1, 326.

V

The Democracies

The territory to the east of Kosala and north of Aṅga and Magadha was occupied mainly by the various clans, namely, the Vajjis, Licchavis, Videhas, Mallas, Bhaggas, and Koliyas. All these clans lived side by side and most probably belonged to the same stock, and this accounted for the similarity of beliefs and practices that prevailed among them. Information about the ways in which the several clans except the Licchavis opposed the introduction of Buddhism among them is extremely scanty. It is only about the Licchavis that we can give a running account. Though the territory of this clan lay outside the limits of the brāhmaṇic middle-country, yet brāhmaṇism was here the prevailing religion. Belief in the brāhmaṇic pantheon, ceremonial worship of deities, performance of sacrifices, observances of ascetic practices, etc., wereall current among its members. They however were not so orthodox as to prevent the non-brāhmaṇical religions from taking root in their

Prevalence of brāhmaṇism among the Licchavis.

country. We find that a brāhmaṇa named Kāraṇapāli used to perform the religious functions of the Licchavis (*Licchavīnaṃ kammantaṃ kāreti*). There is also reference to another brāhmaṇa named Piṅgiyāni receiving cloths from the Licchavi youths as a token of their respect for him[1]. There were a good many shrines on the outskirts of Vesāli and the regular worship of the images of the deities enshrined there was carried on by the Licchavis[2]. Again the fact that the Licchavis worshipped many gods and goddesses of the brāhmaṇic pantheon at the time when their country was being ravaged by famine and pestilence is very significant. These instances are sufficient to show that the Licchavis were imbued to a large extent with the spirit of brāhmaṇism. But inspite of this fact, the path of progress of Buddhism among the Licchavis could not have been as thorny as among the people who were orthodox from the brāhmaṇic standpoint.

When Buddha came among the Licchavis, Jainism had already run through a career of about 250 years from the time of Parśvanātha and had adherents in many of the Licchavis.

1 *Aṅg. Nik.*, III, p. 236.

2 *Dīgh. Nik.*, II, p. 102; Mallas also had such shrines e. g. *Makuṭabandhana.*

This long career of Jainism in the kingdom of Vesāli was not there the only source of its strength. Nigaṇṭha Nātaputta, the reformer of Jainism, belonged to a distinguished family of the Nāta clan with wide influence in the land. This also operated as a source of strength to the religion, as it made it difficult for Buddha and his followers to carry on their missionary work. We have in the *Nikāyas* accounts of a few adherents of Nigaṇṭha Nātaputta either disputing with Buddha or coming into contact with him or his followers in the course of their missionary work. In the first account we find that Saccaka, who as a disputant was held in high respect by the Licchavis, sustains a defeat in a religious disputation with Buddha. It is not however clear whether he became a Buddhist convert as the result of the defeat[1]. In the second account in the *Aṅguttara Nikāya*, Abhaya and Paṇḍitakumāraka enquired of Ānanda about the means of destruction of *dukkha* as pointed out by Buddha and were not satisfied with the answer[2]. On another occasion he approached Buddha with the question whether

Jainism among the Licchavis before Buddha's advent.

1 *Majjh. Nik.*, I, pp. 236, 250.

2 *Aṅg. Nik.*, I, pp. 220-222.

ogha (flood of passions etc) could be overcome either by moral purity or severe penance. Buddha replied that it was only full control over mind, body, and speech that could save a person from *ogha*[1]. The most notable conversion made by Buddha among the lay Jainas was that of Sīha who was a military official of the Licchavis and had a great influence in the country. Inspite of Nigaṇṭha Nātaputta's dissuasion, he met Buddha, and impressed by his teachings, became an *upāsaka*. The weaning of Sīha from the Jaina faith gave a rude shock to Nigaṇṭha Nātaputta's followers who out of jealousy circulated the false report that Sīha had killed animals for feeding Buddha and the bhikkhus[2].

Inspite of active oppositions of this nature, Buddha continued his work of conversion in right earnest. The high encomiums showered on Buddha by the Licchavis at a meeting of their assembly, the feeling of wonder expressed by Mahānāma at the sudden change of the Licchavi youths under Buddha's influence[3], and the desire of Oṭṭhaddha Licchavi with a large retinue to

1 *Aṅg. Nik.*, II, pp. 200-202.

2 *Vinya*, VI, 31, 12.

3 Dr. B. C. Law, *Kṣattriya Clans in Buddhist India*, pp. 88,89.

hear Buddha's discourses[1], show that Buddha could create a favourable impression on the minds of the local people and achieve some success in his missionary activities. As a mark of their devotion to Buddha they dedicated to him not only the Mahāvana Kūṭāgārasālā but also a large number of *Cetiyas* which were also highly appreciated by him as places for meditation[2]. Of these *Cetiyas*, the one at Gosiṅgasālavana was particularly liked by him and his chief disciples Sāriputta and Moggalāna who passed there many a day in meditation[3]. The conversions made by Buddha among the Licchavis were not commensurate with the acts of generosity mentioned above, as the cases of conversion mentioned in the *Nikāyas* are not many. Ānanda's exclusion of Vesāli from the list of places where the laydevotees lived in large numbers also point to the same conclusion[1]. The names of Mahāli, Mahānāma, Ugga-gahapati, Nandaka the

1 *Dīgh. Nik.*, I., p. 151.

2 See *Dīgh. Nik.*, II, p. 102. "*Ramaṇīyā Ānanda Vesāli, ramaṇīyaṃ Udenaṃ cetiyaṃ, ramaṇīyaṃ Gotamakaṃ cetiyaṃ, r. Bahuputtaṃ c., r. Sārandadaṃ c., r. Cāpalaṃ c.*"

3 *Majjh. Nik.*, I. p. 212 ; *Aṅg. Nik.*, V, pp. 133-4

1 *Dīgh. Nik.*, II, p. 169.

minister, Piṅgiyāni brāhmaṇa and a few others are mentioned as converts to Buddhism. Oṭṭhaddha Licchavi and Bhaggava paribbājaka were much impressed by the teachings of Buddha but they did not adopt the religion. On account of the attachment of Sunakkhatta Licchaviputta to other beliefs and practices, Buddha had to be disappointed in him. He joined the order as a bhikkhu and remained as such for about three years. He expected to see the exhibition of his miraculous powers and to have from him the solution of some of the indeterminable problems, all of which Buddha deliberately avoided on principle. This exasperated Sunakkhatta who left the order and commenced speaking ill of it broadcast. This disparagement by Sunakkhatta became the topic of many discussions between Buddha and the Licchavis to whom he explained his position by stating that the benefits of the religion could not be derived by one who had attachment to other teachers and their doctrines and practices[1].

One of the most important events in the history of Buddhism transpired at Vesāli. It was here that Buddha gave his consent to the formation of the order of nuns at the importunities of Ānanda

1 *Dīgh Nik.*, I, pp. 150ff; III, pp. 2ff.

and Mahāpajāpati Gotamī. The latter had already advanced a little as a lay-devotee in the path of sanctification at the time of conversion of Rāhula and Nanda. It was after the death of King Suddhodana that she in the fulness of her grief resolved to embrace the life of a recluse. She formed a band of recluses by bringing together a few ladies who had been bent on retirement from the world for some reason or other. With them she travelled under great physical stress and strain from Kapilavatthu to Vesāli where Buddha was staying and obtained his consent to the formation of the order of nuns by agreeing to comply with the eight ordinances laid down at the time by Buddha for the bhikkhuṇīs[1]. She made a steady progress in spiritual culture under the guidance of Buddha and soon attained the highest stage of sanctification.

Consent to the formation of the order of nuns.

Buddha passed through Vesāli in the course of his last tour. The only notable conversion made on this occasion was that of the famous courtezan Ambapāli who gave away her Ambavana to the Buddhist saṅgha. It was

Buddha's last visit to Vesāli.

1 *Aṅg Nik.*, IV, p. 274.

while dwelling at Cāpala Cetiya situated on the outskirts of Vesāli that Buddha resolved to end his mortal existence in three months.

During Buddha's residence at Vesāli he brought into operation for the discipline of the bhikkhus a few additional measures, which are as follows :—

(1) The bhikkhus were practically prohibited from taking fish or flesh by the framing of the rule that they could take them if the fish or the animals had not been seen, heard, or suspected to have been killed for the bhikkhus (vi, 31. 14).

(2) In view of the scarcity of food at Vesāli at a particular time, certain rules were relaxed allowing the bhikkhus to keep food and cook it indoors, eat such articles of food as they could pick up, take food before meal-time etc[1]. When there was plenty in the land after some time, the rules were restored to their former severity.

(3) The bhikkhus were allowed to have a *Kappiyabhūmi* outside their dwelling-place for the temporary storing of food (vi, 33).

(4) The number of robes of the bhikkhus was limited to three.

(5) An abnormal increase in the number of cases of religious suicide led to the promulgation

1 *S. B. E.*, XVII, p. 118.

of the rule prohibiting absolutely the commission of suicide generally (*Pārā.* III).

Of the *Pātimokkha* rules, ten were framed at Vesāli, comprising three under *Pārājikā*, two under *Nissaggiya Pācittiya*, and three under *Pācittiya*.

Buddha's work among the Videhas.

The kingdom of Videha became in the pre-Buddhistic days an important centre of brāhmaṇic culture on account of King Janaka's enthusiasm, and patronage of learning and spiritual culture which converted his court into an important meeting-place of learned men specially from the western countries of Kosala and Kuru-Pañcāḷa[1]. The *Makhādeva* and *Mahājanaka Jātakas* and the *Brahmāyu Sutta* of the *Majjhima Nikāya*[2] testify to the prevalence of brāhmaṇism in Videha at the time of Buddha. The *Nikāyas* are silent as to Buddha's missionary work in the place and the volume of opposition met by him there in the propagation of his religion. It is only in the *Majjhima Nikāya* that we find that he stayed at Makhādeva-ambavana of Mithilā and converted on a certain occasion

1 *Bṛhadāraṇyaka Upaniṣad,* III; Oldenberg's *Buddha*, p. 398.

2 *Majjh. Nik.,* II., pp. 74ff; 133ff.

Brahmāyu a distinguished and an old brāhmaṇa teacher.

Not so however fruitless was his work among the Bhaggas. Buddha succeeded in converting three distinguished inhabitants of the Bhagga country, namely Nakulapitā, Nakulamātā, and Bodhirājakumāra. There might have been other converts but their names do not appear in the *Nikāyas*. Buddha and his chief disciple Moggalāna visited this place on two or three occasions and stayed at Suṃsumāragiri Bhesakalāvana-migadāya. Buddha delivered a few discourses, at the instance of Nakulapitā and Nakulamātā, two of his most favourite lay-disciples, detailing the duties of house-holders[1]. The discourses delivered here by Moggalāna relate to the means of overcoming passions (*māratajjanīya*)[2]. It was while Buddha was residing in this country that Bodhirājakumāra requested Buddha to stay in his newly built palace Kokanada for a day sanctifying it by his presence, and give him opportunity of formally taking refuge in

Buddha among the Bhaggas.

1 *Aṅg. Nik.*, II, p. 61 ; III, p. 295 ; IV, pp. 85, 268 ; *Saṃ. Nik.*, IV, p. 116.

2 *Majjh. Nik.*, I, pp. 95, 332.

Buddha, Dhamma, and Saṅgha[1]. Three of the minor *Pātimokkha* rules, one under *Pācittiya* and two under *Sekhiya* were framed here.

Buddha among the Koliyas.

In his missionary work Buddha was more successful among the Koliyas than among the Bhaggas. This was due partly to the contiguity of the Koliyas to the Sākyas and partly to the connection of Buddha with the Koliyas through his mother and wife. The first visit paid by Buddha to this country was from Vesāli in the fifth year of his ministry when a fight became imminent between the Sākyas and the Koliyans over the right of drawing water from a stream[2]. It was when the armies of the two clans were arrayed in the battle-field that Buddha intervened and brought about an amicable settlement by his thoughtful and pacifying discourses. Many members of both the clans were struck by Buddha's greatness and were moved so much by his teachings that they retired from the world to become bhikkhus. Of those who were converted to Buddhism at this place, the names of Puṇṇa-govatika and Seniya-

1 *Majjh. Nik.*, II, p. 91.

2 Burlingame's *Buddhist Legends*, III, pp. 70ff ; *Jātakas*, V, pp. 412-413 ; Hardy's *Manual*, pp. 317-20.

kukkuravatika should be mentioned, as they were typical brāhmaṇic ascetics believing in the efficacy of severe penances[1]. Kakudha Koliyaputta became a *saddhivihārika* (novice) of Moggalāna,[2] while Suppāvāsā Koliyadhītā praised by Buddha as the chief of the *panītadāyikānaṃ* (givers of sweet food)[3], and Pāṭaliyagāmaṇī, who required a pretty long discourse dealing with the various contemporary doctrines and the excellences of Buddhism to be convinced, became lay-devotees[4].

Buddha among the Mallas.

The prominence attained by the Mallas of Kusinārā in the Buddhist literature is due to the accident of Kusinārā being the site of Buddha's *parinibbāna*. The reason underlying the objection made by Ānanda to the selection of the place by Buddha for his *parinibbāna* was that it was unimportant as a centre of Buddhism. The mandate issued by the Assembly of the Mallas that persons not according welcome to Buddha would be fined 500 *kahāpanas* shows that there was among the Mallas a party

1 *Majjh. Nik.*, I, p. 387.
2 *Aṅg. Nik.*, III, p. 122.
3 *Ibid.*, I, p. 26; II, p. 62.
4 *Saṃ. Nik.*, IV., pp. 340-358.

opposed to Buddha and his religion. Malla Roja belonged to this party but on coming into contact with Buddha, he could not resist turning a *upāsaka*[1]. Of the two well-known converts from this clan, one was Dabba Mallaputta, the distributer of food and assingnor of residences to the monks at Rājagaha[2], while the other was Cunda kammāraputta who by serving to Buddha his last meal has been immortalized in the Buddhist literature[3].

The Malla country is the scene of two important discourses delivered by Buddha. One of them is the *sutta* in the *Aṅguttara Nikāya* meant to explain to Tapassu gahapati the great charm inhering in the spiritual exercises practised by a monk, by virtue of which they could spurn the pleasures of worldly life. It was the attraction of this happiness in the life of a monk that persuaded even youngmen to turn recluses. Buddha explained the successive stages by which the highest spiritual culture could be reached through this life of meditation and discipline[4]. The other discourse is the *Kinti sutta* of the *Majjhima*

1 *Vinaya*, I, pp. 247, 248.
2 See *ante*, p. 99.
3 *Dīgh. Nik.*, II, pp. 126-8.
4 *Aṅg. Nik.*, V, p. 263.

Nikāya in which Buddha explained that he was out as a preacher not from any selfish motive but for the spiritual uplift of men who had by previous *karma* an innate inclination to the attainment of deliverance from the worldly miseries and required some assistance and guidance for the achievement of their object[1].

[1] *Majjh. Nik.*, II, pp. 238-243.

VI

Other Eastern Countries

1. ANGA. In the estimation of the orthodox brāhmaṇas, Aṅga occupied a place similar to that of Magadha, for it was beyond the Sadānīrā and was looked down upon along with Magadha as a country unfit for the performance of sacrifice and bad enough to be a place whither fever should be driven away from Brahmarṣi-deśa[1]. Aṅga like Magadha had renowned brāhmaṇa teachers, two of whom are mentioned in the *Nikāyas*. One is Soṇadaṇḍa brāhmaṇa living at Campā with 300 students and having a permanent source of income granted him by king Bimbisāra[2], and the other is Pārāsariya brāhmaṇa dwelling at Kajaṅgala[3] with Uttara māṇava and other students[4]. Aṅga felt

Similarity of conditions in Aṅga and Magadha in regard to religion.

1 *Śatapatha-Brāhmaṇa*, I. 4, 1; *Atharva Veda*, v, 22, 14.

2 *Dīgh. Nik.*, I, pp. 111ff.

3 For identification, see Cunningham's *Ancient Geography* (2nd. ed.), pp. xliii, 548, 723; *J. R. A. S.*, 1904.

4 *Majjh. Nik.*, III, p. 298.

also the influence of Nigaṇṭha Nātaputta as apparent from the fact that Anāthapiṇḍika's son-in-law belonged to a family with Jaina persuasion. There were also in Aṅga paribbājakārāmas where the paribbājakas stayed from time to time in the course of their tour[1]. The importance of the country in the history of the spread of Buddhism is on account of its being the easternmost place reached by Buddhism within Buddha's life-time[2]. According to the *Vinaya*, the eastern limit of the Buddhist *majjhima-desa* is Kajaṅgala situated within Aṅga at a distance of about 66 miles to the east of Campā. It was visited by Buddha and made the scene of the last *sutta* of the *Majjhima Nikāya* on *Indriya-bhāvanā*.

It is not definitely stated anywhere in the *Nikāyas* and other treatises as to the time, when Buddha paid his first visit to the country of Aṅga. On more than one occasion Buddha had been to Aṅga dwelling at Campā, Āpana, Assapura and Kajaṅgala. It was during one of these visits

Buddha's activities in Aṅga.

1 *Saṃ, Nik.*, V, p. 189 ; *Majjh. Nik.*, I, p. 339.

2 It is mentioned in the *Saṃyutta Nikāya* (V, pp. 89, 168, 169) that the easternmost place visited by Buddha in the course of his missionary tour was Setaka, a nigama of Suhma in Rāḍha.

that he converted the father-in-law of Anāthapiṇḍika's daughter together with other members of his family. During his absence at Campā on this occasion he left Anuruddha to carry on the missionary work[1]. Soṇadaṇḍa was converted at a time when Bimbisāra, Pasenadi and Pokkharasādi had already become Buddha's disciples. The conversion of the two kings and the distinguished brāhmaṇa teacher was cited by Sonadaṇḍa as a ground, justifying his desire to approach Buddha to listen to his teachings[2]. We find that during Buddha's life-time there were at Aṅga several lay-devotees, as evidenced not only by passages in the *Majjhima* and *Anguttara Nikāyas*[3] but also by separate mentions of their names in various places in the Buddhist scriptures. The most notable of them were Pessa-hatthārohaputta and Vajjiyamāhita gahapati. The former was a great admirer of the spiritual exercises and though a house-holder he tried to practise the four *satipaṭṭhānas*[4], while the latter was praised by

1 Kern's *Manual*, p. 38.

2 *Digh. Nik.*, I, p. 116.

3 *Campeyyakā upāsakā*; *Kajaṅgalā upāsakā*, see *Majjh. Nik.*, III, p. 298; *Aṅg. Nik.*, IV, p. 59.

4 *Majjh. Nik.*, I, p. 340. "presentness of memory

Buddha for his insight into the Buddhist *dhamma*, enabling him to silence those paribbājakas who spoke ill of Buddha in his presence[1]. The *Vinaya* and the *Thera-gāthā* supply us with names of a few bhikkhus who were inhabitants of Aṅga. One of them is the well-known Soṇa-Kolivisa who was ordained a bhikkhu at Rājagaha, the others were Nandaka and Bharata whose psalms have been preserved in the *Thera-gāthā*[2]. We also meet with the name of a bhikkhuṇī belonging to Kajaṅgala and engaged in instructing a few lay-devotees in the principles of Buddhism[3].

The framing of a few Vinaya rules in Aṅga.

While Buddha was at Campā on a particular occasion, some of the bhikkhus completed a few official acts irregularly, unlawfully and without a full chapter of monks. This led Buddha to detail the various formal acts the bhikkhus were to perform, mentioning

in regard (i) to the body (ii) to sensations (iii) to rising thoughts ; and (iv) to *Dharma*". Kern, *op. cit.*, p. 67.

1 *Aṅg. Nik.*, V, pp. 189-192.

2 *Psalms of the Brethren*, p. 135 ; *Vinaya*, MV., V. 1 : it was on account of the very delicate feet of the bhikkhu Soṇa Kolivisa that the rule of using shoes by the bhikkhus came to be introduced.

3 *Majjh. Nik.*, III, p. 298.

the occasion, the procedure to be followed in each case, circumstances which would make them invalid and the punishments that would be inflicted on them for breaches of the rules[1].

Kāśī, an important place.

2. KĀŚĪ. The importance of Kāśī as a great centre of brāhmaṇic culture and learning is recognised in both the Brāhmaṇic and Buddhistic literature. The frequent mention of the place in the *Jātakas* is indicative of its great importance in those days. The Ṛṣipattana of Kāśi has been immortalized in the Pāli as well as the Buddhist-Sanskrit literature as a resort of a large number of ṛṣis in ancient times. The selection of the locality by Buddha for the delivery of his first discourse at the commencement of his missionary career is quite in line with its sacred tradition. In this land of orthodox brāhmaṇism, Buddha's missionary work was naturally hampered by opposition from the brāhmaṇas. For this reason his success here was not so marked as it was in Magadha and Kosala. Buddha's ministration commenced with the conversion of two foreign traders Trapusa and

1 *Vinaya*, MV, IX.

Buddha's first converts.

Bhallika who were travelling with a caravan along the trade-route from Dakkhiṇāpatha to Ukkala[1] a town in the kingdom of Gandhāra. Their conversion at Uruvela was later on commemorated by the erection of *stūpas* in their native villages[2] in Gandhāra. Buddha after enlightenment turned his thoughts first to his comrades in asceticism then residing at Isipatana near Benares. He started from Uruvela and

1 & 2 *Lalitavistara* (Lefmann's edition), Vol. III, pp. 303, 310, 313: *Uttarāpathe Ukkalaṃ nāmādhiṣṭhānaṃ. ......Tehi dāni yathā Keśasthālī nāma adhiṣṭhāno tahiṃ keśa-stūpaṃ kārāpitaṃ. Bālukkho nāma nagaraṃ tahiṃ nakha-stūpaṃ kārāpitaṃ...... Trapusabhallikānāṃ Śilukṣa nāma nigama āvāsitānāṃ......adyāpi Gandhāra-rājye adhiṣṭhānaṃ Śilānāmena jñāyati*". There has been a great difference of opinion with regard to the identification of Ukkala and the birth-place of Trapusa and Bhallika. Though the phonetic similarity between Utkala (Orissa) and Ukkala is very great and the identification of Ukkala with Orissa is alluring, yet in view of the evidence supplied by the *Mahāvastu* and supported by Yuan Chwang, Ukkala should be identified with a place in Gandhāra. Yuan Chwang noticed the remains of two of the stūpas mentioned above in the course of his journey from Balkh to Bamian (Watters' *Yuan Chwang*, I, pp. 111-113).

passed through Gayā, Aparagayā and reached Vaśālā where he was invited to a meal by a *huhuṅka* brāhmaṇa to whom he pointed out as to what makes a true brāhmaṇa and tried to convert him to Buddhism. Thence he passed through Cundadvīlaṃ and Sārathipura, crossed the Ganges and reached Benares[1]. Here at Isipatana he visited his five comrades who would not accept Buddha's arguments regarding the the futility of extreme self-mortifications in taking them to their spiritual goal. Their conviction had to be slowly overcome by Buddha through teachings from day to day impressing upon their minds the impermanence of all worldly things. They were enjoined to live as recluses, practising *jhanas* and self-control[2]. It was for them that he delivered his famous discourse, the *Dhammacakkapavattana* which is believed to have embodied truths found by Buddha under the Bodhi tree. It explains the *majjhima paṭipadā* or in other words the practice of control over *citta* which included *dhyāna*, attainment of *paññā* or true knowledge and perfection in the *sīlas*

1 *Mahāvastu*, III, pp. 324-329; *Lalitavistara*, p. 406.

2 *Majjh. Nik.*, I, pp. 173-175; *Saṃ. Nik.*, III, p. 66.

by pursuing the golden mean. The discourse shows the hollowness of extreme self-mortifications practised by the five brāhmaṇas as the only path leading to *mukti* (salvation). The accumulated effect of the discourse and the teachings was the conversion of the five brāhmaṇas to Buddhism.

Buddha accompanied by the five new bhikkhus passed from Isipatana to Benares and stopped on the bank of the river Varaṇā under a *nigrodha* tree where he met Yasa a rich seṭṭhi's son, who had already become sick of this world. Buddha found his mind a *tabula rasa* fit to receive his doctrines. He therefore addressed to him his discourse on *dāna* (charity), *sīla* (moral precepts) *sagga* (heaven), etc., suited so much to householders[1]. Yasa was ordained as a bhikkhu after which his fifty-four friends followed suit.

Yasa's conversion.

Thus far successful in his mission, Buddha entertained the idea of spreading his religion far and wide by utilizing the services of these sixty converts as preachers. After sending them to their respective tasks in different places, he himself went to Uruvela for preaching his religion.

Buddha's missionary idea.

1 *Vinaya*, MV. i, 6 ; *Mahāvastu*, vol. III, pp. 405ff ; Rockhill's *Life of Buddha*, pp. 38-39.

Buddha spent his first *vassa* at Isipatana and it was long before he visited it for the second time, for he came to this place after the 12th *vassa* on his way from Verañja to Vesāli[1]. But though his visits to this place were not frequent, it was nevertheless a very important centre of Buddhism through the missionary efforts of some of the most prominent of his disciples namely, Sāriputta, Moggalāna, Mahākoṭṭhita, Mahākaccāyana. When Buddha was staying here during his second visit, he delivered a discourse on the true meaning of *avijjā*[2], and advised the upāsaka Dhammadinna to follow practices enjoined in the *suttantas*. If these practices were too difficult for him to follow, he was asked to place faith in *Buddha, Dhamma and Saṅgha*[3], for faith alone could make him a *sotāpanna*, that is one who is in the first stage of sanctification.

Isipatana as a centre.

The delivery of the first discourse by Buddha at the deer-park brought the place into prominence. As it was the first scene of Buddha's missionary activities he himself clothed it with a

1 Kern's *Manual of Indian Buddhism*, p. 36 ; *J. R. A. S.*, 1891.

2 *Saṃ. Nik.*, V, p. 429.

3 *Ibid.*, V, p. 407.

sacred memory and ranked it among the four places of pilgrimage most sacred to a Buddhist[1]. The inscription on the Asoka pillar containing the warning to the *saṅghabhedakas* (schismatics) shows that it continued at the time to be a resort of many contentious Buddhist monks. The beginning of a monastic establishment here are found in the *Nikāyas* where it is stated that bhikkhus often sat in a *maṇḍalamālā* and had discussions over *abhidhamma*[2], the interpretation of verses uttered by Buddha[3], the meaning of *avijjā* and such other topics. As Mahākoṭṭhita figures so often in the discourses as taking part in the discussions described therein, it seems reasonable to infer that he was permanently associated with the locality.

The only Vinaya rule framed here relates to the delegation of the power of initiation to the disciples. Buddha had hitherto been performing the initiation personally with the simple formula "*Ehi bhikkhu, svākkhato dhammo, cara brahmacariyaṃ samma dukkhassa antakiriyāyāti* (Come O bhikkhus, well taught is the doctrine, lead a holy life for the sake of the complete

1 *Dīgh. Nik.*, Mahāparinibbāṇa Suttanta.
2 *Aṅg. Nik.*, III, pp. 392-393.
3 *Ibid.*, III, p. 399.

extinction of suffering), but with the increase of his disciples sent out from Benares it was no longer feasible for him to do so because the converts were growing larger in number and the conversions had to be made at distant places. So he had to delegate the power of initiation to his disciples and required the converts to be shaven, put on yellow robes and utter thrice the formula for taking refuge in Buddha, Dhamma and Saṅgha.[1]

Vatsa.

3. VATSA. Buddha had been to the country of the Vatsas on two or three occasions and passed his ninth *vassa* at Kosambi. His tenth *vassa* was passed in a neighbouring forest called Pārileyyaka whither he retired in disgust at the quarrel that took place between the two groups of bhikkhus of Kosambi, viz., the *Dhammadharas* and the *Vinaya-dharas*[2]. At Kosambi he usually stayed at the hermitage Pāvārika-ambavana built by Pāvāriya, a rich seṭṭhi. There were other hermitages, two of which had been constructed by the seṭṭhis Kukkuṭa and Ghosita. Sāmāvatī was converted by Khujjutarā praised by Buddha as the chief of the learned upāsikās. The queen's devotion to

1 *Vinaya*, MV, vii. 15 ; i. 12. 3-4.

2 See Bk. II of this work.

Buddha was resented very much by another queen as also by her father Māgandiya, a minister of the king of Kosambi, having a great aversion to Buddha. It was during the absence of king Udena at the city that Māgandiya plotted against the life of Sāmāvatī and burnt her to death. King Udena was shocked at this incident and turned an adherent of Buddhism as this was the religion that could evoke so much of religious devotion in the queen[1]. Of the other lay-devotees, we may mention the name of Sandaka the *paribbājaka* who was converted against the will of his followers by Ānanda[2]. The only bhikkhu whose name is recorded in *Nikāyas* as belonging to the city is Piṇḍola Bharadvāja praised by Buddha as the chief of the *sīhanādikānaṃ* (lit. Lion-roarers). He was the son of the royal chaplain of Kosambi and was versed in brāhmaṇic lore[3].

While Buddha was residing at Kosambi, he felt the necessity of framing rules for averting chances of future dissensions in his order. He

1 *Buddhist India*, p. 36; Burlingame, *op. cit.*, I, pp. 277ff.; *Yuan Chwang*, I, p. 369; *Divyāvadāna*, p. 529ff.

2 *Majjh. Nik.*, I, p. 513.

3 *Aṅg. Nik.*, I, p. 25; *Saṃ. Nik.*, V, p. 224.; *Psalms of the Brethren*, pp. 110-111.

detailed, as recorded in the tenth book of the Mahāvagga, the circumstances in which a schism could take place and dwelt on their evil consequences[1]. Of the *Pātimokkha* rules, six were framed here, one under *Saṅghādisesa* and five under *Pācittiya.*

Cedi.

4. CEDI. The country of the Cedis to the west of Kosala lay, it seems, beyond the pale of Buddhism during Buddha's lifetime. Sahajāti, a place in Cedi, attained some prominence as a centre of Buddhism after the death of Buddha. In the *Aṅguttara* and *Saṃyutta Nikāyas* we come across the name of this place as the scene of some of the discourses delivered by the bhikkhu Mahācunda and as the resort of many bhikkhus[2].

1 See Bk. II of this work.

2 *Aṅg. Nik.,* III, p. 355; V, pp. 41, 157; *Saṃ. Nik.,* V, p. 436.

VII

Western And Northern Countries

Dr. Oldenberg's statement that Buddhism was confined only to the *prācya-deśa* is due, I think, to the difficulty in the consultation of unedited texts. He drew support from a passage of the *Mahāparinibbāṇa Suttanta*[1] in which Ānanda enumerated a few towns to Buddha for selecting one of them as the place of his *parinibbāṇa*. As these were the towns where the Buddhist devotees lived in large numbers, the westernmost of them was taken by Dr. Oldenberg as the farthest western limit of Buddha's missionary activities[2]. But a close study of the of the *Nikāyas* shows that Buddha did travel outside the *prācya-deśa* as far west as Verañja, Madhurā[3] and as far north as the country of the Kurus[4]. Another evidence in support of our

Dr. Oldenberg's statement that Buddhism was confined to the *prācya-deśa* criticised.

1 *Dīgh. Nik.*, II, p. 146.

2 Oldenberg's *Buddha*, Excursus I.

3 *Majjh. Nik.*, II, p. 83 ; *Vinaya, Suttavibhaṅga* I, ; 4.

4 *Majjh. Nik.*, I, p. 55.

contention that Buddhism was not confined to *prācya-deśa* is that many disciples of Buddha hailed from *paccantima janapada* or border countries. The reason why the designation *paccantima-desa* was applied to places like Saṃkassa and Ujjeni which are far away from the Indian Frontiers is to be found in the fact that they formed the border-land between *majjhima-desa* of the Buddhists and other places. The rules of discipline framed by Buddha were meant generally for those monks who resided within *majjhima-desa*, boundaries of which are given in the *Vinaya*[1]. Though the boundaries are not identifiable at present except on the eastern side yet it is known that places where Buddhism flourished like Saṃkassa, Avanti, Gandhāra etc. were distinguished as *paccantima janapadas*. Buddha himself relaxed some of the rules of discipline in regard to the monks of those places in view of the physical conditions within which they lived. This relaxation of the rules shows that

Paccantima janapada an integral part of the area within which Buddhism spread during Buddha's lifetime.

1 *Vinaya*, I, v. 13; ix. 4. 1; *J. R. A. S.*, 1904, pp. 83ff.; *Jātaka*, I; Bhandarkar's *Carmichael Lectures*, 1918, p. 43.

Buddha had to take note of the convenience and needs of the monks of the distant regions indicated by the expression *paccantima-janapada.* This proves clearly that the religion in the contemplation of Buddha was not one confined to the eastern territories alone as supposed by Dr. Oldenberg but it was as well a religion that had its roots in the regions lying outside the *majjhima-desa.* This is corroborated by the fact that within a century after Buddha's *nibbaṇa,* Avanti and Pāṭheyya rose to be important centres of Buddhism, so much so that the presence of monks from these distant places was regarded as indispensable at the meetings held for settling points of dispute raised by the Vajjian monks of Vesāli.

A. WESTERN COUNTRIES. Though the whole of western India was placed outside the *majjhima-desa* of the *Vinaya,* Buddhism made a fair progress there during the life-time of Buddha and played an important role in the later history of Buddhism, and that although Buddha wandered generally within the *prācya-deśa,* the religion however was not confined to the region, as supposed by Dr. Oldenberg, but spread over many regions of Western India counting among its adherents people from the western countries such as Roruka, Bharukaccha, Suppāraka, Avanti, Ujjeni, Aparānta, having their monastic establishments at some of these places. The westernmost point reached by Buddha in his peregrinations was Verañja a place near Madhurā in the 12th year after his enlightenment.

Buddha at Verañja.

When Buddha was at Sāvatthi, some brāhmaṇas of Verañja (situated probably west of Madhurā) were there on some business. They had a talk with him about the fruits of good and evil *karma*[1]. On one occasion Buddha was invited by Verañja brāhmaṇas to go to their native country, which Buddha did at the outset of the twelfth *vassa*[2]. We find from a passage in the *Aṅguttara Nikāya*[3] that Buddha once stopped on his way from Madhurā to Verañja (*antarā ca Madhuraṃ antarā ca Verañjaṃ*) and delivered there a discourse to the house-holders on the ideal husband and wife. These house-holders were on their way from Verañja to Madhurā. This shows that Verañja was situated near Madhurā on the analogy of similar passages

1 *Majjh. Nik.*, I, pp. 290-291.

2 Burlingame's *Buddhist Legends*, II, p. 193; Kern's *Manual of Indian Buddhism*, p. 36; *J. R. A. S.*, 1891.

3 *Aṅg. Nik.*, II, p. 57.

found in the Pāli texts where localities situated at a short distance from one another were described exactly in the way in which Madhurā and Verañja have been in the passage quoted above. Buddha and his bhikkhus had a bitter experience at Verañja. It was during their residence there that a famine broke out and the bhikkhus were put to a great difficulty in procuring their daily food. They were neglected by the people of the locality and would have starved but for the charity of some horse-dealers of the northern country who stopped there in the midst of their journey and supplied them with steamed grain in *pattha* measures[1]. Buddha took up his residence at Nalerupucimandamūla where a Verañja brāhmaṇa came and questioned him the reason of his not showing marks of respect to the aged brāhmaṇas. To this question Buddha made a suitable reply justifying his behaviour and converted the brāhmaṇa to Buddhism[2]. At the very same place he had a similar talk with Pahārada Asurinda regarding the eight excellences of his *dhamma* and *vinaya*[3]. He left Verañja at the

1 *Vinaya*, III, p. 6; Burlingame's *Buddhist Legends*, II, p. 193.

2 *Aṅg. Nik.*, IV, p. 172; *Vinaya*, III, pp. 2ff.

3 *Aṅg. Nik.*, IV, pp. 197ff.

end of the *vassa* and accompanied by Ānanda passed through Soreyya, Saṅkassa, Kaṇṇakujja, Payāgapatiṭṭhānaṃ, crossed the Ganges and reached Benares[1]. He met here Mahākaccāyana for the first time and by converting him paved the way for the establishment of a centre of Buddhism in Avantī.

Mahākaccāyana was one of the most distinguished apostles of the Buddhist faith and made a substantial contribution to its prosperity. He was the son of the royal priest of king Caṇḍa Pajjota of Avantī. He was the nephew of ṛṣi Asita (or Kāladevala) the great seer of the Vindhyācala who paid his homage to Siddhārtha when a child. It was at Asita's advice that the young ascetic Nālaka (former name of Mahākaccāyana) came to Benares to pay a visit to Buddha and being very much impressed by the unsurpassed erudition of the Teacher, became a Buddhist monk along with his companions[2]. This group of bhikkhus with Mahā-

Mahākaccāyana, founder of the centre in Avantī.

1 *Vinaya* III, p. 11. (From Benares, Buddha went to Vesāli where he spent his 13th vassa).

2 *Mahāvastu*, II, p. 30; III, p. 382; *Romantic History of Buddha* (translated from the Chinese *Abhiniṣkramaṇa Sūtra*) by S. Beal, p. 276; *Sutta Nipāta* (P. T. S.), Nālaka Sutta, vs. 696ff.

kaccāyana as their head returned to their native country and founded āśramas there at Kururaghara-papāta-pabbata and Makkarakaṭa in Avantī. Of the notable converts made here, names of Puṇṇa, Soṇa Kuṭikaṇṇa of Aparānta, Isidatta a caravan guide of Velugāma, and Kaṇḍarāyaṇa brāhmaṇa may be mentioned[1]. In the *Thera-* and *Theri-Gāthā,* we come across names of a few other monks and nuns of Avantī whose psalms have been preserved in the collection[2] and in the *Majjhima Nikāya* we meet with the conversion of king Madhura Avantiputta by Mahākaccāyana by delivering the famous discourse on caste-system after the parinibbāṇa of Buddha[3].

A remarkable feature of the activities of Mahākaccāyana is that he as an expositor was engaged more in giving detailed expositions of Buddha's enigmatic sayings than delivering independent discourses of his own. People used to come to him for solving their doubts in regard to utterances of Buddha : Kālī upāsikā requested

1 *Psalms of the Brethren* by Mrs. Rhys Davids; *Aṅg. Nik.*, I, p. 68; *Saṃ Nik.*, IV, p. 288.

2 *Psalms of the Brethren*, pp. 41, 42, 107, 149, 292. *Psalms of the Sisters*, pp. 30, 31.

3 *Majjh. Nik.*, II, pp. 83ff.

him to explain a stanza from *Kumāripañha*[1] of the *Sutta Nipāta* (i. p. 126), the Hāliddikāni gahapati from the *Māgandiyapañha* of the *Aṭṭhakavagga* and *Sakkapañha Sutta* of the *Dīgha Nikāya* (*Sutta* No. 21) and so forth[2].

It was under the guidance of Mahakaccāyana helped by Soṇa Kuṭikaṇṇa that Buddhism inspite of adverse circumstances[3] gradually obtained a footing in Avanti. Though the country was situated at a long distance from Magadha, yet on account of its facilities of communication with the ports of Western India and the principal cities of Magadha and Kosala it became an important centre of Buddhism.

The centre of Buddhism in Avanti, it seems, laid special stress on the ascetic practices allowed by the Buddhist code for which it is remarked in the *Vinaya* that the bhikkhus of Avanti were followers of *dhūtavāda* precepts[4].

Though names of western countries other than Avanti are not found in the *Nikāyas*, we come across in the *Vinaya* and *Divyāvadāna* Roruka and Aparānta as places where Buddhism spread during Buddha's life-time.

1 *Aṅg. Nik.*, V, pp. 46ff.
2 *Saṃ. Nik.*, III, pp. 12, 13 ; IV, p. 115.
3 *Aṅg. Nik.*, III, p. 256.
4 *Vinaya*, CV., II, p. 299.

Rudrāyaṇa, king of Roruka, first received through Bimbisāra, the message of the advent of Buddha in Magadha. Bimbisāra sent him inscribed on a plate some of the principles of Buddhism which made a great impression upon Rudrāyaṇa's mind, so much so that he became a Buddhist upāsaka and afterwards a bhikkhu[1].

Roruka.

The notable figure of Aparānta is Puṇṇa who belonged to Suppāraka, a port of Aparānta. His firm resolution to propagate Buddhism inspite of adverse circumstances was commended by Buddha, who on account of this sturdiness in the cause of the religion considered him the fittest person to be entrusted with the work of preaching there his religion[2].

Aparānta.

B. NORTHERN COUNTRIES. The farthest place in the North visited by Buddha in the course of his missionary tour was that of the Kurus,—the ancient home of the highest brāhmaṇic culture. Buddha delivered two important discourses in two of the brāhmaṇa villages of the country, namely, Kammāssadhamma and

The land of the Kurus.

1 *Divyāvadāna*, pp. 550ff; *Psalms of the Brethren*, pp. 90-91.

2 *Ibid.*, pp. 45ff., *Ibid.*, p. 70.

Thullakoṭṭhita. The association of the country with these two discourses has made it memorable in the annals on the spread of Buddhism. These discourses are the *Satipaṭṭhāna Sutta* and the *Mahānidāna Suttanta*[1]. The first deals with the first principles of the Buddhist system of *yoga* and teaches how a person can reach a very high stage of sanctification by the simple process of constant *satipaṭṭhāna* (self-possession) without having recourse to the more arduous methods prescribed in the brāhmaṇic *yoga-śāstras*. The second discourse explains the ten-fold[2] chain of causation (*paṭiccasamuppāda*) leading to misery or salvation. A few other discourses relating to the means of cessation of *dukkha*, worthlessness of sensual pleasures, the eight *vimokkhas*, etc. were also delivered at the place[3].

It appears from the *Raṭṭhapāla* and *Māgandiya suttas* of the *Majjhima Nikāya* that some

1 *Majjh. Nik.*, I, pp. 55ff., *Dīgh. Nik.*, II, pp. 55 ff; 290ff.

2 In the chain the usual first two links have been omitted, and *viññāna* and *nāmarūpa* have been made co-existent instead of one being derived from the another. Cf. *Saṃ. Nik.*, II, pp. 92-93; Mrs Rhys Davids' *Buddhism*, p. 94.

3 *Saṃ. Nik.*, II, p. 107; *Aṅg. Nik.*, V, pp. 29ff.

of the brāhmaṇas of the Kuru country held Buddha in great esteem and resorted to him to listen to his teachings. So great was Bharadvājagotta brāhmaṇa's respect for Buddha that he used to offer a seat to him in his sacrificial hall in the face of protests by Māgandiya paribbājaka[1]. Raṭṭhapāla, a member of the most respectable brāhmaṇa family of Thullakoṭṭhita approached Buddha along with a large number of brāhmaṇa gahapatis to listen to Buddha's discourses. Raṭṭhapāla was so much impressed that he at once made up his mind to become a bhikkhu. He had some difficulty in having the consent of his parents to his ordination but ultimately he succeeded and became a bhikkhu. After the attainment of *arahathood*, he paid a visit to the land of his birth and made a great impression upon the mind of the Kuru king by giving an exposition of some of the principles of Buddhism[2]. The *Nikāyas* do not mention any other convert of the Kuru country except Māgandiya paribbājaka who was at first so very averse to Buddhism[3].

Buddha had also among his disciples the

1 *Majjh. Nik.*, I, p. 502 ; cf. *ante*, II, pp. 55ff.
2 *Majjh. Nik.*, II, pp. 65-72.
3 *Ibid.*, I, p. 512.

people of the more distant Madda country, the notable of them being the bhikkhu Mahākappina and the two bhikkhuṇīs Khemā and Bhaddā Kapilāni. Buddha converted Khemā, the queen of Bimbisāra, in the seventh year of his missionary career after the institution of the order of nuns at Vesāli. She attained the highest stage of sanctification and was designated by Buddha as the chief of the highly wise nuns (*mahāpaññānam*)[1]. Her fame spread all over Magadha and Kosala as *paṇḍitā, viyattā, medhāvinī, bahussutā, cittakathī, kalyāṇapaṭibhānā'tī* (wise, experienced, intelligent and erudite)[2]. She had a discussion with Pasenadi Kosala on indeterminable problems and fully satisfied him by her expositions[3]. The conversion of Khemā opened up a new chapter in the history of Buddhism. Not only did it contribute to the popularity of the Buddhist order of nuns but also made easy the path of the spread of Buddhism in Sāgala, the capital of the Maddas[4], sprung as she

The land of the Maddas.

1 *Aṅg Nik.*, I, p. 25 ; *Manorothapūraṇī*, I, p. 345.

2 *Saṃ. Nik.*, IV, p. 375.

3 *Ibid.*, pp. 375-380.

4 Cunningham's *Ancient Geography*, (*2nd ed.*), pp. 206ff, 686.

was from the royal dynasty of the Madda country. Besides Khemā the two other notable converts, who hailed from the Madda country, are Mahākappina of the royal family of Kukkuṭavatī, mentioned by Buddha as the chief of the *bhikkhu ovādakānaṃ*[1] (admonisher of bhikkhus) and Bhaddā Kapilāni of the chief of the Sāgala brāhmaṇa families and wife of Mahākassapa, referred to by Buddha as the foremost of the nuns who attained the knowledge of their previous births (*pubbenivāsa-anussarantīnaṃ*)[2].

1 *Manorathapūraṇī*, I, pp. 318-324.

2 *Ibid.*, pp. 375-6; *Psalms of the Sisters*, pp. 47-49.

BOOK II

Schools of Buddhism

The
Evolution of the Schools of Buddhism

INTRODUCTION

The origin of the various schools, not long after Buddha's death, was rather a healthy sign of Tathāgata's religion. After Buddha's death there was none at the time able to take his place as a religious teacher. His charming doctrine attracted thousands of men seeking eagerly a solution of the various problems relating to life in this world and the next. There were among these the highly learned followers who were descended from brāhmaṇa families and imbued with an intimate knowledge of brāhmaṇic philosophy, learned members of various religious orders like the Jaṭilas, Jainas, Ājīvikas. They were of a very speculative turn of mind and could not remain satisfied with the then current interpretations of the teachings of Buddha as the common folk were, as a rule. These seekers after truth demanded a more thorough elucidation of the significant words of the Teacher, the leading Buddhist teachers of the time being unable to furnish explanation. Naturally these Buddhist preachers took to hair-splitting argumentations but could not arrive at definite conclusions. The fundamental propositions about which they all reed were[1] :—

(1) All is momentary (*sarvaṃ kṣaṇikaṃ*)

(2) All is without self (*sarvaṃ anātman*)

(3) All is suffering (*sarvaṃ dukkhaṃ*)

But round this nucleus of agreement were ranged several divergences of opinion as to both tenets (*dhamma*) and rules of discipline (*vinaya*) which were responsible for divisions in the fraternity[2]. The development of the six systems of Hindu philosophy from the *Upaniṣads* as their common basis furnishes a parallel to the growth of schools of Buddhism out of a single original cult. "The founders ot the Hindu schools" says Prof. Max Müller[3] "always pretend to find in the *Upaniṣads* some warranty for their tenets, however antagonistic in their bearing. The same applies to the numerous sects that have existed and still exist in India". This remark applies *mutatis mutandis* to the various Buddhist sects.

1 D. T. Suzuki's *Outlines of Mahāyāna Buddhism*, p. 140 (Item 3 is not mentioned in this book).

2 See *Aṅg. Nik.*, I, p. 60.

3 *History of Sanskrit Literature*, pp. 162, 163.

Genesis of Indian sects.

Each sect laid claim to the orthodoxy and special strength of its views and beliefs[1] by culling out and emphasizing those sayings of Buddha that lent support to its particular doctrines, while the sayings that were not so tractable or positively antagonistic were either impeached or passed over in silence.

Factors peculiar to Buddhism for the origin of schools.

The formation of about twenty Buddhist schools within one or two centuries preceding or following the reign of Asoka was due mainly to the following factors :-

(1) *Want of provision for the supreme headship of the Buddhist church after the Founder's death.* Buddha thought that the prescription of heavy punishments for schisms in the church would check them effectively and that his *Dhamma* and *Vinaya* would be self-sufficing in keeping intact the religion established by him, obviating thereby the appointment of religious heads. In this supposition the Teacher no doubt delimited the need for the supreme headship, as the

1 For illustrations, see *Points of the Controversy* by Mr. Shwe Zan Aung, pp. 27 ff.

future history of the Buddhist church has proved, and magnified the unaided strength of *dhamma* and *vinaya*. According to the *Sāmagāma Sutta*[1], Buddha hears of dissensions in the Jaina community as soon as the leader Nigaṇṭha Nātaputta was dead. He was afraid of like dissensions in his church after his death but consoled himself that there was no difference of opinion among his followers in regard to the *dhamma*[2] preached by him and to ensure further safety of his church (in this behalf), he delivered a religious discourse on the cause of schism and the means to avoid them[3]. He placed too much reliance on his *dhamma* and the attachment of his followers to his *dhamma* and *vinaya* which he supposed would be of the implicit

1 *Majjh. Nik.*, II, p. 105.

2 Buddha's *dhamma* is thus detailed by him :—(i) *Four satipaṭṭhānas*; (ii) *Four sammāppadhānas*; (iii) *Four iddhipādas*; (iv) *Five indriyas*; (v) *Five balas*; (vi) *Seven bojjhaṅgas*; (vii) *Eight-fold path.* See *Dīgh. Nik.*, xvi, 50; *Majjh. Nik.*, II, pp. 77, 103, 104; *Lalitavistara* (Bibl. Ind.), a book of the Sarvāstivādins, pp. 34-37; and *Saṅgiti-Paryāya,* one of the seven Abhidharma books of the Sarvāstivādins in *J. P. T. S.* 1904-5, pp. 71, 75.

3 See *Kinti Sutta* in *Majjh. Nik.*, II, p. 103.

type for ever[1]. He instructed his disciples that after his death his teachings would be their Teacher. This is recorded in the *Mahāparinibbāṇa Suttanta*[2] and forms also the subject of a dialogue between Ānanda and Vassakāra brāhmaṇa, the minister of Magadha[3]. Vassakāra asks Ānanda, "Has any bhikkhu been specified (by Buddha) as would after Buddha's death become the refuge (i. e. leader) of men under whom everybody would seek shelter." Ānanda answers in the negative. He asks again, "Has any bhikkhu been selected by the *saṅgha* as would become their leader etc." To this also Ānanda answers in the negative. Vassakāra was curious to learn the cause of the prevailing concord of the church inspite of there being no leader (lit. refuge). Ānanda replies "we are not without a refuge (*appaṭisaraṇā*), *dhamma* is our refuge. There is a treatise called *Pātimokkha* which has been formulated by the omniscient Teacher and which all the monks living in the same parish (*gāmakkhetta*) have

1 See *Pāsādika Suttanta*, (*Dīgh. Nik.*, xxix), p. 121.

2 *Dīgh. Nik.*, xvi, 6, 6, 1. "*Yo mayā Dhammo ca Vinayo desito paññatto so va mama accayena satthā.*"

3 *Majjh. Nik.*, *Gopaka-Moggalāna Sutta* (No. 108); Oldenberg's *Buddha* (Eng. transl.), p. 108.

to recite in a monastery where they assemble on the *uposatha* days. Should there occur any difference or doubt in the recitation, the bhikkhus present should explain them in accordance with the *dhamma* (hence they have their refuge as *dhamma*)." In answer to another question put by Vassakāra, Ānanda explains that though there was no supreme head of the Buddhist fraternity, there was in each parish a qualified head who was respected by the people under his charge and whose guidance would be strong enough to keep the great many parishes connected together in religious concord. This conversation makes it clear that each parish was under the control of the seniormost and best qualified monk that the parish could furnish[1]. The bhikkhus residing under his superintendence met together on the *uposatha* days and held religious discussions among themselves in order to elicit the true

1 In the *Mahāparinibbāṇa Suttanta* (*Dīgh. Nik.*, II, p. 77) it is enjoined upon the bhikkhus that they should offer due respect to the *Saṅgha-pitara or Saṅgha-pariṇāyaka* (the head of the parish) who are bhikkhus of long standing and experience for the well-being of this saṅgha.

Childers in his *Pāli-Dictionary* (s. v. saṅgha) says that a *Saṅghatthera* is usually selected as the President

meaning of Buddha's words. In the course of their discussions, they interpreted the terse expressions of the Teacher in different ways and introduced additional materials in the interpretations, passing them in the name of Buddha to give them stamp of authenticity. This happened in most of the parishes scattered over the whole of northern India. There was none at that time in the whole of the Buddhist community who could dissolve the numberless divergences thus originated into one uniform whole and convert the threatening centrifugal forces then at work into centripetal, conducive to the well-being of the whole saṅgha.

(2) *Grouping of disciples around a noted thera.* Buddha awarded prominence to some of his disciples by extolling them for their attainment of proficiency in certain branches of the Buddhist *dhamma*[1]. Of them, the following

of an assembly. He cites, for instance, Kassapa, the then Saṅghatthera was the President of the first council. He also points out that a Saṅghatthera is not always the one who is the longest ordained for Sabbakāmin who was the longest *upasampanna* bhikkhu was not the President of the Second Council. See also *Aṅg, Nik.,* IV, 21; V, p. 353.

1 *Aṅg. Nik.,* I. xiv, 1.

need mention for our purpose,—

(i) Sāriputta, the foremost of the highly wise (*mahāpaññānam*)

(ii) Mahāmoggalāna, the foremost of the possessors of miraculous powers (*iddhimantānam*).

(iii) Anuruddha, the foremost of the possessors of divine eyes (*dibba-cakkhukānam*).

(iv) Mahākassapa, the foremost of the followers of *dhūta* precepts (*dhūtavādānam*).

(v) Puṇṇa Mantāniputta, the foremost of the preachers of *dhamma* (*dhammakathikānam*).

(vi) Mahākaccāyana, the foremost of the expositors (*saṅkhittena bhāsitam vitthārena atthaṃ vibhajjanantānam*).

(vii) Rāhula, the foremost of the students (*sikkhākāmānam*)

(viii) Revata Khadiravaniya, the foremost of the forest-recluses (*āraññikānam*).

(ix) Ānanda, the foremost of the vastly learned (*bahussutānam*) ; and

(x) Upāli, the foremost of the masters of *Vinaya* (*vinayadharānam*).

Buddha used to observe the mental proclivities of the person to whom he imparted a religious lesson and selected a discourse that appealed to him most. He followed the same course, while prescribing to his disciples their duties for the attainment of *arahathood*. He also indirectly pointed out to his disciples the preceptor most suited to each in view of his peculiar mental leanings. This practice led to the grouping of students around a teacher or his direct disciples ; hence the remark made by Buddha that "*dhātuso sattā saṃsandenti samenti*"[1] on the principle that like draws like. In the *Majjhima Nikāya*[2], we read of ten chief theras, viz. Sāriputta, Moggalāna, Mahākoṭṭhita, etc., each having ten to forty disciples under their tuition. Buddha on a certain occasion pointed out that the group of bhikkhus formed round each of these *theras* was possessed of the same special qualifications that characterised the *thera* himself. Thus the bhikkhus accompaying Sāriputta were *mahāpaññāvantā*, those accompanying Mahāmoggalāna were *mahiddhikā*, those accompanying Mahākassapa were *dhūtavādā*, those accompanying Devadatta were sinfully inclined (*pāpicchā*) and so on[3]. Yuan Chwang noticed about a

1 *Saṃ. Nik.*, II, p. 157.
2 *Majjh. Nik.*, III, p. 118.
3 *Saṃ. Nik.*, II, pp. 155, 156.

thousand years later that on auspicious days the Abhidhammikas worshipped Sāriputra, the Vinayists Upāli, the Śrāmaṇeras Rāhula, the Sūtraists Purṇa Maitrāyaṇīputra, the Samādhists Mahāmoggalāna, the bhikkhuṇīs Ānanda, the Mahāyānists Mañjuśrī and other Bodhisattvas[1]. In the first four classes of bhikkhus, the aforesaid affinity between them and their leaders is obvious. In the next three classes, the affinity existed all the same though it may not be apparent on the face of it. For the Samādhists followed Mahāmoggalāna because he was the master of *iddhi par excellence* which could be obtained only through *samādhi*, and the bhikkhuṇīs followed Ānanda because to him the order of nuns owed its origin. The Mahāyānists do not come within our purview at present. The principal points of resemblance between the followers and their preceptors were the ties that bound them together but these were the points which constituted the features by which the chief qualities of the preceptors were distinguished. These distinctions among them did not lie in any differences of doctrines which they professed but in the degrees of proficiency attained by each, in particular directions of Buddhistic *sādhana*. But

1 Watters' *Yuan Chwang*, I, p. 302.

the divisions though not proceeding from radical differences in doctrine grew stereotyped in course of time, and fusion between them later on became an impossibility due to the separatist frame of of mind that their existence as separate orders naturally developed. Thus the division which had commenced without any doctrinal differences gradually gave rise to the latter and grew into full-fledged schools. History shows that this process of develoment actually came to pass. For instance, the school of the Sarvāstivādins who were connected with the original division of *abhidhammikas* with Sāriputta at their head affiliated themselves to Sāriputta's disciple Rāhula at whose time however the doctrinal differences had not yet appeared, similarly the Sthaviravādins affiliated themselves to Upāli, Mahāsaṅghikas to Mahākassapa and the Sammitīya to Mahākaccāyana.

(3) *Division of monks into bodies, each of which was meant to preserve a particular portion of the Buddhist scriptures.* Throughout the Pāli literature, we often come across terms like these :—

(i) *Suttantikas* or masters of *Suttanta* (belonging to the *Sutta-piṭaka*) ;

(ii) *Vinayadharas* or repositories of the rules of discipline ;

(iii) *Mātikādharas* or those versed in *mātikā* (i. e. *abhidhamma*) ;

(iv) *Dhammakathikas* or the preachers of the Buddhist doctrine ;[1]

(v) *Dīgha-bhāṇaka, Majjhima-bhāṇaka* &c., (i. e. reciters of the *Nikāyas*)[2].

The object of this is obvious. In those days, when writing was hardly used for recording in books the sayings and preachings of Buddha, the means that was utilized for preserving and handing them down to posterity was reciting them regularly and committing them to memory. This was akin to the method that had been in vogue in India from the earliest Vedic period, the need of which mainly gave rise to the numerous Vedic schools. A similar cause produced a similar result among the Buddhists and we find that the memorizing of different portions of the Piṭaka was entrusted to different sets of bodies hardened and separated from one another in course of time and bearing names descriptive of their functions[3].

1 *Dīgh. Nik., Mahāparinibbāṇa Suttanta*, iv ; *Aṅg. Nik.*, II, p. 117.

2 *Sum. Vil.*, p. 15.

3 *Vinaya*, IV. 15. 4. (*S. B. E.* xiii, p. 339). "On the Pavāraṇā day the greater part of the night has passed

It should not be inferred from this that side by side with these bodies, there were not religious students who specialised in a number of branches of the Buddhist scriptures and received epithets like *āgatāgamā*, *bahussutā*, *tipeṭakin*, *pañcanekāyika*. But the existence of such scholars with such wider scopes of knowledge does not preclude that of bodies of scholars having as their special duties an accurate memorising of special branches of the sacred lore. This is confirmed, and that its origin dates back as early as the first council is evidenced, by the fact that in that council Ānanda was requested to recite the *Suttas* while Upāli the *Vinaya*. This would not have been the case if Ānanda or Upāli was not generally famed for proficiency in the particular branches of the Piṭaka. Elements of such specialisation have found to have existed still earlier in Buddha's life-time as can be noticed in a quarrel that took place between a *dhammakathika* and a *vinayadhara*[1].

away while the bhikkhus were in confusion : the bhikkhus were reciting the Dhamma, those versed in Suttantas were propounding the Suttantas, those versed in Vinaya were discussing the Vinaya, the Dhamma preachers were talking about the Dhamma".

1 See *Infra*.

Commonness of duties gave rise to unity among the *dhammakathikas* on one side and the *vinayadharas* on the other in such a marked way that each group made the cause of one individual member its common cause and participated in the dispute. This is sufficiently indicative of the crystallization that had commenced in each group round its common function and the awakening of a consciousness of common interests that bound together its individual members. Indications of stages previous to this crystallization into bodies are found in the *Vinaya* in connection with the arrangements made by Dabba Mallaputta for the residence of the bhikkhus[1]. Dabba Mallaputta made such an arrangement that the bhikkhus adopting the same mode of life (*sabhāgā*) resided in the same place in order that the *Suttantikas* could recite *suttantas* among themselves, *Vinayadharas* discuss the rules of discipline with one another, the *Dhammakathikas* talk mutually about questions of doctrine and so on. Instances are not rare of a feeling of rivalry among these bodies, each member of which wished and was pleased to see the body to which he belonged take

1 *Vinaya*, II, pp. 75, 76.

precedence over other bodies in having seat or food in assemblies or in thanksgiving after a meal[1].

These separate bodies, which existed for a particular function necessary for the whole Buddhist community e. g. the preservation of a particular portion of the Piṭaka by regular recitations, imbibed in course of time, doctrines, which could be looked upon as peculiar to the body holding them and in this way, the body developed into a separate religious school of Buddhism. Such instances are found in the Theravādins who had developed into such a school from the *Vinayadharas*, and the Sautrāntikas from the *Suttantikas*. It must not be thought that all the divisions mentioned above in this connection developed into religious schools, but what I mean to point out is the fact that such divisions supplied from among them bodies which in time grew into full-fledged schools.

(4) *Elasticity of the rules of discipline.* The rules of conduct were in the course of being defined but were not codified at the time. The Sākyaputtiya samanas like other contemporary

1 *Vinaya*, CV. IV, 6, 2; MV. IV, 15, 4.

religious orders possessed a set of rules known as the *Pātimokkha* for their guidance and the disciples had to recite those rules every fortnight in the presence of the congregation, the bhikkhus residing in forests (*āraññakas*) not being excepted[1]. The *Pātimokkha*, as we have it now, obtained its present shape after various additions and alterations according to the exigencies of times and circumstances. For instance, Buddha made some exceptions in favour of the bhikkhus who were placed at a disadvantage by reason of the locality in which they resided. In the border countries (*paccantima janapada*) such as Avanti, the converts were few and intractable, hence, Buddha at the request of Kaccāyana and Puṇṇa Mantāniputta made some exceptions in their favour in regard to the rules for the formation of an assembly for the ordaining of monks and the wearing of leather-made shoes etc., prohibited to the bhikkhus dwelling in the middle country[2]. Buddha's primary object was the emancipation of all beings and as a means to that end, he laid the greatest stress on the

1 *Majjh. Nik.*, II, pp. 8, 9. "*Te* (*āraññakā sāvakā*) *anvaddhamāsaṃ saṅghamajjhe osaranti pātimokkhuddesāya*".

2 See *Vinaya*, I, pp. 197, 198; *Divyāvadāna*, p. 21.

control of mental functions[1] permitting greater latitudes in the discipline of body and speech according to the circumstances of each individual than were allowed by the contemporaneous sects of Jainas, Ājīvikas, etc. In the *Mahāparinibbāṇa Suttanta*[2], one of his instructions was that the saṅgha might, if necessary, abolish the minor rules, making thereby the *Vinaya* (or rules of conduct) subject to changes as time and circumstances required[3]. Besides elasticity, there were other causes for changes in the *Vinaya* rules, one of which was hinted at by the Chinese traveller Fa Hian in the course of his remarks bearing on the Mahāsaṅghika schism : "Certain bhikkhus (of Vaisāli) broke the rules of Vinaya in ten particulars saying that Buddha had said it so"[4]. Another cause of such

1 *Majjh. Nik.*, Vol. I, p. 56.

2 *Dīgh. Nik.*, II, p. 154. "*Ākaṅkhamāno Ānanda saṅgho mama accayena khuddānukhuddāni sikkhāpadāni samuhantu*". Cf. *Milindapañha*, p. 143.

3 *Aṅg. Nik.*, I p. 230. Vajjiputtaka bhikkhu said to Buddha that it would be difficult for him to practise the 250 rules which were recited every fortnight. Buddha asked him whether he would be able to practise the three sikṣās viz. *adhisīla, adhicitta* and *adhipaññā,* to which he replied in the affirmative.

4 Beal's *Records of the Western Countries*, I, p. liv.

division is mentioned in a Sanskrit treatise as lying in the fact that the seceders sought "different interpretations for the commandments of the departed master"[1].

(5) *Dialectical differences.* According to Profs. Beal and Minayeff[2], the practice of preserving the sacred lore in one's own vernacular contributed also to the formation of schools. At present, evidences are not strong enough to put this conclusion on a solid basis and we are now not in a position to point to any particular school as the result of the operation of this factor alone.

(6) *Austerities and ritualism.* It is well known from Buddha's life that his attainment of Buddhahood led him to adopt 'middle path' which eschewed austerities as a means of attaining religious goal. We are also aware that just after his renunciation he became a disciple of two *gurus* under whose guidance he led a life of severe austerity for a few years which only opened his eyes to the fact that such austerities could never fulfil his mission. For this reason

1 Rockhill's *Life of the Buddha*, p. 177.

2 Minayeff's *Intro. to Pāli Grammar*; Beal's *Abstract of four Lectures on the Buddhist Literature in China*, p. 49.

austerities could not be expected to figure in the doctrines preached and recommended by him to his disciples. But in spite of this position we find in some of the earliest portions of the Piṭaka such as the *Majjhima* and the *Aṅguttara Nikāyas* that Buddha is praising ascetics[1] who were given to the practice of *dhūta*-precepts[2] involving austerities. This is an inconsistency which can be explained in two ways, first, by holding that the passages were interpolated in later times by those disciples who were in favour of such practices, and secondly, by the position that Buddha changed his attitude later on in view of the strong tendency of the people who took to or believed in the efficacy of the austerities and who could not be satisfied with a religion barren of such practices. In either case, we have to admit that austerities crept into Buddhism in early times and the adoption of these by Buddhists led to the formation of schools.

Likewise ritualism which Buddha from the commencement of his career as such eschewed as a thing with which the religion preached by him should have no connection could not be kept in

1 *Aṅg. Nik.*, III, pp. 344ff.

2 See Kern's *Manual of Buddhism*, pp. 75-76.

abeyance for a long time. The passages[1] found in the early portions of the Piṭaka advocating certain rites may, like the references to austerities, be explained in the way indicated above. Whatever might be the explanation, it is certain that by degrees rites and ceremonies entered into Buddhism giving it an appearance which could in no way be distinguished from the elaborate rituals of brāhmaṇic worships barring of course differences in the rituals themselves. The introduction of this feature could not certainly have been welcome to the founder of the religion but it was a feature that was demanded in an increasing degree by the large mass of the laity as well as by a great body of their religious teachers. The schools or groups of Buddhists that adopted the rituals naturally fell apart from those that did not do so and ritualism was taken as a feature distinguishing certain schools from the rest.

The above factors have been generalised from the history of the Buddhist church during the three and half centuries after Buddha's death, and have been mentioned as the chief ones that led to dissensions, and development of schools. It is clear from Buddha's sayings that he had

1 See *Dīgh. Nik.*, *Mahāparinibbāṇa Suttanta.*

apprehension for future dissensions among his followers. He often laid stress upon the importance of *samaggā parisā*[1] i. e. the unity of the Buddhist monks as the means of keeping it strong and uninjured in the face of oppositions made by its opponents in various ways. To remedy the evil of breaches in their own camp, he charged his favourite disciples Ānanda, Sāriputta and Moggalna[2] ā with the duty of settling disputes whenever they took place among the monks in order that it might be nipped in the bud. In his opinion it was only the wicked and selfish bhikkhus who achieved their selfish ends by introducing new principles of Dhamma and Vinaya which proved sources of heated contentions[3]. He was however not very particular in regard to existence of differences in *abhidhamma* (i.e. *atireka-dhamma* or minor points of doctrine)[4], *ajjhājīva* (minor rules of ivelihood), andl *adhipātimokkha* (minor rules of discipline), which he regarded as inevi-

Buddha's apprehension for future dissension among monks, and the remedies.

1 *Dīgh. Nik.*, *Mahāparinibbāṇa Suttanta*, p. 76; *Aṅg. Nik.*, I, p. 243; II, p. 70; IV, p. 21.

2 *Aṅg. Nik.*, II, p. 239.

3 *Ibid.*, V, pp. 73, 75.

4 See *Atthasālini*, p. 2.

table in all religions[1]. When it was necessary to check the currency of dissentient views with regard to doctrine, a neutral bhikkhu was sent to a sane and reasonable member belonging to the party which held the views in order to convert him to the orthodox opinion and if the attempt failed no other steps need be taken[2]. As regards the other two classes of differences just mentioned, there were punishments[3] to check them but as they have no bearing on the present subject they may be passed over. To stimulate the bhikkhus to stand united, he held out before them the prospect of a happy and glorious life like that of god Brahmā that will fall to a monk's lot to lead in after-life as the result of any act of his that served to re-unite bodies of monks separated from one another, while he declared the monk sowing dissension among his brethren as doomed to perdition for a *kalpa*[4].

Every quarrel or difference of opinion among the bhikkhus was not characterised by Buddha as *saṅghabheda.* A breach in the saṅgha

1 Cf. *Points of the Controversy*, p. 351.

2 *Majjh. Nik.*, II, p. 238.

3 See *Adhikaraṇasamathas* in *Vinaya*, CV. IV, 14.

4 *Aṅg. Nik.*, V, pp. 73, 75, 78 ; *Vinaya*, CV. vii, 5.

accompanied by the conditions laid down in the *Vinaya* was designated *saṅghabheda*. It is thus described in the *Vinaya*, "For not only is a formal putting forward and voting on the false doctrine essential to schism as distinct from mere disagreement, but the offending bhikkhus must also be quite aware that the doctrine so put forth is wrong, or at least doubtful, and also that the schism resulting from his action will be or will probably be disastrous to the Dhamma. In other words, the schism must be brought about by deliberately putting forward a doctrine known to be false, or at least doubtful, or with the express intention or hope of thereby injuring the Dhamma" [1]. This definition obviously represents the opinion of the conservative school of the Theravādins who naturally looked down upon those who differed from them on religious points and ascribed an evil motive to their entertainment of the differing views. It is very reasonable that the dissenters may have an honest belief on their own views clear of the evil motive of injuring the Dhamma. It will, therefore, be apparent from a neutral standpoint that evil intention is not essential of *saṅghabheda*. The real essentials are :—(1) Belief in a dissentient

1 *Vinaya Texts* (*S. B. E.*), pt. III, p. 271n,

religious view regarding either one or more points of faith or discipline; (2) the entertainment of the view by eight or more than eight fully ordained monks; (3) the division taken among the aforesaid eight or more monks must show a majority on the side of the dissenters[1].

The conditions as laid down in the Vinaya, leading to a *saṅghabheda*; and how it is distinguished from *saṅgharāji*.

Saṅgharāji is a disunion confined to eight monks. This restriction as to number forming the essential of *saṅgharāji* shows that it might at any moment develop into a *saṅghabheda*, by drawing an additional monk into the difference. Of course, *bonafide* belief and the full ordainment of monks are necessary requisites.

During Buddha's life-time dissensions of minor character took place in the Buddhist saṅgha, only two of which attracted his attention and which were called by him *saṅghabheda* and condemned to be as heinous a crime as

1 *Vinaya*, CV. VII, 5, 1; *Milindāpañha*, p. 108: "No layman can create a schism, nor a sister of the order, nor one under preparatory instruction, nor a novice of either sex. It must be a bhikkhu under no disability, who is in full communion and co-resident" (*S. B. E.*, vol. XXXV, p. 163).

patricide or matricide[1]. The first dissension occurred at one of the monasteries of Kosambī[2] where a bhikkhu through ignorance of the law committed a breach of discipline. The monks attached a magnified gravity to the offence and punished him by *ukkhepana* (excommunication). The accused, on the other hand, attributed the offence to his ignorance of the law which did not deserve the severe penalty inflicted on him. The justice of the cause gained for him several adherents who worked to have his penalty set aside. This caused a division not only among the monks but also among the lay-devotees and ultimately led to Buddha's mediation before the differences could be settled. This dissension, it is true, did not last long owing to the presence of the Teacher who removed the doubts of both the parties by his lucid explanations but yet it argues the existence of germs of dissension which bore fruits of far-reaching importance in later times.

Germs of dissensions in the fraternity during Buddha's life-time; (i) Division at Kosambī.

1 *Vinaya*, MV. x, 3, 1; *Kathāvatthu*, xiii, 1.

2 *Ibid.*, MV. x; *Majjh. Nik.*, I, Kosambī-Sutta; *Dhammapada Aṭṭhakathā*, Kosambī-vatthu.

(ii) Devadatta's division.

The next dissension originated with Buddha's cousin, Devadatta, who in his advocacy for more austere discipline requested the Teacher to introduce the following five rules[1] in the monasteries :—

(The brethren) shall (1) live all their life in the forest ;
(2) subsist solely on doles collected out-doors ;
(3) dress themselves in rags picked out of dust heaps ;
(4) dwell always under tree and never under a roof ; and
(5) never eat fish or flesh.

The Teacher declared that he could not make the rules obligatory upon all the monks on the ground that it would conduce more to their welfare to make the observance of these rules optional. Devadatta took this opportunity to create a division in the *saṅgha* (congregation) and departed to Gayāsīsa with five hundred followers.

We have reason to believe that this secession of Devadatta from the original brotherhood gave birth to sects which existed up to the end of the

1 *Vinaya*, CV. VIII,1 ; *Jātakas*, I, p. 34 ; Oldenberg's *Buddha* (Hoey's transl.), pp. 160, 161.

fourth century A. D.[1] and a remnant of whose practices was found by Yuan Chwang to be in three saṅghārāmas in Karnasuvarṇa. The two foregoing instances of division in the saṅgha during Buddha's life-time illustrate that the Buddhist church could not keep itself intact inspite of his personality and sublime teachings.

Within the period of Buddha's ministry which covered less than half a century and the few localities to which Buddhism was confined at the time, the various forces were already at work for the formation of schools. It can therefore be well imagined that in the absence of the great Teacher, the monastic order, which though well-organized with precautions against schisms, had to give way to the growth of as many as twenty schools or more. The appended chart[2] shows the number of schools and the way in which the united church of Buddha gradually become subdivided. The time of emergence of

1 Beal's *Records of the Western Countries*, vol II.

2 This chart is based mainly upon the tradition as preserved in the Pāli works. I have used Rockhill's *Life of the Buddha*, Mrs. Rhys Davids' *Points of the Controversy* and Prof. Geiger's valuable Appendix B to his *Translation of the Mahāvaṃsa* where all the references to the varying lists of schools have been collected and arranged.

the schools cannot be definitely specified at present. Mrs. Rhys Davids has tried in her Introduction to the *Points of the Controversy* to assign an approximate date to the origin of each school on the strength of the Ceylonese traditions. Some of the conclusions drawn by her require however further corroboration to put them beyond the range of doubt.

The Mahāsaṅghika School

It was about a century after Buddha's death that we meet with the great division in the Buddhist church, a division between the conservative and the liberal, the hierarchic and the democratic. It is in this division that germs are traceable of the Mahāyānic doctrines which in the later history of Buddhism gained ground and eclipsed the Hīnayānic schools. Details about this schism are found in the Ceylon chronicles[1] as well as in Pāli[2] and Buddhist Sanskrit works[3] (extant in Tibetan and Chinese translations) which unanimously record that a schism occurred in the Church through the Vajjian monks who deviated from the orthodox rules of discipline in regard to ten points and instituted a new school under the name of Mahāsaṅghikas. We learn

1 *Mahāvaṃsa*, Ch.IV; *Dīpavaṃsa*, Ch. IV, pp. 33ff.

2 *Vinaya Texts* (S. B. E.), Vol. III, pp. 389-414.

3 Rockhill's *Life of the Buddha*, pp. 173ff. for the version of the school of Sarvāstivādins (translated from Tibetan); Beal's *Four Lectures on the Buddhist Literature in China*, pp. 83ff. for the version of the school of Dharmaguptas (translated from Chinese).

further from the *Kathāvatthu*[1] of Moggaliputta Tissa and the *Samavadhoparaca cakra*[2] of Vasumitra that the school had also a number of tenets which were peculiar to itself. The ten points[3], which the Theravādins considered as breaches of the rules of discipline which caused the conflict between them and the Mahāsaṅghikas are :--

Schism of the Mahāsaṅghikas.

(1) *Siṅgiloṇa kappa*—or the practice of carrying salt in a horn for use when needed, which contravened according to one view the rule against the storing of articles of food (*Pācittiya* 38).

(2) *Dvaṅgula kappa*—or the practice of taking food after midday, lit. when the shadow (of the dial) is two digits wide (*Pāc.* 37).

(3) *Gāmantara kappa*—or the practice of going to a neighbouring village and taking a second meal there the same day, committing thereby the offence of over-eating (*Pāc.* 35).

(4) *Āvāsa kappa*—or the observance of *uposathas* in different places within the same parish (*sīmā*) (*MV.* II, 8, 3).

1 See Mrs. Rhys Davids' *Points of the Controversy*, p. xix.

2 Transl. by Prof. Wassilief in his *Der Buddhismus.*

3 *Vinaya*, CV. XII, 1, 10; 2. 9. *Cf.* Rockhill, *op.*

(5) *Anumati kappa*—or doing an act and obtaining sanction for it afterwards (*MV.* IX, 3. 5).

(6) *Āciṇṇa kappa*—or the use of precedents as authority.

(7) *Amathita kappa*—or the drinking of milk-whey after meal (*Pāc.* 35).

(8) *Jalogipātum*—or the drinking of fermenting palm-juice which as not yet toddy (*Pāc.* 51).

(9) *Adasakaṃ nisīdanaṃ*—or the use of a borderless sheet to sit on (*Pāc.* 89).

(10) *Jātarūparajataṃ*—or the acceptance of gold and silver (*Nissagg.* 18)[1].

The above ten points as given in the Pāli and other texts are also stated by Yuan Chwang in his account of the Council at Vesāli. A remarkable difference between Yuan Chwang's

cit., pp. 171, 172 and Beal, *op. cit.*, pp. 83-94.

1 For a discussion on the interpretations of the terms, see Minayeff, *Recherches*, I, pp. 44-50.

The first three rules seem to be relaxations of stringent rules, made by Buddha regarding the storage of food and eating to suit the conditions created by famine in Vesāli. The people of Vesāli continued to observe the relaxed rules though they were abrogated later on by the Theravādins in their *Vinaya.*

account and the traditions in the Pāli and other texts is noticeable in connection with the Mahāsaṅghikas at the meeting of the Council at Vesāli. According to the former, the Mahāsaṅghikas renounced all their deviations from the orthodox rules and took to those that were approved by the Theravādins, while according to the latter, the seceders did not in practice adopt the rules which they should have done according to the decisions of the council, in which they were outvoted. Inspite of their defeat, they remained as stubborn as before and asserted their separateness from the Theravādins by convening a council of their own. Watters disbelieves the tradition of the texts and relies on Yuan Chwang's account as true, and Kern also arrives at the same conclusion after comparing the various traditions[1].

The *Kathāvatthu*, which received its final shape in Asoka's council, had been growing by accretions since the holding of the council at Vesāli[2]. This work attributes a few differences in tenets to the Mahāsaṅghika school. Bhavya, Vasumitra, Vinītadeva and Tārānātha trace the

1 Kern's *Manual*, p. 109; Watters' *Yuan Chwang*, II, pp. 75-77.

2 See *Points of the Controversy*, pp. xxxi ff.

origin of this school in Mahādeva's five articles of faith which were,[1]—

"(1) An arahat may commit a sin under unconscious temptation.

(2) One may be an arahat and not know it.

(3) An arahat may have doubts on matters of doctrine.

(4) One cannot attain arahatship without the aid of a teacher.

(5) 'The noble ways' may begin with a shout that is, one meditating seriously on religion may make such exclamation as "How sad" and by so doing attain progress towards perfection."

The first four of the above articles of faith have been found in the *Kathāvatthu*[2], the commentary of which states them to have been held by the two branches of the Mahāsaṅghika school known as the Pubbaseliyas and Aparaseliyas[3]. Prof. Poussin after examining the works of Bhavya, Vasumitra and others sums up, regarding the five articles of faith, thus,—"Several traditions indicate that there was a council concerning the five points, and that this

1 *J. R. A. S.*, 1910, p. 416.

2 *Kathāvatthu*, ii, 2 ; ii, 3, 1 (ii, 1, 5) ; ii, 4 ; ii, 6.

3 *Kathāvatthuppakaraṇa Aṭṭhakathā*, see the references noted above.

controversy was the origin of the Mahāsaṅghika sect[1]." Yuan Chwang relates that Mahādeva enunciated five dogmas, as enumerated above, which formed the subject of bitter controversy among the bhikkhus. At the instance of the reigning king, an assembly of arahats and non-arahats was summoned, in which the arahats voted against the five dogmas[2] whereas the inferior brethren sided with Mahādeva and started the Mahāsaṅghika school at Pāṭaliputra[3]. This testimony of the Chinese traveller regarding the ten points of the breaches of the rules of discipline and the five dogmas of Mahādeva goes a very great way to prove that a schism did happen in the Buddhist church at or about the time of the second Buddhist Council. The agreement between Vasumitra's work and the *Kathāvatthu* in regard to the essential tenets of the Mahāsaṅghika school proves beyond doubt that the school existed before the time of composition of the *Kathāvatthu*, *i.e.*, at or about the time of the Second Council.

1 *J. R. A. S.*, 1910, p. 414.

2 They were the adherents of the Sthaviravāda school which a few years later branched off into many schools of which the Sarvāstivādins were the foremost.

3 Watters' *Yuan Chwang*, I, pp. 268, 269.

Two traditions for the origin of the schism accounted for.

The two classes of tradition preserved in the Buddhist literature, one attributing the schism of the Mahāsaṅghikas to the ten points of the breaches of the rules of discipline, and the other to Mahādeva's five articles of faith, may be accounted for in this way: The former appears in the Ceylonese chronicles and various versions of the Vinaya, while the latter in the Tibetan and Chinese versions of later Buddhist Sanskrit books dealing with the history of schools. One feature deserves our attention in this matter, namely, that in some works the differences as to the rules of discipline alone are referred to, while in other works the differences in regard to the doctrines to the exclusion of those regarding the rules of discipline are recorded. This can be accounted for, perhaps, either by the particular leanings of the authors of those works, or by the exclusive nature of the subject with which the works were concerned; for instance, the various versions of the Vinaya mention only the differences as to the points of discipline, and the Ceylonese chronicles composed by the Ceylonese bhikkhus whose principal care was for the Vinaya rules[1] put

1 Watters' *Yuan Chwang*, II, p. 234.

aside matters of doctrine, while the later Buddhist Sanskrit writers confine themselves to doctrines alone. Yuan Chwang was for the first time interested in the record of divergences in regard to both discipline and faith ; and that was because as an annalist he was more catholic than either of the two classes of authors. It should, however, be borne in mind that very probably the schism with the Mahāsaṅghikas had its first beginnings in the breaches of the then current rules of discipline encroaching in course of time on matters of doctrine.

The principal objective of the Mahāsaṅghikas in seceding from the main body of orthodox Buddhists becomes apparent to us by a glance at the subject matter of the rules regarding which they differed and the doctrines which they turned to profess. To put it in a nutshell, they wanted to have an amount of latitude and freedom regarding certain of their actions which the strictness and narrowness of orthodoxy was not ready to allow, and to carry into their organization and general governance a democratic spirit which set at nought what appeared to them an unreasoning servility to the monastic authorities, which could not be supported in a reasonable management of the monasteries. The exclusive power and privileges which by lapse of time the arahats came to claim for themselves at the expense of the bhikkhus of lower order were looked upon by the Mahāsaṅghikas as a reappearance in a different garb of the selfish exclusiveness of the brāhmaṇas, against which the rise of Buddhism was, as it were, a revolt. To yield to this meant but to yield to the same evil which the brāhmaṇas wanted to perpetuate and the Buddhists wanted to eradicate. It was in this sort of logic that the Mahāsaṅghikas found a justification for their conduct and it is upon this that they found a force which could unite them into a body. The first to begin the campaign against the above tendencies of the arahats came naturally from the monks belonging to a clan which was noted throughout its existence for its democratic spirit, *viz.*, the Vajjians. An expression of this spirit noticed at the very inception of the schism was found in the strong opposition that was made by them to the procedure by which it was decided by the orthodox arahats to make their decision at a council binding upon the opposing party. According to the procedure, only the *arahats* could be present in the Council and not the non-*arahats*. When by the application of this method of decision, the new party was outvoted, the latter rejected the decision of the majority and convened another council which was called Mahāsaṅgīti[1] because it included both the *arahats* and non-*arahats* of the new party and from which the party itself took the name Mahāsaṅghika.

Alteration made by the Mahāsaṅghikas in *dhamma* and *vinaya.*

The seceders, according to the chronicles, revised the Dhamma and Vinaya in their own way and the doctrines which were thus supported in the revised collections were known as the Ācariyavāda[2] as distinguished from the Theravāda of the first council. The *Dīpavaṃsa* says that the Mahāsaṅghikas did not stop after changing the Vinaya rules; they went further by laying down for themselves new doctrines contrary to the established ones. When according to the usual procedure at the Mahāsaṅgīti held by them, they recited for the settlement of the texts for their purposes the *Sūtras* and the *Vinaya*, they made alterations in the texts and their

1 Beal's *Records of the Western Countries*, Vol. II, p. 164, runs thus "And because in the assembly, both common folk and holy personages were mixed together, it was called the assembly of the great congregation."

I am indebted to Dr. B. M. Barua, M. A., D. Lit., for some suggestions in this connection.

2 *Dīpavaṃsa*, Ch. iv.

arrangement and interpretations. They also replaced portions of the text by others according to their liking, and even rejected certain parts of the canon though they had been accepted according to tradition by Mahākassapa's council. They refused to include *Parivāra, Abhidhamma-ppakaraṇa, Paṭisambhidā, Niddesa,* and the *Jātakas* within the Piṭaka collection[1]. The importance and accuracy of the decision by which the Mahāsaṅghikas discriminated between the original portions and the later interpolations are found in the full support that the decision obtains from modern researches bearing out their discrimination *in toto.* The *Parivāra* (*pāṭha*), which is a sort of index to the Vinaya and meant as a manual for the bhikkhus has been proved by many Buddhist scholars to be a composition of a later date than that of the canon[2]. The *Abhidhamma* literature also has been proved to have developed after the Council of Vesāli and received its final form in Asoka's Council[3]. Lastly the three works, the *Paṭisambhidā*, the *Niddesa* and the *Jātakas* are found to have been

1 *Dīpavaṃsa*, Ch. v, vs. 32-38.

2 Rhys Davids, *Hibbert Lectures*, p. 42 ; Oldenberg's *Intro. to the Vinaya Piṭaka*, Vol. I, p. xxxiv.

3 Oldenberg, *op. cit.*, p. xxxiv.

added to the canon without any discrimination long after its close. It would have been proper if the *Paṭisambhidā* had been put in the Abhidhamma collection and if the *Niddesa* which is only a commentary on the *Sutta Nipāta* as also the *Jātakas* which form a commentary on the canonical Jātaka book had been excluded from the Piṭaka collection.

Literature of the Mahāsaṅghikas.

Yuan Chwang relates that the Mahāsaṅghikas accepted the canon as rehearsed in Kassapa's Council but they included some discourses which had been rejected by it as non-canonical, and that the Mahāsaṅghikas divided their canon into five parts, *viz.*, Sūtra, Vinaya, Abhidharma, Miscellaneous, and Dhāraṇīs[1]. It is from the Chinese travellers Fa Hien and Yuan Chwang that we learn that this school had a complete canon of its own. Fa Hien took away from Pāṭaliputra to China a complete transcript of the *Mahāsaṅghika Vinaya* in 414 A. D., and translated it into Chinese two years later[2]. According to Yuan Chwang, the Vinaya of the

1 Watters' *Yuan Chwang*, II, p. 160; Kern's *Manual of Buddhism*, p. 4.

2 Takakusu, *Records of the Buddhist Religion*, p. xx.

Mahāsaṅghikas was the same as the one rehearsed in the first council. The Pāli authorities also mention that the difference between the orthodox school and the Mahāsaṅghikas lay only in the ten rules of discipline. From this we see that the differences between the versions of the Vinaya of the two schools were negligible[1]. In Nanjio's *Catalogue*, we find mention of an Āgama called *Ekottarāgama* (corresponding to Pāli *Aṅguttara Nikāya*) and two Vinayas, *viz.*, *Mahāsaṅghika Vinaya* and *Mahāsaṅgha-bhikṣuṇī Vinaya* existing in Chinese translations[2]. We have at present practically no information regarding the *Abhidharma* literature of the Mahāsaṅghikas. Yuan Chwang's biography furnishes us with a reference enabling us to be sure as to the existence of treatises forming part of their Abhidharma literature. The reference is furnished by the passage in which it is stated that Yuan Chwang studied certain Abhidharma treatises of the Mahāsaṅghika school with two monks at

1 Watters' *Yuan Chwang*, II, p. 160—Watters finds expressly mentioned in the Chinese translation of the Questions of Sāriputta that the Vinaya settled in Mahākassapa's Council was called the Mahāsaṅghika Vinaya.

2 Nanjio's *Catalogue of the Chinese Tripiṭaka,* Cols. 247 and 253 and Ms. No. 543.

Dhanakaṭaka, the centre of the Pūrva- and Apara-śaila schools[1]. Similarly, the Sūtras are merely mentioned as *Mahāsaṅghika-nikāya-āgama* in the Chinese work *She-ta-sheng-lun*, ch. 1 (No. 1183)[2]. We expect much light on the present point from the information which, we hope, the Chinese scholars would in the near future place at our disposal. Thus far can, however, be said regarding the *sūtras* that they were common to all the Buddhist schools in the form appearing in the Pāli *Sutta-Piṭaka*. The only work now available of the Mahāsaṅghika school is the *Mahāvastu* partly in prose and partly in verse. It is professedly the Vinaya of the Lokottara-vāda school[3], a branch of the Mahāsaṅghikas, and depicts the life of Buddha like the *Lalita-vistara* and the *Abhiniṣkramaṇa Sūtra* of the other schools.

The *Mahāvastu* has been edited by Prof. Senart about which he and M. Sylvain Lèvi furnish us with some information. It was properly speaking a book belonging to the Lokottara-vādins of Bamian in Kashmir. The versified

1 Watters, *op. cit.*, II, p. 217.

2 *Ibid.*, II, p. 161.

3 *Mahāvastu*, ed. by Senart, p. 2.

portion of the work is in a language approaching Sanskrit while the prose portion is in Sanskrit. At present further information about the linguistic medium which might have been used by the Mahāsaṅghikas in their literature at the different localities where they spread is not forthcoming except this that Csoma Körösi tells us from a Tibetan source that their '*sūtra on emancipation*' (*i. e.*, the Prātimokṣa-sūtra) was in a corrupt dialect, and Wassiljew informs us from the same source that their literature existed in Prākṛt.

The linguistic medium of Mahāsaṅghika literature.

Up till now the manuscripts explored from Central Asia have been shown to be the remnants of the literature of the Sarvāstivādins and the later Mahāyānic schools. Nowhere do we find in the published portions of the manuscripts any mention of the Mahāsaṅghikas. The history of this school shows that it suffered much in its early days at the hands of the orthodox Buddhists because it was the outcome of the earliest schism in the Buddhist church. It held in high esteem and even claimed Mahākassapa, the president of the first council, as its patron-saint and founder, and believed that the new doctrines

The popularity and centres of influence of the Mahāsaṅghika school.

and rules of discipline were deducible from the canon settled by him[1]. One of the main obstacles in the way of its general popularity was its failure to secure the support of any king ; for royal patronage usually counted for much in the establishment of a religion on a secure footing. Yuan Chwang records a tradition that a hundred years after the death of Buddha, a dispute regarding doctrine took place in the Buddhist church and 'King Aśoka' (most probably Kālāsoka of the *Mahāvaṃsa*) sided with the heretical party the Mahāsaṅghikas. The orthodox monks left Pāṭaliputra and went to Kashmir. The king afterwards changed his mind and repented of having supported the heretical party. This is, no doubt, an echo of the legend in the Mahāvaṃsa[2] that king Kālāsoka, being misled by the seceders, the Vajjiputtakas, supported them, but afterwards, by the warning of his sister Nandatherī, changed his mind and supported the cause of the orthodox party, the Theravādins. The tradition of the *Mahāvaṃsa* corroborated by Yuan Chwang shows that the

1 *J. A. S. B.*, 1838, p. 143 ; Wassiljew, *Der Buddhismus*, pp. 294, 295 ; Eitel's *Handbook of Chinese Buddhism*, p. 88.

2 *Mahāvaṃsa*, Ch. IV, vs. 37-44.

Mahāsaṅghikas lost the support of the then reigning king of Magadha which they had at first secured. It is evident that their first centre was at Pāṭaliputra[1] where they continued to reside side by side with the Theravādins and the later religious schools. We learn from Yuan Chwang that he saw followers of different schools dwelling in the same monastery, from which it seems that the acrimony of their early hostile relations diminished a good deal at the time of Yuan Chwang's visit. I-tsing (671-695 A. D.) informs us that the Mahāsaṅghikas were found in his time mostly in Magadha (Central India) and a few in Lāṭa and Sindhu (Western India) and some in a few places in Northern, Southern and Eastern India[2]. Before I-tsing, both Fa Hien and Yuan Chwang had come across the adherents of this school though not so frequently as those of the others. The earliest notice of this school is found in the inscription on Mathura Lion Capital (about 120 B. C.)[3] mentioning that it had a very strong opponent in Buddhila, an

1 Watters, *op. cit.*, I, p. 269, 'the majority of inferior brethren at Pāṭaliputra began the Mahāsaṅghika School'.

2 Takakusu's *Records of the Buddhist Religion by I-tsing*, Intro., p. xxxiii.

3 *Ep. Indica*, vol. IX, pp. 139, 141, 146.

adherent of the Sarvāstivāda school. The school acquired some followers in Afghanistan as is evidenced by the Wardak vase discovered there, containing relics of Buddha that had been presented to the teachers of the Mahāsaṅghika school during the reign of Huvishka by one Kamagulya of the place, whose father had probably built the vault within which the Wardak vase was deposited[1]. Yuan Chwang confirms this evidence by his reference to three monasteries at Andarab where he arrived after three days' journey from the country of Wardaks[2] (near Ghazni). There was another centre of the school at Karle, in the Bombay Presidency, famous in the history of Buddhist architecture for its possession of the largest and finest cave-temples[3] which are still standing as memorials of their past glory. That this cave was in the possession of the Mahāsaṅghikas is shown by two inscriptions at the cave-temples, one recording the gift of the village of Karajaka by Gautamīputra Śātakarṇi to the monks of the

1 *Ep. Indica*, Vol. XI, p. 211.

2 Watters' *Yuan Chwang*, II, pp. 267, 269.

3 See for its description Fergusson's *Indian & Eastern Architecture*, pp. 117ff; Fergusson and Burgess, *Cave Temples of India*, pp. 232ff.

Vāluraka caves for the support of the school of the Mahāsaṅghikas[1], and the other of the time of Vāśishṭiputra Siripulumāyi recording the gift of a nine-celled hall to the same school by an inhabitant of Abulama[2]. Though the Mahāsaṅghikas did not receive much attention from the Buddhist writers and donors, the Karle caves show that the school commanded a great popularity in that part of the Bombay Presidency where the caves exist; for, otherwise the cave-temples could not have been so richly decorated with such fine specimens of sculptural and architectural beauty by a series of donors through centuries anxious to express their religious devotion and zeal in the best way that their resources could command. The offshoots of this school, the Lokottaravādins and the Caityavādins wielded also much influence in Buddhist society for a long time paving the way for the advent of Mahāyānism which later on came to be diffused over the whole of India.

It will appear from what has been stated previously that though germs of Mahāyānism are traceable in the doctrines of the Mahā-

1 *Ep. Indica*, vol. VII, pp. 64ff.

2 *Ibid.*, pp. 71ff.

saṅghika school, it was affiliated to Hīnayānism and possessed a *piṭaka* similar to those of other prominent Hīnayāna schools. The Mahāsaṅghikas claimed for themselves more orthodoxy than the Theravādins and believed to have preserved more accurately the *piṭaka* as settled by Mahākassapa in the first council. The little that we know about their doctrines from the *Kathāvatthu*, the *Mahāvastu* and the works of Bhavya, Vinītadeva and Vasumitra[1] points to the fact that they subscribed to the cardinal principles of Hīnayāna schools. A comparative study of the *Mahāvastu* of the Mahāsaṅghikas with the Pāli *Vinaya* of the Theravādins shows the great doctrinal affinity existing between the two schools. One of the objects common to both the treatises being the delineation of the early part of Buddha's missionary career, the same discourses have been recorded in each, the difference lying only in linguistic garbs. These discourses embody the essence of Buddha's teachings ; and faithfully preserved, as they are, in the *Vinaya* of the two schools, it is apparent that the Mahā-

The doctrines of the Mahāsaṅghikas.

1 Prof. Masuda's translation of Vasumitra's work from the Chinese has been mainly relied on here. (*Calcutta University Journal of Letters*, I, pp. 7ff.)

saṅghikas and the Theravādins had no difference of view regarding what constituted the most important portion of Buddha's teachings. The discourses dwelt on the four aryan truths and their interpretations[1]; the eightfold path leading to emancipation[2]; the absence of soul as a separate entity[3]; the *karma* being the motive force in transmigration[4]; the theory of *paṭiccasamuppāda*[5]; the method of imparting spiritual teachings by gradual stages commencing from the simple *dānakathā, sīlakathā etc.* and ending in the higher truths[6]; thirty seven *Bodhipakkhiya dharmas*[7] etc. The schools however differed in in their Buddhalogical speculations, and the corollaries issuing therefrom. Prof. Takakusu has ably shown in his article on 'Docetism'[8] the way in which the idealizing process was carried on by the Buddhists, giving rise to the belief of the Mahāsaṅghikas and others that Buddha was

1&2 *Mahāvastu*, III, pp. 331-333; *Vinaya*, I, pp. 10-11.

3 *Ibid.*, pp. 335-337, 447; *Ibid.*, 13-14.

4 *Ibid.*, II, p. 363; III, 65, 66, 168.

5 *Ibid.*, pp. 448-9; *Vinaya*, I, pp. 1-2.

6 *Ibid.*, III, pp. 257, 408; see *supra*, pp. 47, 48.

7 See R. Kimura's *Developed Doctrines* etc. p. 27.

8 *Encyclopædia of Religion and Ethics*, vol. IV.

lokottara (superhuman) and had no worldly attributes (*sāśrava dharmas*), and the mortal being popularly known as Sākya Gautama was required only for *lokānuvartana* (conforming to worldly ways) for the benefit of this world. The corollaries based on this belief are that Buddha is omnipotent, speaks truths and nothing but truths. His *rūpa-kāya* (physical body), life, energy, and powers are limitless. He is always self-possessed and in *samādhi* (trance)[1]. The most important doctrine that resulted in this way lay in the theory of the Bodhisattvas. The Mahāsaṅghikas by idealizing Buddha had to make room for a class of beings called the Bodhisattvas who by passing through various trials and by making immense self-sacrifices rose to higher stages of Bodhisattvahood. These acts are classified as the four *caryās* (practices)[2], the ten *bhūmis* (stages)[3] and the six *pāramis*[4]. It was these Bodhisattvas who could attain Buddhahood in course of time. The Bodhi-

1 *Mahāvastu,* I, pp. 167-9 ; II, pp. 147, 220 ; *Calcutta University Journal of Letters,* I, pp. 7ff.

2 Viz., *prakṛticaryā, praṇidhānacaryā, anulomacaryā,* and *anivartanacaryā.*—*Mahāvastu,* I, pp. 46ff.

3 *Mahāvastu,* I, pp. 77ff.

4 *Ibid.,* III, p. 226.

sattvas in the various births were believed to be born without passing through the embryonic stages. They could not entertain feelings of enmity and hatred (*vihiṃsasaṃjñā* and *vyāpāda-saṃjñā*), and were above sensual desires (*kāma-saṃjña*). In conformity with this belief they supposed that Rāhula was self-born (*aupapāduka*) as Bodhisattvas could not be subject to *kāma*[1].

The attainments of Sākya Gautama were regarded by them as the ideal to be kept in view by every Buddhist, for according to them it was for the enlightenment of worldly beings that the *lokottara* Buddha adopted the human form to enable people to imitate his examples and ultimately attain Buddhahood. It was this point which brought about the schism between the Mahāsaṅghikas and the Theravādins. According to the latter, the *summum bonum* of a Buddhist should be *arahathood* and not *Buddhahood* as it is exceedingly rare that a Buddha appears in the world. It is possible for the Buddhists to become *arahats* in large numbers but it is exceedingly difficult for them to attain Buddhahood. The Mahāsaṅghikas believed in the plurality of Buddhas, as will be evidenced from the first line

[1] *Mahāvastu*, I, p. 153.

of the *Mahāvastu*[1] and according to them the *summum bonum* of a Buddhist should be *Buddhahood* and not *arahathood.* In accordance with this principle as also for other reasons stated previously they did not look upon the position of an *arahat* as the highest stage of sanctification[2].

It was the Mahāsaṅghikas who originated the worship of *caitya* and favoured that great religious merit could be acquired by even a single circumambulation of a *stūpa*[3]. Traces of *stūpa* worship are also found in the Pāli works but as such worship is not in consonance with the principles of the Theravādins, it seems that in later times the former borrowed it from the Mahāsaṅghikas.

1 *Mahāvastu*, I, p. 1; III, p. 229.

2 See *supra*, pp. 232, 233.

3 *Mahāvastu.*, II, pp. 362ff.

The Theravāda School

I do not wish to reiterate the points that have already been found out after laborious researches by Pāli scholars and published in their works. I wish here to confine myself only to certain points about the language or dialect used by the Theravādins in their literature. Before proceeding to the task, I want to point out that the Theravādins were otherwise known as the Vibhajjavādins and wherever we see references to the latter, they can be applied to the former without any feeling of doubt. Dr. Oldenberg was uncertain as to the identity of the two names and the classes they denote, but after comparison of the lists of schools supplied by the Northern and Southern Buddhist sources, he found out that Vibhajjavāda was but another name of Theravāda.[1] This conclusion finds corroboration in the Ceylonese chronicles which state the very same thing. There would have been no room for this doubt if he had noticed that in the *Majjhima Nikāya*, Buddha declares himself to be a *vibhajjavādin* and not an *ekāṃsavādin*, indicating that

1 Oldenberg's *Intro. to the Vinaya Piṭaka*, I, p. xlii.

his method of teaching was analytic and not synthetic.[1] Again in the same *Nikāya*, Buddha on hearing the doctrines of Ālāra Kālāma and Rudraka Rāmaputra says that he possesses a better knowledge than those teachers because he knows the *ñānavāda* as well as the *theravāda*.[2] These two references go to prove that the doctrine represented by the Pāli scriptures was Theravāda. It was also called Vibhajjavāda owing to the particular mode of teaching the *dhamma* adopted by the Pālists. Profs. Kern, Rhys Davids and others have endorsed the view that the whole Pāli literature represents the tenets of the Theravāda school. Though much has been said by scholars regarding the doctrine and and literature of the Theravādins *alias* Vibhajjavādins, nothing has been definitely stated as to the position of the Pāli language in relation to Buddhist literature. Many a tough problem in the history of Buddhism can be solved by studying the history of Buddhist schools, *viz.*, the original language of the Tripiṭaka and the time and place of origin of the Pāli language. The passage occurring in the *Vinaya*,[3] "*Anujā-*

1 *Majjh. Nik.*, II, pp. 99, 197.
2 *Ibid.*, I, p. 163.
3 *Vinaya*, CV., v. 33. 1.

nāmi bhikkhave saka niruttiyā Buddhavacanam priyāpunitum" (I permit, O bhikkhus, to learn the words of Buddha in one's own dialect) carries a very great weight in regard to our present subject. It is stated by Wassiljew and Csoma Körösi[1] on the strength of Tibetan sources that the Sarvāstivādins recited their '*sutra on emancipation*' (*prātimokṣa sūtra*) in Sanskrit, the Sāṃmitīyas in Apabhraṃśa, the Mahāsaṅghikas in a corrupt dialect (a prākṛt) and the Sthavira or Theravādins in Paiśācī. These four dialects are also mentioned in the *Mahāvyutpatti* while enumerating the subjects of a grammar.[2] The Sanskrit manuscript *Vimalaprabhā*[3] of the mediæval period contains a remark that the Piṭakas were written in 96 countries in 96 languages.[4] The manuscript gives in detail the names of the countries, and the language current in each of them. It also records a tradition that

1 Wassiljew, *Buddhismus*, pp. 264, 295; Csoma Körösi in *J. A. S. B.*, Vol. VII, p. 142.

2 *Mahāvyutpatti*, p. 64.

3 MS. No. 4727 mentioned in the Descriptive Catalogue of Sanskrit Manuscripts in the Government Collection, A. S. B., Vol. I, p. 77.

4 The number 96 seems to be a rough way of indicating a large number.

soon after the death of Buddha, the *Saṅgītikārakas* wrote down the doctrine of the three *yānas* in book-form. Under the direction of Tathāgata (*tathāgata-niyamena*), they preserved the *three piṭakas in the Magadha-bhāṣā, the Sūtrāntas in Sindhubhāṣā, the Pāramitās in Sanskrit, the Mantras and Tantras in Sanskrit, Prākṛt, Apabhraṃśa and uncultured Śabarādi mlecchabhāṣā and so forth.* The manuscript further mentions that the Buddhists did not pay much attention to Sanskrit regarding metres and grammatical rules, indicating thereby that it had in view the mixed dialect (*gāthā* as it is usually termed) used in some of the Buddhist Sanskrit books like the *Lalitavistara, Mahāvastu,* etc. The above statements of Indian writers of old have an evidentiary value as will be seen presently. Scholars like Stein, Grunwedel, Le Coq, Leumann, Hoernle, Sylvain Lévi by their unflinching zeal in the search of manuscripts in Central Asia have brought to light many things confirming the assertions of the mediæval writers. These scholars have saved from eternal oblivion remnants of manuscripts in so many languages as Sanskrit, Prākṛt, Kuchean, Khotanese, Proto-Tibetan and Eastern Iranian. Some of the fragments of Sanskrit and Prākṛt manuscripts as also a few discovered in Nepal have their counterparts in the Pāli piṭakas.[1] Among them are found almost complete portions of the piṭakas, *e.g.*, the Sanskrit versions of the *Udānavarga* and the *Prātimokṣa Sūtra*, and the Prākṛta version of the *Dharmapada*. Prof. Kern in his introduction to the translation of the *Saddharma Puṇḍarīka*[2] has shown that the various versions of a passage in Sanskrit, Pāli and Prākṛt reveal that they are not based upon one another but upon a common original, which is now lost. Dr. Hoernle in editing the fragments of the manuscript *Saddharma Puṇḍarīka* remarks that the Sanskrit text found in Nepal bears many similarities to the former but with some variations, from which it may safely be concluded that "the text of the *Saddharma Puṇḍarīka*, to which both the Central Asian and the Nepalese manuscripts go back, was written in a language that had far more Prākṛtisms than either of the two versions."[3] Hence we see that

1 E.g., *Āṭanāṭiya Sūtra*; *Saṅgīti Sūtra*; *Pravāraṇā Sūtra*; *Candropama Sūtra*; *Śakti Sūtra*; *Śuka Sūtra*; etc. Hoernle's *Manuscript Remains of Buddhist Literature in Eastern Turkestan*, pp. 18, 36, 41, 46.

2 *S. B. E.*, vol. xxi, pp. xi-xv.

3 Hoernle's *Manuscript Remains of Buddhist Literature in Eastern Turkestan*, p. 161.

the two versions are based upon an original work in Prākṛt. He has also shown by comparing the fragments of Sanskrit manuscripts with passages in the Pāli Sūtra and Vinaya Piṭaka that there was a complete Sanskrit canon which was independent of the Pāli canon but with a commonness from which it could be safely inferred that both the Sanskrit and the Pāli canon were based upon a common original. This original very probably dates back to the lifetime of Buddha and was the one which was recited in the first council. The manuscript *Vimalaprabhā* says that just after the demise of the Tathāgata, the *Saṅgītikārakas* put down the Tripiṭaka in the *Magadhabhāṣā*. That this tradition had a kernel of truth in it appears from these facts:—

All the versions of the Piṭaka were based upon one common original in Magadhabhāṣā.

(1) Buddha preferred preaching in the spoken dialect of the masses in order that his doctrines might be readily intelligible to them; (2) he was born and bred up in a place, the current dialect of which, if not the same as that prevailing among the masses of Magadha among whom he preached, must at least have been influenced by the latter in view of the widespread influence that is, as a rule, exercised by the principal dialect of the metropolis; (3) it is not likely that

Buddha who used a dialect at Kapilavastu up to about his 29th year should have found the dialect of Magadha unintelligible to him; on the other hand he used the dialect of Magadha easily and fluently, from which it is allowable to infer that the dialect of Kapilavastu was not at least separated from the dialect of Magadha by a gulf which required previous education or preparation to bridge up; and (4) his early missionary tours were generally within the limits of the country of Magadha. In the present state of our knowledge it is not possible to state anything more definite than what has been said above about the dialect in which Buddha preached. Buddha's preachings that were learnt by heart at the time and handed down to posterity no doubt existed in the very dialect used by him which has been termed the *Magadhabhāṣā*. It is very likely that this dialect has been dragging out its thin thread of existence under the layers of various other dialects or languages that have accumulated in the Pāli Piṭaka in its present form; and many of the various antiquated words and expressions that meet our eyes in the said Pāli text and which differ from the genuine Pāli words and expressions in several respects can with probability be credited to the *Magadhabhāṣā*.

Dr. Oldenberg agrees with us in holding that the Pāli version of the Tripiṭaka was not the original version but a redaction of same. He then takes up the question as "to what part of India did the Pāli originally belong, and from whence did it spread to Ceylon." The solution he arrives at is that Pāli was the original language of Kaliṅga, *i.e.*, of countries south of the Vindhya mountains. This solution is based on the resemblance of the Khaṇḍagiri inscription to the Pāli language. It is asserted by Dr. Oldenberg that the Pāli Tripiṭaka was taken to Ceylon from Southern India probably from Kaliṅga or Andhra with which countries Ceylon stood in close connection; and he attaches little importance to the Ceylonese tradition that Mahinda took the Pāli canon to Ceylon.[1] These inferences of Dr. Oldenberg are open to doubt for reasons which are given below:—

Time and place of origin of the Pāli language of the Theravādins.

(1) Franke by an exhaustive and comparative study of the inscriptional Prākṛts and Pāli has come to the conclusion that the home of literary Pāli was at Ujjayinī surrounded by

1 Oldenberg's *Intro. to the Vinaya Piṭaka*, I, p. liv.

localities where the inscriptional dialects are more akin to Pāli than the dialects of the inscriptions found in the East, South, and South-west.[1]

Franke's result of comparative study of inscriptions.

(2) There were two centres of the earliest form of Buddhism, one at the well-known metropolis Pāṭaliputra and the other at Ujjayinī. The establishment of the second centre of Buddhism was mainly due to Mahākaccāyana, one of the great disciples of Buddha. He was a native of Ujjayinī, being a son of the priest of king Caṇḍa Pajjota of the place. After completing his brāhmaṇic education, he succeeded to his father's office. It is said that he was sent by king Pajjota to fetch Buddha, but was on his arrival there ordained, after which he returned as a bhikkhu to his native land Avanti.[2] Buddha could not come with Mahākaccāyana but he said that Mahākaccāyana

Csoma Körösi's statement as to the Paiśācī dialect seen in the light of conclusion of Grierson and others as to the development of Pāli from Paiśācī.

1 Otto Franke's *Pāli und Sanskrit*, pp. 131, 132, summarised by Grierson in his paper 'Home of Literary Pāli' in the *Bhandarkar Commemoration Volume*, p. 117.

2 *Majjh. Nik.*, III, pp. 267ff.; *Saṃ. Nik.*, IV, p. 60; *Divyāvadāna*, pp. 37-39; *Mahāvastu*, III, p. 382.

would be able to satisfy the king with his exposition of the law. Another noted disciple of this part of the country was Puṇṇa Mantāniputta who was a trader and an inhabitant of Sunāparānta. On one occasion he went with a caravan to Sāvatthi where he heard a discourse from Buddha, resolved to become a Buddhist monk and became a disciple of Mahākaccāyana. From the conversation that Puṇṇa Mantāniputta had with Buddha, it appears that people of Sunāparānta were rough and rustic in their manners and Buddha was afraid lest he (Puṇṇa) should receive rough treatment at their hands.[1] However, it is said that Puṇṇa won many people to his side. Mahākaccāyana once sent information to Buddha through a disciple of his, Soṇa Kuṭikaṇṇa, that the number of bhikkhus at Avantidakkhiṇāpatha was not very large. The activities of these two chief disciples of Buddha for the propagation of Buddhism in Western India met with some success even as early as the 5th century B.C.[2] The Chinese travellers, who saw followers of the Theravāda school at several places in eastern India and Ceylon,

1 *Vinaya*, MV., v, 13, 2.

2 Upāli's name is associated with this school in the tradition given by Csoma Körösi.

found them also at Surat and Bharukaccha,[1] Lāṭa and Sindhu.[2] Csoma Körösi and Wassiljew furnish us with the information that the Theravādins preserved their literature in the Paiśācī dialect.[3] Prof. Konow places the home of Paiśācī at Ujjayinī or more properly, about the Vindhya mountains.[4] He also points out that Pāli closely agrees with Paiśācī. Sir G. Grierson holds the view as well that Pāli is a literary form of Paiśācī[5] but does not agree with Prof. Konow regarding the home of the dialect; he is of opinion that its place of origin was in the North-west at and near Takṣaśilā, and states that the dialect very probably passed from the North-west to Rajputana up to the Konkan coast. The tradition preserved by

1 Watters' *Yuan Chwang*, II, pp. 241, 248. Yuan Chwang refers to the Theravāda School as the Mahāyānist Sthavira School; for a discussion on the subject see Watters, *op. cit.*, II, p. 235.

2 Takakusu's *Records of the Buddhist Religion*, p. 7.

3 Wassiljew, *Der Buddhismus etc.*, pp. 294, 295.

4 *Z. D. M. G.*, lxvi, (1910), pp. 114ff, summarised by Sir G. Grierson in the *Bhandarkar Commemoration Volume*, pp. 119, 120. See also *J. R. A. S.*, 1921, pp. 244-45, 424-28.

5 *Indian Antiquary*, 1915, p. 227 fn.

Somadeva,[1] Daṇḍin[2] and Subandhu that the *Bṛhat-kathā* was written in Paiśācī by Guṇāḍhya, an inhabitant of the region about Ujjayiṇī, favours the view that Paiśācī was for sometime the spoken dialect of Ujjayiṇī. But the strongest ground for the view is philological which has been exhaustively dealt with by Prof. Konow and need not be repeated here. The close resemblance that subsists between Paiśācī and Pāli may be seen by a glance at the two passages, mentioned below, one in Paiśācī and the other its Pāli rendering.[3]

(3) The great importance attached by the Pāli writers and Chinese travellers to Mahinda for the propagation of Buddhism in Ceylon should not be dismissed as baseless. The integrity of the chapter of the *Mahāvaṃsa* detailing Asoka's missionary activities and supplying us

1 Somadeva's *Kathāsarita-sāgara,* Intro.

2 Daṇḍin's *Kāvyādarśa,* p. 35. See also Bühler's article in the *Indian Antiquary*, vol. I.

3 Paiśācī (*Kumārpāla-carita*):—

Paññāna rachiyā guna-nithinā raññā anañña-puññena
Cintetabbam matanādi verino kiha vijetabba.

Its Pāli rendering:—

Paññānam rājinā guna-nidhinā raññā anañña-puññena
Cintetabba madanādi verino kehi vijetabba.

Mahinda's connection with the place of origin of Paiśācī and his journey to Ceylon therefrom, embarking from an western port.

with names of missionaries has been corroborated by the discovery of a casket on which are inscribed names of two missionaries sent to the Himavanta which are identical with those given by the *Mahāvaṃsa.* In these circumstances, it would be unreasonable to doubt the statement regarding Mahinda's mission to Ceylon unless they are negatived by other stronger evidences. Dr. Oldenberg disbelieves that Mahinda received his Buddhistic education at Ujjayinī. He bases his opinion on the *Mahāvaṃsa* which states that Mahinda studied the Tripiṭaka at Pāṭaliputra[1] when Mahinda was twenty years old. But there is nothing in the *Mahāvaṃsa* to indicate that Mahinda accompanied his father on his way to Pāṭaliputra for assumption of royal power. On the contrary we learn that Mahinda's mother continued to live at Vidisā,[2] owing to her subsidiary position among Asoka's wives. Asoka had two other wives referred to in the Buddhist-Sanskrit works as living with him at Pāṭaliputra. It was usual with the Hindu kings and chiefs

1 Oldenberg's *Intro. to the Vinaya Piṭaka*, p. li.

2 *Mahāvaṃsa*, Ch. xiii.

to be polygamous, but it was the principal wife alone who enjoyed a status in the eye of the laws relating to inheritance.[1] Children born of wives other than the principal either lived on appanages or retired from the household life.[2] It was due to this custom, I believe, that Mahinda joined the Buddhist order and continued living with his mother at Avanti instead of coming to Pāṭaliputra with Asoka. It was not until his twentieth year that he was called by Asoka to the metropolis where he was asked to be ordained and to devote himself to the study of the Tripiṭaka. It is this fact which has been mentioned in the passage of the *Mahāvaṃsa* which has been utilized by Dr. Oldenberg as pointed out already. There is nothing in this passage to show that the Tripiṭaka studied by him was in the Pāli language. The passage of the *Mahāvaṃsa* is silent on this point and Dr. Oldenberg supplied it on the strength of the resemblance that the language of the Khaṇḍagiri inscription bears to the Pāli language. If he did so, it was not as the result of the development of the Pāli piṭaka from the spoken dialect of Kaliṅga as Dr. Oldenberg supposes, nor as the

1 V. A. Smith's *Early History of India*, p. 191.

2 *Ibid.*, p. 185.

result of Mahinda being educated at Pāṭaliputra, for Mahinda had his early education at Ujjayiṇī. The Pāli piṭaka was more easily intelligible to Mahinda than any other for the reason that he was educated in a place where Paiśāci was the current dialect and Pāli was the literary one and used in the piṭaka which in course of time supplanted the Paiśācī piṭaka. The carrying of the Pāli piṭaka to Ceylon for the first time by Mahinda has been disbelieved by Dr. Oldenberg. But there are reasons for doubting Dr. Oldenberg's conclusion. Mahinda when he was charged by Asoka with the duty of propagating Buddhism in Ceylon came to Avanti where he stayed immediately before his journey to Ceylon. Dr. Oldenberg states that Pāli piṭaka was taken to Ceylon by a certain person from a port in Kaliṅga. But as I have already shown, there is no reason to doubt the tradition of Mahinda's sailing to Ceylon for the purpose and as it is a historical fact that he stayed at Ujjayiṇī before sailing out, it would be natural that he would choose to start from a port on the western coast which was near Ujjayiṇī than from one on the far off eastern coast overcoming the difficulties of communication that existed in those days in going to a distant place. It may be said in a general way that in ancient times Ceylon had closer connection with western India than the eastern in almost all matters. Now as to the question of choice of the piṭaka which Mahinda took to Ceylon: From what has been said above as to the early education of Mahinda, his connection with Ujjayinī as his birthplace, and his stay there up to his twentieth year during which time he became familiarised with Paiśācī as the spoken dialect, it is, I think, reasonable to infer that his choice would fall upon the Pāli piṭaka, Pāli being the literary form of Paiśācī, the piṭaka in that language gradually supplanting its progenitor the Paiśācī version.

To sum up: In view of the combined arguments advanced by Sir G. Grierson, Profs. Sten Konow and Franke that Pāli is the literary form of Paiśācī which obtained currency in the region about Ujjayinī, and, in view of the statement made by Csoma Körösi and Wassiljew on the authority of Tibetan sources that there was a Paiśācī version of the piṭaka, it is only natural to infer that the piṭaka using Pāli as its medium was based upon the one in Paiśācī. It has also been shown from Csoma Körösi and Wassiljew's statements that the Theravādins had their literature in Paiśācī,—a fact which is significant for my purpose, because of the vital connection of the Theravādins with Avanti, and their exodus to Ceylon from there. The early education of Mahinda makes it apparent to us that he must have been more inclined to the literary dialect of his birthplace than to any other and it was only natural that he should take the Pāli version with him to Ceylon because it was the version of his country that was growing into popularity and throwing the Paiśācī version into the shade.

The Sarvāstivāda School

Buddhism has at present two principal divisions, namely, Hīnayāna and Mahāyāna, the former being subdivided into Vaibhāṣika and Sautrāntika, and the latter into Mādhyamika and Yogācāra[1]. Each of these four schools has its origin in the teachings of one great teacher, promulgated over 2,000 years ago, and has developed in its own way through several centuries. The present section aims to unfold the history of one of them, the Vaibhāṣika, formerly known as the Sarvāstivāda school, the appellation of Vaibhāṣika having been given to the school by Hindu philosophers in view of the fact that its doctrines were based upon the Vibhāṣā-śāstras compiled at the council of Kaniṣka[2].

Almost all the treatises dealing with the schools exclusively or *inter alia* record their number as eighteen as traditionally fixed, affili-

1. For the tenets of the four schools, see Mahāmahopādhyāya Dr. Satis Candra Vidyābhūaṣṇa's *Mediæval Logic* (1st ed.), pp. 66 ff.

2 Dr S. C. Vidyābhūṣaṇa, *op*, *cit.*, p. 66.

ating them to one or other of the two primitive schools, Sthaviravāda and Mahāsaṅghika. Deviations from this sort of classification are found in the Tibetan work *Bhikṣu-varhhagrapṛtstha*[1] and the *Records* of I-tsing[2]. They affiliate the eighteen schools to the four original ones, viz. (1) Ārya-sarvāstivādin, (2) Mahāsaṅghika, (3) Ārya-sāṃmitīya, and (4) Ārya-sthavira. The duration of existence of these four as independent schools was comparatively longer, and the number of adherents larger[3]. Other schools were short-lived, or coalesced into one another in spite of their points of difference. The most primitive school was the Sthavira-vāda, the doctrines of which have been fully preserved in the extant Pāli literature. The school that can claim priority in age and preservation of pristine originality next to the Sthavira-vāda is the Sarvāstivāda. Its literature is vast but to our misfortune the whole of it is yet in manuscripts[4], some of which are in Buddhist-Sanskrit and

1 Rockhill, *Life of the Buddha*, p. 180, fn.

2 Takakusu's *I-tsing*, pp. 7-8.

3 *J. R. A. S.*, 1891.

4 A few of these Mss. in Buddhist Sanskrit are deposited in the Library of the Asiatic Society of Bengal.

the rest in Chinese and Tibetan. The two schools mentioned above were associated with the names of two great emperors, Asoka and Kaniṣka, through whose effort and patronage, they gained ground and produced a rich and extensive literature. The principal seat of the Theravādins was Magadha while that of the other was Kashmir in conformity with the location of the courts of the respective sovereigns from whom each drew its support.

An account of the Council of Kaniṣka[1] is furnished by the Chinese traveller Yuan Chwang.

Council of Kaniṣka.

It was held in Kashmir about 400 years after the death of Buddha at the instance of Kaniṣka. The king evinced interest to learn the truths of Buddhism but he was perplexed by the variant interpretations given of Buddha's teachings by the monks[2]. In concert with the head of the

1 Watters, *Yuan Chwang,* I, pp. 270 ff. In later Tibetan works the Council is referred to and some particulars are also given but they do not agree in details with Yuan Chwang's account. See *Ibid.*, p. 278 (citing Tārānāth, 58 and *Vasubandhu-chuan*, No. 1463); Wassilief, *Der Buddhismus*, pp. 183 ff.

2 The modern N. W. Frontier Province and Gandhāra were inhabited by many sects of Hindus and

Buddhist church Pārśva, the king, convened a council with a view to record the different interpretations, and selected Kashmir as the place of meeting. Five hundred *arahats* were called out for membership, the Sarvāstivādins forming the majority. The President of the meeting was Vasumitra who was also a Sarvāstivādin, believing in the realism of material existence in the past, present, and future[1], and composed the two Abhidharma *pādas* (supplements) of the school[2]. Pursuant to the resolution of the council were compiled the Vibhāṣās (commentaries or discussions) being the opinions of the different schools on the Sūtra, Vinaya, and Abhidharma, known respectively as the *Upadeśa Sūtra, Vinaya-Vibhāṣā Śāstra*, and *Abhidharma-Vibhāṣā Śāstra.* But as the decisions of the disputed points rested on the President[3], the accepted version should naturally be in most cases that of the

Buddhists. Kashmir was the stronghold oi the Mahāsaṅghika and Sarvāstivāda Schools. See Watters, *Yuan Chwang*, I, pp. 202, 283.

1 Cf. Mrs. Rhys Davids, *Points of the Controversy*, p. xix.

2 *Abhidharma Prakaraṇa Pāda* and *Abhidharma Dhātukāya Pāda* ; see *infra*, pp. 288ff.

3 Watters, *Yuan Chwang*, I, p. 271.

Sarvāstivādins[1]. It is for this reason that the Vibhāṣās denoted the literature of the Sarvāstivādins and specially the Abhidharma commentaries, and the appellation Vaibhāṣika was given them by later writers[2].

It was only after this council that the Sarvāstivāda school rose to its highest importance.

Duration of existence of the Sarvāstivāda or the Vaibhāṣika school.

But the seed sown during the reign of the great Buddhist emperor Asoka when the activities of the school were confined within Magadha and Kosala now grew into an extensive foliage sending forth its branches beyond these limits under the fostering care of Kaniṣka. With the spread of Buddhism into Kashmir by the first Buddhist missionary Majjhantika sent by Asoka under the advice of Moggaliputta Tissa, the Sarvāstivādins thought

1 V. A. Smith, *Early History of India*, pp. 267, 268. Mr. Smith is of opinion that the Council was of the Sarvāstivādins and the literature written at that time, viz., the Mahā-vibhāṣā, belonged to this school.

2 Prof. Takakusu in his article on the Sarvāstivādins (*E.R.E.*, xi, p. 198) says that the *Vibhāṣā* is the name of the commentary compiled some time after Kaniṣka's reign to explain the *Jñānaprasthāna Sūtra* of *Kātyāyanīputra.*

it advisable to depute their representatives to Kashmir in view of its growing importance as a proselytizing centre. Yuan Chwang[1] also tells us that Asoka not only sent Buddhist monks but also built monasteries at that place. Now as the school of Buddhism planted here came from Pāṭaliputra and through the members of Moggaliputta's church, it would naturally follow that the first church founded in these places was that of the Theravādins. With the growing importance of the place as a centre of Buddhism, other schools also made their way to Kashmir, and it is not unlikely that the Sarvāstivādins owing to their closer connection with the Theravādins would follow next. But it should be remembered that the Sarvāstivāda school of Kaniṣka's time brought in further changes in the doctrine for which it has been distinguished from the older school, which was named the Ārya-sarvāstivādin[2]. However, the original Sarvāstivāda school had its birth before Asoka's council (3rd century B. C.), for,

1 Watters, *Yuan Chwang*, I, p. 269.

2 Rockhill, *Life of the Buddha*, pp. 183 ff. quoting *Bhikkhu Varhhagrapṛtstha* which puts Mūla-sarvāstivādin as one of the four schools seceding from the Ārya-sarvāstivādin.

the *Kathāvatthu*[1] which obtained its final shape in this council took notice of same for refuting its tenets. The school does not seem to have gained much importance at this time or a century later, as the Sanchi or Bharhut inscriptions[2] did not mention it or any other schools which abounded in the later inscriptions. About the beginning of the Christian era, it came to be recognized as one of the principal schools not only in Kashmir and Gandhāra but also in Central India. The adherents of this school began to be the recipients of donations in the shape of monasteries, images, etc., from monks, laymen, kings, and queens[3].

Fa-hien (319—414 A. D.) noticed the existence of this school in Pāṭaliputra and China while Yuan Chwang (629—645 A. D.) found it "chiefly in Kashgar, Udyana, and several other places in the Northern Frontier, in Matipura, Kanauj, and a place near Rājagṛha in

1 Mrs. Rhys Davids, *Points of the Controversy*, p. xix.

2 *J.R.A.S.*, 1892, p. 597. (Bühler's letter).

3 *Epigraphia Indica*, Vol. ii, p. 212 (Kamari Inscription); Vol. viii, p. 111 (also Vol. ix, p. 29) (Set Mahet Image Inscription of the time of Kaniṣka or Huviṣka); Vol. ix, pp. 135 ff. (The Inscriptions on the Mathura Lion-capital).

Northern India and also in Persia in the West." Since this time the geographical expansion of the school continued further until in I-tsing's time the adherents of the school were also found in Lāṭa, Sindhu, Southern and Eastern India, Sumatra, Java, China, Central Asia, and Cochin China.[1] Śaṅkarācārya (eighth century A. D.), set himself to refuting the doctrines of the Sarvāstitvavāda from the standpoint of a Vedāntin[2], while Mādhavācārya in the fourteenth century tried to give an exposition of the doctrines of the Vaibhāṣikas[3], by which title the Sarvāstivādins were afterwards known. Thus we see that the school, originating in the third century B. C., attained its highest development in the reign of Kaniṣka and lasted up to the fourteenth century; and counted as one of the four premier schools of Buddhism, it stood on the same level with one of them, namely, that of the

1 Prof. Takakusu, *J.P.T.S.*, 1904-5, p. 71 citing Legge's *Fa-hien*, p. 99; *J.R.A.S.*, 1891, p. 420; and I-tsing's *Records*, pp. xxii-xxiv.

2 *Vedānta Sūtras* (translated in *S.B.E.*, Vol. xlviii, pt iii), pp. 500-516.

3 *Sarva-darśana-saṃgraha* (translated by Cowell and Gough), Ch. II. See also *Ṣaḍ-darśana-samuccaya*, and *Advaita-brahma-siddhi*, pp. 67 ff.

Theravādins, who, by being compelled by force of circumstances to take shelter in Ceylon, have survived up till now[1].

Wassiljew[2] on the authority of the Tibetan sources makes the statement that the literature of this school was in Sanskrit. The later works of this school, composed or compiled after the council of Kaniṣka, were no doubt in Sanskrit[3], e.g. the *Prātimokṣa-sūtra*, *Udāna-varga*, prose portion of the *Lalitavistara*, *Divyāvadāna* etc. but the earlier works seem to have been written in a Prākṛt dialect.. This can be inferred from the following considerations. The council of Kaniṣka was held in Kashmir, the literary dialect of which at this time was Sanskrit. Though the Vibhāṣās compiled at this council have not come down to us, yet the fact that they were composed at the place inhabited

Language used in the works of this school.

1 Cf. *E.R.E.*, xi, p. 198—"The existence of the Sarvāstivādins can be traced during more than fifteen centuries of Indian history".

2 Wassiljew, *Der Buddhismus*, p. 294. I am indebted to Dr. B. M. Barua, M. A., D. Litt. for this information and a few other suggestions here.

3 See Hoernle's *Manuscript Remains of Buddhist Literature etc.*, pp. 166ff.

by people among whom Sanskrit was prevalent as the literary language, and to whom, in a large measure, the Vibhāṣās were intended to appeal, is a strong reason for supposing that they were most probably compiled in that language. To this should be added the consideration that all the seven titles of the seven works on Abhidharma of the Sarvāstivādins in their Chinese version have been restored by Prof. Takakusu to Sanskrit originals. The names of those works appearing in the list furnished by *Mahāvyutpatti*[1] and *Abhidharma-koṣa-vyākhyā*[2] are also Sanskrit showing a great probability of the compilations of the works of this school in Sanskrit.

The discovery of manuscripts in connection with the excavations in Central Asia under the supervision of Dr. Stein lends support to the view and rouses the hope that more light would be forthcoming upon these obscure points. The finds that are already to hand prove that there was a complete Buddhist-Sanskrit canon belong-

1 Published in the *Bibliotheca Buddhica*; see art. *Āgama*.

2 *Kārikā* III, cited by Prof. Takakusu in the *J. P. T. S.*, 1904-5, p. 75, fn.; see also p. 76, fn., for the titles as restored from the Tibetan sources.

ing to the Sarvāstivādins. The order in which, roughly speaking, Sanskrit and Prākṛt alternated as a literary medium in North-western India, seems to my mind to be that in pre-Buddhist period Sanskrit was generally used as the medium, but with the movement initiated by Buddha and afterwards taken up by Asoka for spreading Buddhism, involving the necessity of appealing to the religious sentiments of the masses through a medium easily intelligible to them, the existing literary works began to be rendered into the Prākṛt versions and new Prākṛt works began to be composed. The prevalence of Prākṛt as the literary medium lasted for a long time and this was followed by a period when Sanskrit re-asserted itself as the medium for literary uses. The factors which contributed to these changes are many, of which only one or two are patent to us and the rest are either obscure or stand even beyond the range of guesses. The only inferences that we can draw in these circumstances are from the fragments of facts that are coming up into view at times, giving rise in our minds to hypotheses which fit in best with the bases of our present knowledge of Buddhistic history of the times; these provisional inferences, however, will have to be modified in the light of facts that future may reveal.

Literature of the school: (1) Sūtras.

The translation of six hundred and fifty-seven Buddhist canonical works from Sanskrit into Chinese is attributed to Yuan Chwang. Sixty-seven of these works make up the *Sūtras*, *Vinayas*, and *Śāstras*[1] of the Sarvāstivādins. In Nanjio's Catalogue[2] under the heading *Hīnayāna Sūtras*, the four *āgamas*, viz., *Dīrghāgama*, *Madhyamāgama*, *Ekottarāgama*, and *Saṃyuktāgama*[3] corresponding to the four Pāli Nikāyas, have been mentioned and the contents of the first three *āgamas* have also been given. By comparing the contents with those of the Pāli recensions of those works it becomes evident that the Chinese translations were made from an original which is not identical with the texts as represented in the Pāli recensions. The differences are not merely in the texts but also in the number and arrangement of the *sūtras*. In spite of the differences, however, the names and the subjects of the *sūtras* are identical with those

1 Watters, *Yuan Chwang*, I, pp. 20, 21; *Śāstras* here refer to the *Abhidharma-piṭaka*.

2 Buniyu Nanjio's *Catalogue of the Chinese translations of the Buddhist Tripiṭaka.*

3 *Divyāvadāna* (p. 333) knows of four āgamas, *viz.*, *Dīrgha*, *Madhyama*, *Saṃyukta*, and *Ekottarika.*

of the Pāli works. The other Chinese works placed under the aforesaid heading (*Hīnayāna Sūtras*) seem to be separate translations of the important *sūtras* comprised in the four *āgamas.* In the *Mahāvyutpatti*[1], the four *āgamas* bear the identical titles and to them a fifth *āgama* is added, namely, the *Kṣudrakāgama.* The Chinese translators do not expressly mention the school to which these *āgamas* or *sūtras* belong, as they have done in the case of the *Vinaya* and the *Abhidharma* except in the case of the translation of the *Buddhacarita* and *Abhiniṣkramaṇa Sūtra*[2], in which the translator remarks that five different schools named the *Life of Buddha* in different ways as follows :—

(1) *Mahāvastu* of the Mahāsaṅghikas,

(2) *Mahāvyūha* or *Lalitavistara* of the Sarvāstivādins,

(3) Buddha's former *Nidāna* or *Avadāna* of the Kāśyapīyas,

(4) *Buddhacarita* of the Dharmaguptas, and

(5) *Vinaya-piṭaka-mūla* of the Mahiśāsakas.

The Chinese translators used, as a rule, to mention the name of the school to which the

1 *Mahāvyutpatti*, Art. *Āgama.*

2 Nanjio's *Catalogue*, col. 163.

works translated by them belonged. Want of this indication in the case of the *āgamas* leads us to infer that the various schools were at one in their acceptance of the texts of the *āgamas*. It is natural that it should be so in view of the sanctity and reverence attached to Buddha's sayings which none of the schools dared to alter without committing sacrilege and, therefore, the differences were confined to the doctrines only, originating in the divergent interpretations of the same texts as also in the variations in the stress laid on particular aspects of their meaning. The collection of these sayings varied in number in the different schools, and this accounts for the varying number of *sūtras* on the same subjects in the compilations of the different schools. Though the *Udānavarga*[1] and the *Dharmapada*[2] are in verse, their Theravāda and Sarvāstivāda recensions agree in the substance of the sayings versified in them, though they disagree as to the length and arrangement of their respective treatments of those sayings. The *Kathāvatthu* collecting the doctrines of different Buddhist schools makes it clear that though

1 Rockhill's translation (Trübner series).

2 In the Kharoṣṭhī recension (ed. by Dr. Barua and Mr. Mitra).

the doctrines differ, they all refer to the same *piṭakas* as their authority, which also goes to support the inference. Further, in the *Kathāvatthu,* the authorities cited in support of the doctrines of each school have been traced in the Pāli piṭakas, proving thereby that there was no variation in the substance of the sayings though there might have been in the recensions. The *Prātimokṣa Sūtra* of the Sarvāstivādins and the fragments of the *Nikāyas* and the *Vinaya* found in Eastern Turkestan also corroborate the above inference[1].

The *Vinaya* unlike the *Sūtrapiṭaka* experienced a very different treatment in the hands of the bhikkhus. We learn from the Chinese translations that there were four *Vinayas* belonging to four different schools, viz., Sarvāstivāda, Mahiśāsaka, Dharmagupta, and Mahāsaṅghika[2].

(2) Vinaya.

There were constant disputations among the bhikkhus on account of disagreement regarding minor rules of discipline,

1 Hoernle, *Manuscript Remains, etc.*, pp. 166, 168, 173.

2 Nanjio's *Catalogue*, col. 246ff. Besides the complete Vinaya of the above mentioned schools, there were supplementary treatises dealing with portions of the Vinaya text.

e. g., cutting and wearing of robes, inclusion of meat and milk in the articles of food, residence in monasteries within towns and cities, worship of *caityas* and images, etc[1]. To heighten the importance of the rules, each school invented episodes in the life of Buddha to serve as the basis of these rules. This accounts for a good many differences among the rules of several schools, but, there were also other causes such as divergences in the circumstances and surroundings that were responsible for the like differences. Though there were alterations in the supplementary portions of the *Vinaya* as adopted by the schools, viz., in the *Mahāvagga* and *Cullavagga*, the original *Pātimokkha* seems to have remained the same in all of them. It is evident from the *Prātimokṣas* of the Sarvāstivāda, the Dharmagupta, and the Theravāda schools that the differences between them are negligible[2]. Dr. Oldenberg has advanced his arguments to prove the *Pātimokkha* to be the

1 See *supra*, pp. 221, 222, regarding Devadatta's school, and quarrel among the Kosambī bhikkhus; Watters, *Yuan Chwang*, I, p. 150; Takakusu, *I-tsing*.

2 *J.R.A.S.*, Vol. xix, O.S., pp. 407-408; *Prātimokṣa Sūtra* of the Sarvāstivādins (ed. by L. Finot in

oldest part of of the *Vinaya*. The frequent mention of the *Pātimokkha* in the *Nikāyas* shows beyond doubt that this formed one of the earliest compositions of the Buddhists. Dr. Oldenberg, after a comparison of the *Vinayas* of the three schools, Mahiśāsakas, Theravādins, and Sarvāstivādins, arrived at the conclusion that all the *Vinayas* were fundamentally the same though later additions were made to some of them[1].

The Tibetan version of the *Vinaya*, an analysis of which is furnished by Csoma Körösi[2], was based according to Wassiljew on the Sarvāstivāda recension of the *Vinaya*[3]. This inference finds support in the fact pointed out by Csoma Körösi that a picture representing Buddha in the middle with Sāriputta and Rāhula on his two sides appears on the first leaf of the Tibetan manuscript. The significance of this picture from our point of view lies in this that Sāriputta and Rāhula were the special objects of worship

the *Journal Asiatique*, 1913. See also Hoernle, *op. cit.*, pp. 356-376.

1 *Vinaya Piṭaka* (ed. by Oldenberg), Intro., p. xxxvii.

2 *Asiatic Researches*, Vol. xx.

3 Wassiljew, *Der Buddhismus*, p. 96.

of the Sarvāstivādins. Rāhula, a disciple of Sāriputta has been mentioned by Chinese authorities as the founder of the Sarvāstivāda school[1]. It also appears from a passage in the manuscript that the Tibetan rendering was made by an inhabitant of Kashmir who was a follower of the Vaibhāṣika school which is nothing but a variant appellation of the Sarvāstivāda.

Thus, we see that the Sarvāstivādins had a complete *Vinaya* in all its divisions, viz., (1) *Vinaya-vastu*[2], (2) *Prātimokṣa sūtra*[3], (3) *Vinaya-vibhāga*[4], (4) *Vinaya-kṣudraka-vastu*[5], and (5) *Vinaya-uttara-grantha*[6]. Prof. Csoma Körösi's analysis of the Tibetan *Vinaya* furnishes details of the first part of the book only, i. e., the *Vinaya-vastu*.

By way of illustration of the degree of similarity and dissimilarity existing between the Tibetan and Pāli versions of the Vinaya, I give

1 Eitel, *Handbook of Chinese Buddhism*, sv. Rāhula. Cf. Hoernle, *op. cit.*, p. 166.

2 Corresponding with the *Mahāvagga* of the Pāli *Vinaya-piṭaka*.

3 & 4 Corresponding with the *Sutta-vibhaṅga* of the Pāli *Vinaya-piṭaka* (including *Pātimokkha*).

5 Corresponding with the *Cullavagga*.

6 Corresponding with the *Parivāra*.

here a rough sketch of the inferences that may be drawn from a comparison of the two versions of the first part of the Vinaya, viz., the *Vinaya-vastu.* I should mention at the outset that throughout the *Vinaya,* we see as a rule that particular events are taken up by Buddha as the subjects of anecdotes pointing to a moral, which has been reduced by him into rules for the guidance of his disciples; and thus the *Vinaya* naturally divides itself into two portions, one giving the anecdotes and the other the rules, though, of course, the former are in every case followed by those of the latter to which they appertained.

In the two versions of the *Vinaya* there is very little disagreement as to the rules but it is found that the same rule has been elicited from different anecdotes. As for example, in the Pāli version, the rule that a person cannot be ordained unless he has obtained the permission of his parents has been educed from the ordination of Rāhula, who had not taken his mother's consent[1]. In the Sarvāstivāda version appears the same rule but the occasion is differently stated, viz., a young man leaves his home

Vinaya, I, p. 83.

secretly and joins the order without the knowledge of his parents[1].

It may also be mentioned as a distinctive feature of the Sarvāstivāda version of the Vinaya that it is more diffuse at places than the Pāli version. Another distinction lies in the fact that certain points occurring in the former are altogether absent in the latter. In leaf 195 of the second volume of the *Vinaya-vastu*, reference has been made to the abstract meditation carried to excess by the priests of the Śākya clan, and explanations given of the terms relating thereto. In leaf 20 of the same volume, five sorts of *ghaṇṭis*, (plates of metals) are mentioned as required at the time of prayer and the recitation of the *Prātimokṣa*. The fourth volume of this book contains 470 leaves in which a complete life of Buddha has been given embodying accounts beginning with the origin of the Śākya race and ending with Devadatta's (*Lhas-byin*) efforts to injure Buddha and cause divisions among his disciples. The subjects of the third volume are not found in the Pāli *Vinaya*, but appear in its *Sutta-piṭaka*. Thus, the Sarvāstivādins mixed up the *Sūtra* and *Vinaya* while the Theravādins

1 *Asiatic Researches*, Vol. xx, leaf 115 of the Tibetan *Dulva*.

kept them separate. The belief current up to now that the one is a redaction of the other is baseless. Both have come from a common source, and by reason of development in different centres, minor accretions have grown round them creating differences in their exterior. The commonness of the names of places, where the various scenes[1] mentioned in the *Vinaya* are laid, supports the above inference while the mention of Kashmir in connection with its conversion to Buddhism found only in the Sarvāstivāda version speaks a good deal in favour of the aforesaid probability of the existence of a close connection between this school and Kashmir[2].

1 Such as Rājagṛha, Śrāvastī, Sāketa, Vārāṇasī, Vaiśālī, and Campā. *Asiatic Researches*, Vol. xx, p. 44.

2 Some points of agreement between the two versions : *Vinaya-vastu*, Vol. I, leaves 1-193 contain the subject of entering into the religious order—*Pravrajita-vastu* corresponding with *Mahākhandhaka paṭhama* of the Pāli *Vinaya*, Vol. I, p. 98.

Leaves 193-357 contain "the description of the confession or self-emendation, and general supplication" corresponding with the Pāli *Uposatha-khandhaka*.

Leaves 357-378 "on passing the *Vassa*" corresponding with *Vassupanāyika-khandhaka tatiya* (*Vinaya*, I, p. 158) and *Pavāraṇa-khandhaka* (*Ibid.*, p. 178).

Yuan Chwang informs us that the Sarvāstivādins of some places allowed the use of the three kinds of pure flesh and the drink of grape syrup as beverage, which was contrary to the principles of Mahāyānism of which he was an adherent. In the Vinaya of the Sarvāstivādins as well as of the Theravādins the eating of meat with some restrictions was allowed by the orthodox[1]. The Sarvāstivādins had a peculiar mode of wearing and colouring their robes not approved by the followers of several schools[2].

Leaves 378-408 (end of the vol.) and leaves 1—10 (of the next vol.) "on the subject of leather and skin" corresponding with *Cammakkhandhakaṁ pañcamaṁ*. (*Ibid.*, I, p. 198).

The second volume of the *Dulva* contains the chapter on medicaments (leaves 11-78) and garments of priests (leaves 78 ff.) corresponding with *Bhesajjakkhandhakaṁ* (I, p. 251) and *Kaṭhinakkhandhakam* and *Cīvarakkhandhakam* (*Ibid.*, pp. 265-310).

1 Watters' *Yuan Chwang*, I, pp. 53, 60; Körösi's analysis in the *Asiatic Researches*, Vol. xx, p. 67 and *Vinaya*, *Mahāvagga*, vi, 31, 14. The admissibility of grape-syrup as a drink is found only in a quotation given by Watters. See Watters, *op. cit.* pp. 237 ff.

2 Watters, *op. cit.*, I, pp. 150ff. Takakusu, *I-tsing*.

It is the Abhidharma literature of the Sarvāstivāda school that deserves special attention.

(3) Abhidharma.

Prof. Takakusu has rendered valuable service by furnishing us with the contents of the seven abhidharma books at present unique and preserved in Chinese translations[1]. The number of books in this collection is just the same is in that of the Theravādins, the difference being that the latter collection consists of seven independent works while the former of one principal treatise the *Jñānaprasthāna Sūtra of* Kātyāyanī-putra with its six *pādas* or supplements[2]. They are,—

(1) *Saṅgīti-paryāya* of Mahākauṣṭhila,

(2) *Dhātu-kāya* of Pūrṇa,

(3) *Prajñapti-sāra* of Maudgalyāyana,

(4) *Dharma-skandha* of Śārīputra,

(5) *Vijñāna-kāya* of Devaśarman, and

(6) *Prakaraṇa-pāda* of Vasumitra.

Prof. Takakusu on a comparison of the Abhidharma works of the two schools comes to the conclusion that the "two sets have no real

1 "The Abhidharma Literature of the Sarvāstivādins" by Prof. Takakusu in *J.P.T.S.*, 1904-5, pp. 67-146; see also his article on the Sarvāstivādins in *E.R.E.*, xi.

2 *J.P.T.S.*, 1904-5, pp. 74ff.

connection." Though there is no apparent connection between the two sets, yet it is clearly noticeable that most of the subjects treated in the two sets are found in the *Sūtra-piṭaka* but the mode of treatment in one is different from that of the other. The first *pāda* reveals a close relation of the Abhidharma works of the Sarvāstivādins to the Suttas of the Theravādins. Prof. Takakusu hints that the first *pāda*, *Saṅgīti-paryāya*, has been modelled on the *Saṅgīti-suttanta* of the *Dīgha-Nikāya*[1]. He remarks that "the contents of the ones, twos, threes, etc. (in the *suttanta* and *paryāya*) are usually different." But it should be pointed out that the contents do agree with one another except that the instances of ones, twos, threes, etc., as given in the Pāli text exceed greatly in number those of the other as explained below[2].

If a text on account of its pithy baldness be

1 *Dīgh.*, *Nik.*, III, *Suttanta* No. xxxiii.

2 E.g. (1) Section on *Eka-dharmas* :—
All beings live on food, etc.,—Takakusu's contents.
Sabbe sattā āhāraṭṭhitikā.
Sabbe sattā saṅkhāraṭṭhitikā. (*Dīgh. Nik.*, Vol. III, p. 211).
(2) Section on *Dvi-dharmas* :—

considered earlier than another on an identical topic presented at length with much elaboration of details, then the *Pāda* should be regarded as anterior in age to the *Suttanta*. The statement of Prof. Takakusu giving an earlier origin to the *Suttanta* cannot from this standpoint be regarded

Mind and matter—(Takakusu).
Nāma-rūpa—(*Dīgh. Nik.*).
Means for entering into meditation and coming out of meditation, etc. corresponding with Nos. i and ix of the *Saṅgīti Suttanta*, I, 9. The *Suttanta* enumerates 33 *Dvi-dharmas*.

(3) Section on *Tri-dharmas* :—

Prof. Takakusu's list can be identified with the following numbers of the *Suttanta*, i, ii, iii, v, vi, xi, xxvi, xxviii, xxxvi, xxxvii, lviii, except the three *āpattivyuṭṭhānas*. In the former list, the total number is 36 whereas in the *Suttanta*, it is 60.

(4) Section on *Catur-dharmas* :—

Prof. Takakusu gives us only 7 fours out of the total 21 fours; 5 of the fours correspond with the following numbers of the *Suttanta* i, ii, vi, xv, xlvii; the number of fours in the latter is 50.

In this way all the *ten dharmas* can be traced but it will be noticed that the *Suttanta* list is much longer than the *Pāda* list.

as unimpeachable. His next remark that the "work was compiled after the council of Vesāli which was held chiefly for suppressing the ten theses of the Vajjian bhikkhus," based on a passage of the *Pāda* referring to the Vajjian bhikkhus of Pāvā, does not rest on a sound basis. Mr. Wogihara was right in rendering the passage to the effect that it was Nigaṇṭha Nātaputta of Pāvā, and not the Vajjian bhikkhus[1]. The Vajjian bhikkhus, again, were inhabitants of Vesāli and not of Pāvā, the residents of which place, namely the Mallas, were partly followers of Nigaṇṭha Nātaputta and partly of Buddha. The object of Sāriputta in putting the *dharma* as the summation of a few metaphysical and religious truths for its followers was to avert the danger of a split in the Buddhist church as had happened in the Jaina *saṅgha* just at that time[2]. The close correspondence between the *Suttanta* and the *Paryāya* specially in their introductory and concluding passages shows that one is based upon the other and that the author is the same for both. Prof. Takakusu preferred the tradition which ascribed the authorship to Mahākausṭhila but the coincidence of the other tradi-

1 *J.P.T.S.*, 1904-5, p. 99, fn.
2 *Dīgh. Nik.*, Vol. III, p. 210.

tion (ascribing it to Sāriputta) with that of the *Saṅgīti Suttanta* leads us to infer that Sāriputta was the author of the work.

The fourth *Pāda*, the *Dharma-skandha*, is said in the colophon to its Chinese translation to be "the most important of the Abhidharma works, and the fountain-head of the Sarvāstivāda system." The subjects treated contain nothing which can be claimed by the Sarvāstivāda as its own. They constitute the essence of Buddhism and if the claim of the Sarvāstivādins be admitted, that of the Theravādins of a similar nature cannot be denied an equal force on the same ground. It is only natural that, as Prof. Takakusu points out, the *Saṅgīti-Paryāya* should often quote this book, traversing as they do the same ground[1].

Thirteen sections, again, of the above book are found in the seventh section of the *Prakaraṇa pāda*, "discussions on one thousand questions"[2], the author of which is Vasumitra. I think that as Vasumitra was a Sarvāstivādin, the section was meant to be a supplement discussing the exposition embodied in the *Dharma-skandha*.

The composition of the second *pāda, Dhātu-*

1 *J.P.T.S.*, 1904-5, p. 115.
2 *Ibid.*, p. 106.

kāya, is attributed to either Vasumitra or Pūrṇa according to different traditions. Preference should be given to the former tradition in view of the fact that this *Pāda* is only an enlarged treatment of the topics contained in section 4 of the *Prakaraṇa-pāda* of Vasumitra.

The fifth *Pāda*, *Vijñāna-kāya*, is said to have been the work of Deva-śarman, an arahat of Viśoka (near Kauśāmbī) who lived some time before the 5th century after Buddha' *parinirvāṇa*. Yuan Chwang informs us that Deva-śarman refuted the views of Moginlin (Moggalāna) who denied the reality of past and future[1], one of the chief principles of the Sarvāstivāda doctrine. This remark of Yuan Chwang finds support in the fact that the first section of this *pāda* records the opinion of Maudgalyāyana about *pudgalas*, *indriyas*, etc., the next section containing *inter alia* a discussion of the theory of *pudgala*[2] (soul). This work was highly appreciated by the Vaibhāṣikas who gave it a canonical position which was denied to it by the Sautrāntikas[3].

The third *Pāda*, *Prajñapti-sāra*[4], gives an

1 Watters, *Yuan Chwang*, I, p. 373.

2 *J.P.T.S.*, 1904-5, p. 108.

3 Watters, *op. cit.*, p. 374.

4 *J.P.T.S.*, 1904-5.

account of the life of Buddha, and its authorship has been ascribed to Mahā-Maudgalyāyana.

Doctrines.

The Sarvāstivādins, as stated already, were like the Theravādins, a conservative school of the Hīnayāna. They held almost the same views as the Theravādins and believed in the non-existence of soul, impermanence of material composites, the law of *karma*, and *nirvāṇa* as "the cessation of passions (*kleśas*) to be attained by transcendental knowledge[1]". Their views about the human life and the universe were also similar to those of the Theravādins. Their chief exponent Katyāyanīputra in his *Jñāna-prasthāna-sūtra* accepts in every detail "the theory of the five *skandhas*, the twelve *āyatanas*, the eighteen *dhātus*, the twelve-linked chain of causation, the three worlds (*kāma*, *rūpa*, and *arūpa dhātu*), the four classes of birth (*aṇḍaja*, *saṃsvedaja*, *jarāyuja*, and *aupapāduka*) and the four cycles (*antarakalpa*, *mahākalpa*, *sārakalpa*, and *śunyakalpa*)"[2]. The only difference between the doctrines of the Sarvāstivādins and those of the Theravādins lies in this that the former admitted

1 Yamakami Sogen's *Systems of Buddhistic Thought*, p. 165.

2 *Ibid.*, p. 178.

the reality of the elements (*skandhas*) that compose a being as against the latter's view of their unreality. Both the schools admitted the continual flux of elements or in other words the momentary existence (*kṣaṇikatva*) of every composite thing with this difference that the one looked upon the elements of the past as disappearing to give rise to the present and the present as giving rise to the future, while the other believed that the elements of the past underwent changes to develop into the present and the present developed into the future. In short, the Sarvāstivādins admitted the reality of elements as existing in all times,—past, present, and future. On account of their belief in the *astitva* theory of elements, they have analysed the material composites into various classes of elements which they have enumerated in connection with the exposition of their philosophy[1]. It appears from the *Lalitavistara*, a treatise originally belonging to the Sarvāstivādins, that the theory of *paṭiccasamuppāda* (chain of causation) found much favour with this school and particularly for proving impermanence and soullessness of beings. In Buddhological specu-

1 For the analysis, see Sogen, *op. cit.* pp. 119ff. and Kimura's *Original and Developed Doctrines* etc. pp. 12ff.

by the *Kathāvatthu* indicates that the school existed in Asoka's time. The next early evidence as to the existence of this school is furnished by the inscription of the early Gupta period discovered at Sarnath. This inscription also shows that the first school that prevailed at Sarnath was that of the Theravādins. It was supplanted by the Sarvāstivādins at about 300 A. D. About a century afterwards this school again was ousted by the Sāṃmitīyas who continued till the time of Yuan Chwang[1]. The Sāṃmitīyas could not prosper in the pre-Christian era but they gradually attained importance in Northern India during the Gupta period reaching climax in the reign of Harṣavardhana.

From the figures supplied by Yuan Chwang regarding the number of Sāṃmitīya monks in various places, it will be seen that though they resided in Ahicchatra, Sankassa, Hayamukha, Visoka, Benares, Karṇasuvarṇa etc., they had their predominance in Malwa, Sind[1] and the neighbouring places, such as Ānandapura, A-tien-p'o, Pi-to-shih-lo and A-fan-tu. The name

1 Dayaram Sahni's *Catalogue of the Museum at Saranath*, p. 30 ; *Ep. Indica*, VIII, p. 172.

2 The number of Sāṃmitīya bhikkus in Malwa and Sind was 20,000 and 10,000 respectively.

Avantaka applied to the Sāṃmitīya school by Vasumitra shows that its centre in Northern Avantī i. e. Malwa must have been very important[1]. The ascription of the origin of this school to Mahākaccāyana, the famous missionary of Avantī, also shows that it must have had some connection with Malwa at the time of its emergence.

Language and literature of the school.

The Sāṃmitīyas, according to the Tibetan tradition, possessed a pīṭaka in the Apabhraṃśa dialect. Modern philologists hold that the Śaurasenī-Apabhraṃsa which prevailed in Malwa and Gujarat was the standard Apabhraṃśa dialect and that it was different from the pure Śaurasenī. It was here that the few Jaina texts now existing in the Apabhraṃśa dialect were written. It is very probable that the Sāṃmitīyas, who had a piṭaka of their own handed down orally from generation to generation, committed it to writing when they flourished in the Gupta period, using as their medium the dialect prevalent in the place i. e. the Apabhraṃśa.

1 Rockhill, *Life of the Buddha*, pp. 182, 194; Wassiljew, *Der Buddhismus*, p. 85.

The statement that Yuan Chwang carried to China fifteen treatises of this school[1] shows that it had a literature of its own. I-tsing observes that it had a separate *Vinaya*, but it is not mentioned in Nanjio's *Catalogue*. Incidentally he tells us that this *Vinaya* had rules regulating the use of the undergarment, girdle, remedies and beds by the members of the sect in a way peculiar to itself[2]. The only treatise that is expressly mentioned as belonging to this school in Nanjio's *Catalogue* and now existing in Chinese translation is the *Sāṃmitīya-śāstra* or *Sāṃmitīya-nikāya-śāstra* containing the tenets of the sect[2]. Most of the passages cited in the *Kathāvatthu* as giving the view of the Sāṃmitīya school have been found to be identical with passages on the subject in the Pāli Sutta-piṭaka. From this it seems probable that the Sutta-piṭaka of the Sāṃmitīyas was a redaction of the original piṭaka from which the Pāli piṭaka has been derived.

For information regarding the doctrines of the Sāṃmitīya school, we have now to depend upon works belonging to the rival schools of the

1 Watters, *Yuan Chwang*, I, pp. 20, 21.
2 Takakusu, *I-tsing*, pp. 7, 66, 140.
3 *E. R. E.*, Vol. XI.

Theravādins and the Sarvāstivādins, viz., the *Kathāvatthu*, the *Abhidharmakoṣavyākhyā*, and the *Vijñāna-kāya-śāstra*[1]. The only remarkable doctrine of the Sāṃmitīyas is that regarding the nature of the 'pudgala'. They admitted the impermanence of material composites but at the same time held the view that there was an entity which should be distinguished from the five *skandhas* but which could not exist independently of those *skandhas.* This entity corresponds to what is called soul in Hindu philosophy but very different from it, as it in their opinion ceased to exist when the five *skandhas* came to an end. It served as the carrier of the five *skandhas* through births and re-births of beings as the Sāṃmitīyas held that there is an *antarābhāva* i. e. an intermediate state between the death of a being and its re-birth[2]. They agreed with the Sarvāstivādins and the Mahāsaṅghikas in hold-

Doctrines.

1 The substance of the last two works is found in Prof. Stcherbatsky's *Soul Theory of the Buddhists* and Yamakami Sogen's *Systems of Buddhisitic Thought.*

2 *E. R. E.*, XI, pp. 168ff. For details about the psychological views of this school, see Mrs. Rhys Davids' *Points of the Controversy*, Intro., pp. xviii, xix.

ing that the stage of an *arahat* is not immune from a fall to a lower stage and that the spiritual progress of a convert is always gradual.

INDEX

Abhaya, 157
Abhayarājakumāra, 57, 73, 89n, 90, 92, 125
abhidhamma, 217, 235 ; Sarvāstivādin, 288ff
abhidhammika, 206, 207
Abhidharmakoṣavyākhyā, 275, 301
ācariya, 112
Ācariyavāda, 234
Acelakassapa, 103
ādesanā, 67
Āgamas (=Nikāyas), 277, 279
āgatāgama, 209
Aggañña Suttanta, Buddhist cosmology in, 10-11
Aggika-bharadvāja, 135, 137
Aggivessana, 61
ahiṃsā doctrine, 7-8, 22
Ajātasattu, 82, 84, 88, 89n, 96, 107, 123
Ajitakesakambalin, 84, 91
Ājīvika, 49, 65, 133
Ālavi, 154
Ambalaṭṭhikā, 125
Ambapālī, 73, 76, 126, 161
Ambaṭṭha, 59, 60
Ānanda, 29, 71, 73, 74, 92, 96, 103, 157, 159, 182, 187, 201, 204ff ; training of, 106
Anāthapiṇḍika, 73, 76, 118, 122, 132, 143, 170, 171 ; spread of Buddhism in Kosala helped by, 143
Andhakavinda, 92, 127
Andhavana, 153
Aṅga, 76 ; Buddha's activities in, 170, 171 ; religious condition of, 169, 170 ; Vinaya rules framed in, 172-3
Aṅgulimāla, conversion of, 71, 144
Āniyatā, 152
Añjanavana at Sāketa, 153
Anuruddha, 73, 96, 103, 204 ; training of, 105
apabhraṃsa, 252, 299
Āpana, 170
Aparānta, 185, 189, 190
Aparaseliyas, 229
arahat, position of, 229, 233

arahathood and Buddhahood, 247-8
araññakūṭikas, 99
ascetic practices, Buddha's attitude towards, 16, 18n
Asibandhakaputtagāmaṇī, 90, 125
Asita, 187
Asoka, 27, 31, 46, 270, 271 ; Mahinda's connexion with, 262 ; Theravādins patronized by, 268
Assaji, 87
Assalāyana, 56
Assapura, 170
Aṭṭhaka, 4, 13
austerities and ritualism in Buddhism, 214-5
Avantaka, another name of Sāṃmitīya, 299
Avantī, 68, 116, 183ff ; Mahinda's connexion with, 261-2
Bāvari, 139, 142
Belaṭṭhaputta. See Sanjaya
Benares, 93. See Kāśī
Bhaddā Kapilāni, 193, 194
Bhaddavaggiya youths, 101, 131n
Bhaddiya, 103,
Bhaggas, 74, 155 ; Buddha among, 164-5
Bhaggava, a paribbājaka, 160
Bhagu, 73, 103
Bhallika, 173
bhāṇakas, ii, 208
Bharukaccha, 185
Bhesakalāvana, near Suṃsumāragiri, 75
Bhikkhunī-pātimokkha, 151-2
Bimbisāra, 69-70, 84, 88-9, 94, 96, 99, 100-1, 115, 171
Bodhirājakumāra of the Bhaggas, 75, 164
bodhisattva, theory of, 246-7
brāhmaṇas, conversion of, 120 127, 136-140, 164, 171, 175, 188, 192, 194 ; Buddha and, 38, 85-7 ; whether superior to kṣatriyas, 11
brāhmaṇa villages, Kosalan, 140 ; Magadhan, 127 ; Sakyan, 147
brāhmaṇic faith, bases of, 4
brāhmaṇism, toleration of, 3-4 ; two main bases of, 12-3 ; Buddha's opposition to, 3ff
Brahmāyu, a distinguished brāhmaṇa, 164
Buddha, personality of, 6-7,27 ; on caste-system, 9 ff ; on sacrifices, 46ff ; on magical

practices, 15; on self-mortifications and ascetic practices, 16; brāhmaṇas and, 4, 38, 85-7, 134-6; Jainas and, 88-91; the four non-brāhmaṇical teachers and, 91ff; first converts of, 174ff; disputations allowed by, 53-4; missionary idea of, 44, 176; works on the life of, 278

Buddhahood and arahathood, 247-8

Buddhism, internal forces in the spread of, 2 ff; external forces in the spread of, 27ff; attraction of, 22-6; a proselytising religion, 40 ff; patronized by, 68 ff; catholic spirit of, 48-50; gradual course of training in, 47-8; rationality in, 22-3; a cause of decline of, 34

Buddhist saṅgha, leader of, 201; no supreme headship in, 199-203; unity in, 199, 200; how differences settled in, 202-3

Bulis of Allakappa, 75

Caityavādins, 243

Campā, 169, 170ff

Caṇḍa Pajjota of Avanti, 72, 187

Caṅki, a brāhmaṇa teacher, 64, 139

Cāpāla cetiya of Vesāli, 162

Caste system, Buddha on, 9 ff

Cātumā, 147

Cave-dwellings at Rājagaha, 97ff

Cedi, 181

cetiyas at Vesāli, 159

Ceylon, Mahinda's connexion with, 261-2

Ciñcā-mānavikā, 134

conversion, evangelical method of, 42; defeat in disputation led to, 55-6, 63-5; no stigma in, 63-4; methods employed for, 47ff

Corapapāta, 97

cosmology, Buddhist and Brāhmaṇic, 10-11

council of Kaniṣka, 268-270

Cunda Kammāraputta, 167

Dabba Mallaputta, 99, 167, 210

Dakkhiṇāgiri, 92, 127

Daṇḍakappaka, 140

Devadaha, 147

Devadatta, 73, 89n, 96, 103, 204, 222, 288; training of, 107

dhammakathikas, 208ff
Dharmaskandha of the Sarvāstivādins, 288, 292
dhūta-precepts, 215
dhūtavādas, 189
dhyāna, experiences of, 53-4
dialectical differences, a factor for the origin of schools, 214
disciples, Buddhism preached by, 20ff ; grouping of, 203-7
discourses, four ways of delivering, 58
Dīghatapassi, a Jaina monk, 56, 90, 125
Dīghanakha, a paribbājaka, 101-2
disputation, allowed by Buddha, 53ff ; essential for a missionary, 54-5 ; an illustration of, 60-2 ; conversion of the vanquished in, 63-4
dissensions in the saṅgha, Buddha's apprehension for, 217ff ; occurring in Buddha's life-time, 220ff ; remedies suggested by Buddha to avoid, 217ff ; of Devadatta, 222-3
ekāṃsavādin, 249, 250
Ekanālā, a brāhmaṇa village, 85, 127
Ekottarāgāma, 237
Esukāri, 64
foot-wear, use of, 116
Gāryha, 152
Gayā, 93, 94
Gayāsīsa, 93, 123, 222
Ghoṭamukha brāhmaṇa, 31, 64
Gijjhakūṭapabbata, 96
Gomatakandara, 97
Gosiṅgasālavana, 159
Home of Paiśācī, Mahinda's connexion with, 261-5
Icchānaṅgala, 140
Indasālaguhā, 94
initiation, rules of, 111-2, 148-6
Isigilipasse Kālasīlā, 97
Isipatana, a centre of Buddhism, 177, 178
Jaina laity, conversion of, 49, 120
Jānussoṇi, 137, 140, 141
Jātakas, 235-6
Jaṭilas, 57, 64, 88 ; conversion of, 93-4
Jetavana, 152
Jīvaka, 73, 123, 124 ; ambavana of, 100
Jñānaprasthāna Sūtra, 288, 294

Kajaṅgala in Aṅga, 169, 170, 172
Kālakārāma of Sāketa, 153
Kālāsoka, 243
Kallavālamuttagāma, 92, 101, 127, 128
Kammassadhamma, 190
Kaṇhāyanas, origin of, 59
Kaniṣka, 46 ; council of, 268-270, Sarvāstivādins patronized by, 268
Kaṇṇakujja, 187
Kaṇṭakivana of Sāketa, 53
Kapilavatthu, Buddha's visit to, 103, 130, 131, 147-8, 161
Karṇasuvarṇa, 223
Kāśi, Buddhism in, 173 ; brāhmaṇic culture in, 173
Kasmir, 30, 286
Kassapas, 57
Kaṭhina ceremony, 151
Katyāyaṇīputra, 289
Khānumata, 85
Khemā, queen of Bimbisāra, 193, 194
Khomadussa, 148
Kimbila, 73, 103 ; training of, 105
Koliyas, 74, 155, 165 ; Buddha among, 165-6
Kosala, 68 ; introduction of Buddhism into, 130-4 ; brāhmaṇism in, 130, 136 ; topics of the discourses delivered in, 136 ; whether outside the limits of orthodox brāhmaṇism, 129-130
Kosambī, 179, 180 ; division at, 221
Koṭigāma, 126
kṣatriyas, whether superior to brāhmaṇas, 11
Kukkuṭa-ārāma of Pāṭaliputta, 126
Kukkuṭavatī of the Madda country, 194
Kuru country, centre of brāhmaṇic culture, 36, 37, 182, 190 ; Buddha in, 190ff
Kururaghara-papāta-pabbata, 188
Kusinārā, 74, 166
kutūhalasālā, 55, 102
Kūṭadanta, 5, 56, 84, 85
kūṭatarka in Buddhist works, 59-60
ladies, spread of Buddhism helped by, 75-7 ; conversion of, 120
lay-society, formation of a Buddhist, 17, 118ff ; spread of Buddhism helped by, 118, 122

Licchavis, 74 ; Brāhmaṇism among, 155-6 ; Jainism among, 156-8 ; Buddhism among, 158ff
Lohicca, 138
Lokottaravādins, 238, 243
Madda country, 193 ; converts from, 193-4
Madhurā, 182, 185, 186 ; Avantiputta of, 188
Magadha, brāhmaṇic unorthodoxy in, 36ff ; religious views in, 13-4, Buddhism in, 82ff, 92ff
Magadhabhāsā, Buddha preached in, 252, 254-5
Magical practices, Buddha's views on, 16
Māgandiya, 180, 192
Mahācunda of Cedi, 181
Mahādeva, articles of faith of, 230ff
Mahākaccāyana, 29, 57, 72, 177, 187, 204ff, 212, 257ff, 299 ; founder of the centre in Avanti, 187ff
Mahākappina, a Madda prince, 100, 193, 194
Mahākassapa, 64, 96, 99, 127, 194, 204ff, 239
Mahākauṣṭhila, 288
Mahākoṭṭhila, 57, 177, 178
Mahāli, a Licchavi, 159
Mahānāma, 146, 158, 159
Mahāpajāpati Gotamī, 74, 161
mahāsālas, 138
Mahāsaṅghikas, tenets of, 229 ; rules of discipline of, 226-7, 236, 237 ; literature of, 236-8 ; linguistic medium of, 239 ; centres of influence of, 239ff ; democratic spirit of, 232-3 ; doctrines of, 244ff
Mahāvana-kūṭāgārasālā, 159
Mahāvira, 7, 125
Mahinda, 261-5
Majjhantika, 270
majjhima-desa, 183, 184. See mid-land
Makkhali Gosāla, 84, 91, 92, 133
Mallas, 74 ; Buddha among, 166ff ; discourses delivered among, 167-8.
Malla Roja, 167 ; conversion of, 68-9
Mallikā, a queen of Pasenadi, 142
mātikādhara, 208
Medalumpa, 147
medicaments, rules of, 151
meditations, Buddhist works on, 18

mettā feeling, 8, 9, 22
mid-land, brāhmaṇic, 36-7
miracles, competition in, 90 ; interdicted by Buddha, 67
Mithilā, 163
missionary work, not known to the Hindus, 42 ; a radical departure made by the Buddhists, 43ff
Moggalāna, 28, 64, 84, 96, 159, 164, 177, 204ff, 217, 288
Moggaliputta Tissa, 45, 271
monasteries, rules of building, 99, 100
monks, formation of groups of, 207-11 ; programme of life of, 17
Moriyas of Pipphalivana, 75
mortifications, Buddha's views on, 16ff, 146
Nādikā, 126
Nāgasena, conversion of, 51
Nālaka (=Mahākaccāyana), 187
Nālandā, 90, 92, 125
Nanda, 41, 73, 103 ; training of, 105
Nandatherī, 240
Niddesa, 234, 236
Nigaṇṭha Nātaputta, 57, 84, 88-91, 144, 146, 157, 170, 200 ; among the Sākyas, 146-8
Nikāyas, ii, iii
Nirvāṇa, signification of, 20, 21
Nissaggiya, 117, 152, 163
Nissayas, 113, 114
Northern countries, spread of Buddhism in, 190ff
nuns, order of, 76-7, 160-1
occult powers, a factor in the spread of a religion, 77-82
origin of Buddhist schools, factors peculiar to, 199ff
paccantima janapada, 183, 184, 212
Pācittiya, 117, 163, 165, 181
Pādas, a study of, 289ff
Paiśācī, home of, 259 ; basic dialect of Pāli, 257-260
Pakudha Kaccāyana, 84, 91
Pāli language, iii, 256 ; origin of, 250 ff ; literary form of Paiśācī, 264-5
pañcanekāyīka, 209
Pañcasālā, 85
Pārājīkā, 117, 152, 163
Pārāsāriya brāhmaṇa. of Kajaṅgala, 169
paribbājaka, 55, 95, 120 ; students as, 64 ; of Kosala,

140-2 ; spread of Buddhism helped by, 63-5
paribbājakārāma, 55, 102, 140 ; in Aṅga, 170
Parivāra, 235
Pasenadi of Kosala, 61, 70-1, 90, 132, 171, 193 ; follower of brāhmaṇic religion, 142 ; conversion of, 142
Pāṭaliputta, 92, 126
Pāṭheyya, 184
Pāṭidesanīya, 117
Pātimokkha, 115, 116, 129, 151-2, 163, 181, 212, 281-2
Paṭisambhidā, 235, 236
pavāraṇā, 150
Payāgapatiṭṭhānam, 187
Pāyāsi, instructed by Buddha, 5
Piṭakas, based upon one common original, 253 ff
Piṇḍola Bharadvāja, 45, 57, 180
Pīpphaliguhā, 98
Pokkharasāḍi, 64, 138, 171
Prācya-desa, predominance of kṣatriyas in, 39 ; Buddhism confined to, 182 ff
Prajñāpti-sāra, 288, 293
Prakaraṇa-pāda, 292
preachers, tenacity, perseverance and tolerant spirit of, 47, 50
preaching, rules of, 67-8 ; Buddha's zeal in, 44 ; merit of, 42 ; ways of, 65-7
precepts, rules of, 149
proselytism, duty of monks, 40 ; outcome of *mettā*, 41
Pubbārāma, 144, 153
Pubbaseliyas, 229
pudgala theory, 297, 301-2
Puṇṇa, 118, 190
Puṇṇa Mantāniputta, 29, 50, 96, 204ff, 258, 288 ; praised by Buddha, 51 ; missionary of Śroṇāparāntaka, 50-1
Purāṇa Kassapa, 84, 91, 92
puratthima janapada, 129, 130
Rājagaha, 83, 94ff,
Rājyaśrī, sister of Harṣa, 297
Rāhula, 103, 125-149, 204ff ; training of, 104 ; founder of the Sarvāstivāda school, 282-3
Raṭṭhapāla, conversion of, 191-2
ritualism and austerities, 214-6
Roruka, 90, 184, 189, 190
Rudraka Rāmaputra, 83
Rudrāyaṇa, king of Roruka, conversion of, 90, 190
Śabarādi mlecchabhāṣā, 252

Saccaka, a Jaina, 60ff, 157
sacrifice, Buddha's attitude towards, 2ff, 84
Sadānirā, 38, 130, 169
Sāgala, 193, 194
Sahajāti in Cedi, 181
Sāketa, 153, 154
Sakulūdāyi, 56, 64, 82, 102, 103
Sākyas, 73-4 ; brāhmaṇism among, 145-6 ; origin of, 59 ; Jainism among, 146-8 ; conversion of, 145ff
Sāmāvatī, queen, 72, 76, 280
Sāṃmitīyas, 207, 251, 267, 297ff ; doctrines of, 300-2 ; centres of influence of, 291ff ; language of, 299-300
saṅgha, internal strength of, 32ff
saṅghabheda, defined, 218ff ; distinguished from saṅgharāji, 219-220
Saṅghādisesa, 117, 152, 181
saṅgharāji. See saṅghabheda
saṅghatthera, 202, 203n
Saṅgīti-paryāya and suttanta, 288, 289-292.
Sañjaya Belaṭṭhaputta, 57, 83-4, 87-8, 101, 102
Saṅkassa, 183, 187
Sanskrit, language of the Sarvāstivādins, 274-6
Sāriputta, 28, 45, 57, 64, 84, 96, 97, 101, 132, 159, 177, 204ff, 296ff
Sarvāstivāda school, language of, 274-6, literature of, 277ff ; doctrines of, 294-6 ; centres of influence of, 272-4
Sattāhakaraṇīya, rule of, 150
Sattapaṇṇi, 97
Sautrāntikas, 211
Sāvatthi, missionary work at, 117
schools, origin of, 197ff ; chart of, 224
Sekhiya, 152, 165
Sīha, 73, 158
sīmā, 115
Sindhubhāṣā, 252
Sītavana Sappasoṇḍikappabbhara, 97
Soṇadaṇḍa, 56, 169, 171
Soṇa Kolivisa of Aṅga, 116, 172
Soṇa Kuṭikaṇṇa, 188ff
Soreyya, 187
Śreṇis, 121
Sroṇāparāntaka, 51
suicides, religious, 192-3

Sunakkhatta Licchaviputta, 160
Suppāraka, 206
Sutraists, 185
Suttantikas, 207, 210, 211
Tapodārāma, 98
Theravādins, 211, 219, 228, 240, 249ff
Thullakoṭṭhita, 190
Tinduka-kandara, 98
tipetakin, 209
training, gradual course of, 47-8
Trapusa, 173
Tripiṭaka, original language of, 250
Udāyi, 131
Udena of Kosambī, 31, 72, 76, 180
Ujjeni, 183ff; home of Pāli in, 256ff
Ukkala, 174
Ukkaṭṭha, 131, 154
Upagupta, 31
upājjhāya, 112; distinguished from ācariya (s. v.), 149
Upāli, 56, 90, 96, 103, 204ff; a Jaina, 135
upāsakas, society of, 139-140; duties of, 164. See lay-society
uposatha, 115
Uruvela, 44, 93; Kassapa of, 94
Vacchagotta, a paribbājaka, 102
Vaibhāsika, 266, 270
Vaiśyas, Buddhism helped by, 121, 122
Vajjians, 31, 155, 184, 233
Vajjiputtakas, 240
Vāmadeva, 4
Vāmaka, 13
Vappa, a Sakyan Jaina, conversion of, 147
Vāsabhakhattiyā, 71
vassavāsa, 116, 150
Vasumitra, 262, 288
Vatsa country, 68; Buddha in, 179-180
Vedas, Buddha's views on, 112
Vekhanassa, 56, 64, 141
Veluvana, 90, 99, 100
Verañja, 182ff; Buddha at, 185-6
Vesāli, missionary work at, 60, 74, 117; Buddha's last visit to, 161-2; Vinaya rules framed at, 162ff
Vessāmitta, 5, 13
Vibbajjavādins, another name of Theravādins, 249, 250
Vibhāṣā śāstrās, 266, 269

Videha, 47, 155 ; Buddhism in, 163
vihāra. See monasteries
Vijñānakāya, 288, 293, 301
Vimalaprabhā, a ms., 251, 254
Vinaya, five divisions of, 283 ; of different schools, 280 ; of the Sarvāstivādins, 280ff ; of the Mahāsaṅghikas, 226-7 ; comparative study of, 284ff
Vinayadhara, 207ff
Vinayists, 206ff
Vinaya rules, abolition of minor, 213 ; elasticity of, 211-4 ; framing of, 108-9 ; for bhikkhuṇis, 151 ; of Devadatta, 222
Visākhā, 73, 76, 144, 153
Western countries, progress of Buddhism in, 184ff
worship of deities, Buddha's views on, 14
Yasa, 30, 73, 101, 176
yoga, 80 ; simple form approved by Buddha, 18-19, 25

ERRATA

p. 23, heading	Read Internal Forces
p. 47	Read VII for VI.
p. 84, l. 18	Read monarchs
p. 101	Read Buddha's
p. 124, l. 6	Read physician
"	" disciples
p. 153, l. 12	Read Kālakārāma
p. 169, l. 1	Read Aṅga
p. 187	Read Mahākaccāyana
p. 207, l. 10	Read development
p. 250, l. 15	Delete 'and'
p. 266, l. 8	Read developed

Printed by N. C. Paul, Esqr. at the Calcutta Oriental Press,
107, Mechuabazar Street, Calcutta.